STALKING THE WARDEN

By

Carlos Patrick Reid

Note:

This book is based upon the experiences of Carlos Patrick Reid while serving the Department of Conservation of Alabama as a Conservation Officer or "Game Warden". While the events described are real and actually happened, the stories in the book are intended merely to illustrate the writers' experiences and are not intended to refer to actual persons, whether living or dead. Some characters in the book are composites. To provide foundation and texture to the books' narrative structure, some parts are based on information from third parties. In lieu of using terminology such as "Jane or John Doe" or "Subject Property or complaint", all character names as well as the names of the properties and locations described in the book, have been made up by the writer. This book should be considered an expression of the writers' observations and opinions with regard to the characters and events depicted in the book, and not as a representation of actual Fact as to any particular individual or event:
STALKING THE WARDEN

Dedication

This one is dedicated to my amazing twin boys, Alex and Neville. I regret the nights and weekends of our time, missed and lost forever. Now you will know that I was playing hide and seek and having fun. Remember in the world of "Poke-Mans"...only Poppa Chu can fly!

Also a special dedication to a soldier
Private Spire, Class #24, MOS 12N
A Company 554th Engineer Battalion
Congrats. Couldn't be prouder!

Author's Acknowledgements

Special thanks to my Game Warden buddies Chester Pugh, Mike McNeil and Kevin McKinstry who provided photos and the others officers who made my tour as an officer an adventure. Every time I hear a rifle shot or see a 64 county tag I think of you all.

About This Work

For 15 years I performed the police patrol of an Alabama Conservation Enforcement Officer. This position is known locally as a *Game Warden*, to Cajuns as *the Man* or to misinformed rural folk as *Game Warrior*. I have taken the opportunity to write this because during this time my true boss…my wife simply couldn't listen to the stories. She was the one who had to sit alone at night and listen to the radio while dreading the report that I had been killed by a violator. I was excited and enjoyed every second of the adventure but the thought of my work was terrifying to her. Now in an effort to explain some of my cynicism and strange expressions and to share with her a part of my secret life, I recount some of the most disturbing events. Here I want to take an opportunity to give you a WARNING. I am an avid reader and when writing this piece I wanted to give you a candid look into the events associated with the profession and also give you a look into lives of these mostly male characters without glamour and heroic bias. It would be easy to make this work a comical and heroic epic with an uplifting message, but I think that's been done. I wanted to honestly display the memorable events even as they highlight the frailty of our species.
PARENTAL GUIDANCE RECCOMENDED: contains disturbing events and strong language.

Contents

PHOTOS CAN BE FOUND ON PAGES:
5, 41, 77, 120, 124, 128, 131, 133, 136, 138,155, 166, 167, 168, 174, 191, 192,193,194,195

INTRODUCTION

The Nightmare

I step forward like a goose-stepping Soviet soldier. Faster and faster, I march onward through the pine forest. My heart is pounding, and as I move, my moist breath makes white clouds from the brisk cold winter air. Puffs of white ghostly fog circle my pale white face and these new born clouds drift around and follow me as I march onward with purpose, like a machine. My heart races as I see water running into a fresh boot track.

I stoop and study the tracks in the muddy brown road. The water is disturbed and cloudy as it pours into the depressions made by the fresh tracks.   I continue looking down. I know that I should be more wary because he should be very close. He must be just ahead. For some reason I am not concerned, but instead I am just fascinated by the drama that I see from these lonely boot prints.

Beside the track is a long drag mark in the mud. It looks as if someone is pulling a bag of sand. I know the truth. It is not a bag of sand. This continuous mark is littered with tan and white hairs and a mixture of blood and leaves. It's the disemboweled corpse of a female deer being pulled along this dirt road by an exhausted poacher... The head and entrails are now several hundred yards behind us. I had found the pile of guts in a little hollow just off the side of this dirt road.

His boot tracks are closer together now, and the tracks are deeper. He is tired and probably wondering if the meat is worth all of this effort and the risk involved with poaching the illegal deer. Who knew poaching was so much work?

Inside I mock him, the ground is soft and he cannot escape. *Muhahahha* a silent blood- curdling laugh erupts across my mind. I have been trailing him for some time beginning at the barbed wire fence that marks the property line. I had followed a well worn trail; a path crushed leaves. These leaves told me that he has used it many times. I have followed him before. He is an old nemesis. I am looking at his tracks and now, I imagine him creeping along, constantly stopping to look for a hidden hunter. His eyes are wide, and beads of sweat and desperation drip down his temples. Camouflaged and well armed, he is vigilant for the owner of the property and the remote possibility that the warden is working this property.

BOOM! (A single blast from a 12 gauge shotgun in a wooded bottom.) I had run through the woods to the place where I had heard the gunshot. At first I had only found a few leaves disturbed and upturned. These few brown oak leaves had been kicked over exposing their dry undersides. They were dry markers on this hidden dew covered trail. Hardly noticeable really, most wouldn't think twice about a few scattered leaves. I looked along the trail of overturned leaves and noticed a sloppily painted red oak leaf, a piece of bone, and then a few steps later- deer hair.

But now after dragging the kill onto the road, it becomes a trail of desperation. He has thrown caution to the wind because he is tired. It is an exhausting task dragging 35 lbs of dead weight. And I know that I will catch him. I am closer now, so if he runs I will hear his booming feet on the dirt road and I will hear the splashes as he cuts through the standing water and slush in an absolute panic to escape me, the warden.

In the military they taught us to never stare at someone you are watching. If you stare long enough, the person will eventually look back at you. Instead, you look to the side keeping the subject in the periphery of your vision. The feeling you get is like someone tapping on your brain… you can feel the stare. It must be some primordial skill or talent that helped humans escape predators. A chill runs Up my spine. S*hit. Someone is doing it to me now*! I can feel his stare. Someone is staring at me. I look up and he is right in front of me.

Just a few steps ahead, a tall, lean black man with a short afro stands calmly watching me. He is wearing a green camouflage jacket that is open in the front exposing a sweat stained white t-shirt. His boots are not laced and are spread open at the top. They are covered in mud. My first impression is that he is a hobo hunter. He is smiling slightly and seems happy. My gaze drops, and now I am looking straight down the muzzle of a double barreled shotgun. Before I can issue my calming greeting, he fires the gun.

I feel the impact of the 9 buckshot pellets, and those hardened lead marbles pass through my paper thin shirt. I watch as my blood begins to pour out of my body. It is surreal, and the scene reminds me of the cowboy in an old western movie, where after a successful gunfight the winner takes a drink and he smiles triumphantly at the crowd. His smile vanishes as water then pours out of the many bullet holes.

My hand grabs for my 40-caliber Beretta that is holstered in my leather utility belt. I struggle with the metal snap. It feels like it is stuck in cement. I pull with all my effort. The pistol won't come free? I yank with all my strength and it finally snaps open. I look up into the face of the man, just as he fires the other barrel of the shot gun. Again, I feel the impact of the pellets. My pistol is free now and I bring it up to shoot the man. I level the 6 inch nickel finished barrel two inches below his heart. I will shoot. The special bullets will hit his heart which will explode and push though his lungs and spine. A volcano of blood and flesh will erupt out of his back spraying the grey- brown dirt road behind him. He will be dead even before his knees fold up; his limp body will pile straight downward into the mud like a puppet with the strings suddenly cut. I tighten my finger on the trigger of my deadly weapon.

He drops the gun and raises both hands into the air and says, "I surrender! I surrender! Please don't kill me!"

My gun is now leveled at his chest. In this split second a million thoughts cross my mind. He is unarmed. Do I shoot him? If I pass out will he just finish me off? Will anyone ever find me? In my heart I know that I am dead. No one can survive these wounds. Do I really want to kill him? Don't I have to kill him? I stand there thinking. I see him look down at my feet. I look down to see my crimson blood pooling at my shiny black boots. There is s*o much blood*. I wonder if anyone will ever find out what happened to me. I look up into the face of my killer. I study his expression. He is smiling now. His eyes are wide and the whites of his eyes give him a crazy look but the most that I gather is his feeling of profound...control? What is it? I shudder as I realize that it is his joy. He is delighted as my life drains into the earth. How could my death bring him so much satisfaction? It is victory and he is feeling satisfaction at winning this little battle.

In a microsecond I am angry. Not for the death of a small deer, or for the loss of my family and life, I am mad because I am losing the game. Beaten! Damn it! I am beaten by my own arrogance. This isn't a game at all. It was real. Every time I left home, violent death was a real possibility.

Now it's a simple stalemate that he will win. He will win unless I kill him. He takes a small step toward me with hands out like he will catch me as I fall. His expression imitates mock concern.

I whisper, "Give me a break, asshole!" I tighten my index finger on the trigger.

The Game Warden

I abruptly awaken breathless, scared and then relieved. I look over at Jackie and she is snuggled in the comforter peacefully asleep. I ease out of bed and wander down the hallway to the kitchen. I click the power button on the Mister Coffee and then wander to the bay window to look out into the darkness. The clock reads 3:00 am. It is 30 minutes earlier than last night. *Shit*. After pouring a steaming cup of 'army' black coffee, I quietly walk to my children's bedroom. I stand there staring at my twin angels sleeping peacefully, each with a chocolate chip cookie resting on the nightstand beside them. This is the emergency cookie, the just in case cookie, and a ritual that guarantees solid uninterrupted sleep. Maybe I should try it. My life couldn't be more perfect except for the fact that I could be violently murdered or accidentally killed every day. I make a mental note to increase my term life insurance in the morning.

I am an Alabama Conservation Enforcement Officer working for the Game and Fish Division of the Department of Natural Resources. My job is to enforce the hunting laws of Alabama. We have all kinds of laws but most are simply related to the matter of taking game. These laws range from the really important laws that protect and insure the viability of the game animal, and the ultimate protection of endangered animals, to the mundane and even silly. By far the majority of the laws are designed to control harvest methods for fairness to the other hunters and to the game. These rules try to provide a 'fair chase' to hunted animals and make sure that the limited resource is shared among the hunters.

For the most part I am a referee in tan shirt, ball cap and green polyester pants searching the woods for hidden players. Sounds simple enough until you mentally make the walk into the forest with me. How exactly does one do this? My jurisdiction is the entire State Of Alabama and its millions of acres of rural woodlands. Depending upon the availability of other officers, I might be asked to drive hundreds of miles away to work a complaint on some unknown lands which I have never even seen. Mostly my area of concern is the county to which I am assigned, Marengo County in west central Alabama. It is 98 square miles of rivers and creeks, swamps and woodlands.   Communication is a must for safety and assistance but my radio is practically worthless and has no signal. When I am on foot I can rarely reach anyone locally, much less my fellow law enforcement officers in neighboring counties. I am thoroughly alone and isolated. The hunters that I search for are hidden, camouflaged, and well- armed with weapons designed to kill big game. I have to find them and watch them in their natural movements or crimes without getting accidentally shot. I have to watch them and catch them in surprise; without catching them in such a horribly compromising position that they feel they have to get rid of an intrusive witness. I don't want to stumble on them committing a felony, chopping up a body and trying to hide it. I don't want to wander into a booby trapped marijuana field or whiskey still. All these are crimes that I will arrest people for but understand that I cannot be surprised. I must not stumble into these kinds of situations without being ready. I am cautious. I am patient. I will follow a dangerous subject back to his vehicle. After he empties his weapon and puts it into the gun rack, I will quietly appear behind and calmly greet him. I am constantly watching his body language. It's okay if he cuts a look at his weapon now uselessly hanging in the gun rack, but no sudden grabs for it please. I am in control and he is safe. All the time making sure that he feels, no, that he knows that he is beaten. I must win every encounter. If I fail I will be reduced to a bloody pulp of humanity never to be found again.

The nightmare I described is caused by my personal anxiety. For years I kept it to myself, but after getting more experience, I confided to one of my fellow officers. I was surprised when another officer admitted that he had his own nightmares. After that, I talked with other wardens and they, too, have their own nightmares. Evidently it isn't uncommon, and it is simply a symptom of the job. I remember in college having dreams about taking a test but not knowing the answers, or another dream where I am getting a call from registration that I was failing a class that I didn't realize I had signed up to take.

Same thing I guess- but now much darker and deadlier. The dreams come in the fall and as the opening of the gun season approaches. After the first day of stalking the 'sneaky' game violators and after making a couple of arrests without incident, then and only then- does the anxiety go away. It will be business as usual *or God forbid…routine.*

Why the Hell would anyone do this kind of work? I guess I was born to be a crime fighter.

The honest truth is that this job can be the most amazing experience that you can imagine. I get paid to hike and patrol in some of the most beautiful country in the world. Ninety nine percent of the time it is one glorious nature fest…birds, deer, raccoons, and butterflies. It is an amazing trek. Nature lover aside, at heart I am still a kid. I am issued a 4- wheeled all -terrain vehicle. For the uninitiated, let me explain this is a motor cycle with big fat wheels that can cross most terrain, the Bat bike. Are you kidding? *(Vroom Vroom!)* I get a 16- foot aluminum boat with a 75 horsepower Mercury motor to run the waterways of two large rivers that join in my county. You guessed it…*Bat boat*. They gave me a boat. It is like having a superpower to fly across water. I use these "amazing toys" to monitor the activity of hunters and fishermen. If I sound like a kid then at heart I know it's true and it is probably a job requirement. I remember being seventeen and playing army with my little brothers and some cute girls from the high school caught me …I was so immature!

I have always been a *Batman* fan. He was the only super hero with no super powers. *Batman* was just a guy driven with a passion for justice and in possession of some cool gadgets. He was a lonely, fragile human with the guts to make a difference. Superman fan, not so much. How can you be a hero if nothing can hurt you? An idealistic kid, maybe, but you must be naïve to even begin to try to do this job. And some would argue that you had to be just a 'damn fool'. That's fine and I definitely understand that opinion but for me it's totally worth it. I have seen some incredible things so vivid that words can't capture the profound beauty. I have always felt at ease in the woods and have more than once stopped and softly placed my hand against the rough bark of a tree finding an almost spiritual comfort. I have felt connected and at home. *Alive*

Reasons for Telling My Story

I remember when I first started the job, people where always telling me that they wanted to take a gun into the woods, even into the parks. *How silly,* I would think. Cocky response, I know, but then I would tell them that they were the top of the food chain and if they were scared in the woods, then they should just go to a movie…maybe a chick flick. We are the "top of the food chain." Damn arrogant and I realize that now. After 15 years of the work, I feel very different. I have startled bobcats, coyotes, feral dogs, and alligators without giving it a second thought. I must admit that I look over my shoulder checking for a way to run and catch my breath when I stumble on another unexpected human in the woods. And I must admit my first mental response is *what in the hell are you up to?* You should be armed. Not from the animals, not from the snakes or bobcats or coyotes. The humans…you need a weapon for the humans. People do some weird stuff in the woods. I am no longer a Game Warden, but wanted to share my adventures and my horrors with some of the rest of you.

Chapter One: Creeps and Perverts

This chapter picked itself. I mean it's not my intent to start my tale with this disgusting subject matter but from the get go, from the start, this stuff kept creeping up. I write this first story because …hell it was the first guy I ever checked. No shit the very first guy. I should have known then that I was cursed!

I remember it like it just happened. I checked my freshly pressed and starched uniform in the mirror. The green polyester pants had creases down the center so sharp you could cut yourself if you bumped into my leg. My khaki cotton shirt was "board" stiff, and my polished badge and name tag flashed like laser beams. I looked up and my hair was meticulously combed…oops...I had missed some shaving cream behind my ear. I glanced down and squinted, I could just make out my features in my mirror shined cowboy boots. Yes, I said cowboy boots. How many police get to wear Texas style boots? I must be dreaming. I put my green baseball cap. The cap with the Department patch and seal centered over the bill. I wink at my reflection and think, *Showtime*. I stop by the hall closet and pull out a black leather belt which has my pistol holster, handcuffs, and flashlight holder. I wrap it around my waist and then secure it to my dress belt with leather ringlets called 'keepers'. I reach onto the top shelf and grasp my stainless steel plated revolver. I enjoy the feeling of strength and firmness as I wrap my fingers around the solid grip. The weapon is all steel and real; I enjoy the solid weight of it and heft it to feel the gravity of the instrument. With one graceful stroke I pull it to my side and slide it down into the waiting holster. I snap the retaining strap down securing the weapons. I grab my powerful coal black flashlight and reverse it and then slide it into the ring shaped holder on the belt. I seat it like I am returning a sword to a scabbard. I reach to the small of my back and check the circular handcuff holder and make sure that the cuffs are securely held in place. Oh my God! I have a utility belt. I am freaking *Batman…* of the woods. I step outside and stroll to edge of my driveway. I wait by the curb…like a school boy waiting for the bus. Standing there in the yellow light of the rising sun, I was God's gift to law enforcement, brand new, sparkling clean, ready to protect and save Mother Nature from evil ne'er-do-wells.

The day begins with me standing all shiny and new and… optimistic in front of my tiny little starter home waiting to be picked up by a game warden named Wesley Knapp. He was about 5 foot 10 inches tall with black hair with gray on his temples. He was a good looking guy who was actually a local celebrity He was the leader of a country band and performed at the local clubs and events. He was cheerful guy and had those laugh lines around his eyes, the kind of lines that tell you that he smiles a lot. He picked me up in a new olive green pickup truck. I could tell he was nervous, I was his first trainee. I would later learn that the supervisor had told him that I was a typical college boy and he was moderately self-conscious about it. He hadn't gone to college, and thanks to me would truly believe that he hadn't missed anything.

He needed a shave and looked tired. Wesley was wearing a full green jump suit over his khaki shirt and green polyester pants. His boots were stiff with mud.

He had been up all night working an illegal night hunting complaint. He was all business at first. I suspect that he was trying to decide if I was worth getting attached too. Luckily, I had just gotten out of the Army from a station in Germany. He was in the National Guard, and it turned out that we had a lot in common. One thing about being in the army is that all soldiers share the same stressful training and life. After completing a tour you can go anywhere in the world and have a buddy. Well, in any bar there will always be some poor sap who did a tour and who is eager to share stories with a brother-in-arms.

We continued on patrol. Well, when I say patrol I mean 'safe for a rookie' patrol. I hadn't been to the academy yet- so I mean an innocent and non-lethal patrol. We drove to an area south of Linden, Alabama following a tip. One thing that a game warden relies upon is feedback from informants. And Wesley was so personable that he literally had mothers calling and informing on their own children, brothers calling on each other, and in- laws calling reporting each other. Usually everyone would get along until someone killed a huge trophy deer or turkey. Then your kin became an illegal son of a bitch who killed it illegally cheating or something. Jealously…envy. Call it trophy envy. For now take it from me that Alabama folks are very competitive. Everything we do is competitive; hunting and fishing, and for that matter sports in Alabama are treated with the passion of a HOLY WAR.

Well this day he had a report that an 80 old Mr. Buckner had killed a turkey illegally from a baited green field. His sister's husband was pissed because he had killed a turkey with an 11 inch beard and 1 ¾ spurs. For now, just trust me that in the sport of hunting he was ahead. Problem was that it was squirrel season- not turkey season, and it was also illegal to bait the turkeys into a killing field. Truth was that 10 miles south of the incident and across the county line, there was a fall turkey season 118 miles across the state line in Florida someone could have shot the bird over a pile of corn. So, it's easy to see that this is one of those times when officers act as referees in the game of turkey hunting. Here we have something akin to offside's, *out of bounds*, and *un-sportsman like conduct*, but instead of a 5 or 15 yard penalty like you see in football…instead of throwing a yellow flag we hand you a ticket ranging in cost from 25 to 500 dollars.

It was now afternoon of my first day and we pulled behind a water tower and hid Wesley's new police truck. We then walked down an old logging road, and Wesley took the lead or point position like a bird dog searching for quail. He was sneaking along looking at the ground and sniffing the air. I for the most part just stumbled along after him. My God it was beautiful. The road was dry but covered in brown pine straw, and a slight breeze stirred up some scattered oak leaves that littered the ground here and there. The trees crowded the road and for the most part kept it shaded. It was like walking in a tunnel running through the forest. The road abruptly turned left and went downhill, and there we found a shooting house on the left side of the road facing a green field. A shooting house is nothing more than a plywood box with a tin roof and with holes or windows cut through it for hunters to shoot from. The little hunting shack is usually just big enough for one hunter and a chair. Wesley walked past the shooting house studying the ground with intense concern. He looks down and sees corn. We were doing a reconnaissance and we didn't expect to see anyone. Remember this was a rookie safe patrol. This time of day, hell it was one in the afternoon, nobody should have been hunting! *Honestly! WHO HUNTS AT LUNCHTIME!* Like an Indian scout, Wesley points at the ground and says, "Bait." I am a few steps behind him standing beside the door of the shooting house. He has thoroughly briefed me not to get out in front of him or out of arms reach. After all, it would not do for his student to get shot on the first day. Well, I am right beside the shooting house when he says "bait." Immediately rustling and struggling noises and breathless sounds emerge from the shooting house. Wesley is looking into the field as a hen turkey runs out. He snaps his head around and looks in my direction as an 80 year old man steps out of the shooting house.   Wesley reaches for his weapon and states

"You are under arrest for hunting over bait."   The old guy confidently replies, "Oh I ain't got no gun!"

He says it with the confidence that only comes from expecting the conversation.

I am right beside him as he exit's the shooting house. Looking at me, he offers his hand and says, "How do you do?"

Being a professional, I politely reach out to accept his hand. I glance at Wesley. Oh my God he is mouthing something. What is he saying??? The old man grabs my hand with his sweaty paw…I look back at Wesley…I remember it now like a movie, and the event is happening now in super slow motion Wesley is shaking his head left and right. He is waving his arms like a ground guide waving off an airplane that has botched its landing. He is silently mouthing and signally with his hands…NOOOOOO! I am confused and look at the harmless old guy with his friendly smile and that's when I notice. His hunting coveralls are unzipped with his Hanes and what is left of his shriveled manhood peeking out…UUGH! I remember it vividly. It was all in slow motion the old guy really pumping my hand and looking at my face. I guess the old guy completely forgot. He was so excited to retort that he wasn't hunting. He had rehearsed it so many times. He was shaking my hand in one of those bone crushing southern handshakes. Wesley was shaking his head and grimacing…NOOOO! NOOO! I turned back toward Wesley and gave him a helpless look as this old guy continued to shake my hand with his nasty grip of death. I felt so violated and inside I made a little whimpering sound. I reached for my pistol but was saved by Wesley.

Wesley spoke up, "Well…sir we have to check and make sure you aren't hunting. Pat you down for weapons and check out the shooting house."

The old man took this as a cue; he released my hand and stepped toward Wesley. I meekly staggered forward and looked into the wood box that we called a shooting house. The floor was littered with all kinds of pornography. I mean some really scanky stuff. I wouldn't even know where you could buy crap like that   This was 20 years ago…no internet…hell the county had just legalized alcohol sales.

While I was looking for a weapon, the old guy offered his hand to Wesley who curtly said, "I will pass."

After we were satisfied that the old pervert didn't have a weapon, we parted ways leaving him standing by the small house. This guy was at least 80 years old and I guess that should have been the end of it, but after we left the old guy in the shooting house, we doubled back down a trail and walked a ½ mile to another field. No use having to make another trip to the area when we could simply go into "sneak mode" and look around now. I checked the next field which also had corn sprinkled around here and there and then I proceeded up the dirt road to a rendezvous point with Wesley. I heard someone in the brush. I crouched behind a tree. I was at least ½ mile away from where we caught great-grandfather time with his hand in his pants. Well, low and behold, the guy has crossed a swamp bottom to this field. At first I thought he had a gun and started to stand up. For a split second, I think *Ha, I got you, you old nasty bastard. You have your gun now and this is a baited area,* then I realize it is a walking cane. He just stood there staring at the field, leaning on his cane and looking for game. He has one hand on his cane and the other...you guessed it, it is in his pants. *Damn. Gross...*He is just digging around like a squirrel buries a nut. He eases into this shooting box and I quietly slip back up the road. I met Wesley at the vehicle and he tells me that he hasn't found anything. I tell him about the other field. He thinks that it's funny. In fact, he thinks it is hilarious! I make a big deal about opening the door with my left hand and holding my right hand out from my body like it's got something nasty on it.

He says, "I got another place to check." I look him in the face. Can we please stop at a gas station so I can wash my hand?"

"Sorry Pat…we have to check this next place." He pulls a lock blade knife from his pocket and opens the sharp blade. "Maybe you should just take it off at the elbow." That's Wesley… always wanting to help.

"Yes Pat, that's the way I am…I guess I am just a giver. Here use my knife…I cleaned it this morning…ha-ha."

I grimace and then make a motion that I am going to wipe my contaminated hand on his shoulder. He makes a mistake and flinches. At that moment I see his weakness and leap.

He drops the knife and squeezes against the driver's door with his face pressed against the window.

As he struggles to open the door to avoid my gross hand, I begin to threaten him. "Put it on you…I am going to put it on you." I say in a creepy voice.

The door opens and he spills out on the ground. He rolls with laughter. He is weeping now.

"Okay, okay. Ha-ha .We can stop at the store in Sweet Water…you can get cleaned up there."

He fakes concern now but I can tell that he can't wait to get back to the jail to tell the deputies. The ice was definitely broken, and Wesley would never be nervous around me again.

You are probably wondering, "How old are these tools?" And I honestly can't blame you. Well what would you have done? I made a mental note to get some gloves. Yea even *Batman* had gloves. *Bat Gloves.* Now I know why but I would never have imagined. I think that I will pause now and go wash my hands

I feel dirty.

The Animals

We had a chronic complainer, and it's true the squeaky wheel gets oiled. So squeaky, that through the years we became very familiar with the hunting club right across the river from Demopolis. While it was in another county, the old warden who worked the county lived 30 miles north and would not work night hunting. I lived less than a mile from this club so I ended up working the complaints.

The private land was bordered by public hunting land which was only accessible by river. It attracted a rare and talented breed of poachers. I mean dedicated people who drove hundreds of miles to access the private lands by water and poach the game. They would use vehicles and boats to sneak onto this prized hunting land. They were worthy opponents for the common warden but for *Batman…please.* I tell you this because we will return to this club when we talk about these poachers but that fact bears only mention here. Well this private land-which was loaded with deer and turkey was hunted by an aristocratic and politically connected bunch of old guys. These guys knew how to stir up trouble if they didn't get proper attention from game wardens. Their goal was to get a security guard for free. The membership list included district attorneys, mayors, a senator and judges but most importantly for a poor warden, the department head was an honorary member and turkey hunted the club land. In this line of work, a turkey hunt with one of our department heads was like crack cocaine to an addict. If you took my boss hunting, well, you got all the love and attention you needed. I tell you this because it is interesting that these guys were 'stick up the butt' deacons of a very large powerful church. True to nature, I always smelled alcohol on them when they were at the hunting camp but goddamn, you had better not ever ask them if they had been drinking. I was talking to one of the old patriarchs and he had invited me to bring my wife and kids to a cookout on a Saturday evening. I innocently asked him if I needed to bring some drinks or alcohol.

He took his cap off and pulled it to his chest covering his heart. Leaning toward me he soundly responded. "No. Absolutely not!"

His attitude was "Why…Why…I never…HOW dare you!"

Now picture me leaning back from his alcohol reeking breath as it blew my hair backward.

"Oh. Sorry. I didn't mean to offend you." I shamefully replied. Truthfully I am

11

thinking *Yeah, right. Sure, you don't drink… asshole…and by the way a breath mint wouldn't kill you!*

This cocky bunch had a problem. They had a chronic problem. Seems no matter how many wild dogs they shot, more just appeared. It was crazy. This went on for years and I bet they killed hundreds of dogs. These old guys would spend all fall planting beautiful green fields to attract deer. I mean hours of bush hogging, and plowing fields. They would spend thousands of dollars on fertilizer and special seed. They were totally committed to the endeavor by investing in every little gadget or legal lure to seduce the trophy deer into their killing fields. They built massive elevated shooting houses, insulating the walls, installing sliding windows, and soft cushioned benches or recliners oriented to view out the windows. In this neck of the woods this was standard practice for these 20th century hunters. They would have the latest technology for heating whether it was smokeless propane heaters or battery powered socks. Every evening these old fellows would drive to the area and unload their 4 wheeled ATV to then drive into the woods. Parking a short distance from the shooting house, the old hunter is pausing only to spray 'doe in heat' urine on his boots. Sometimes they hobble to their hunting spot with their canes or walking sticks. They struggle up the stairs or ladders to these shooting houses. Once there they would load their rifles and then proceed to load their stomachs with fine sipping whiskey. Warm now, they would recline in those comfortable seats and watch the sun sink below the horizon. They are entertained by the birds, squirrels and deer that would feed in the mint green fields below them. They would be sitting in their shooting houses in dreamlike perfection when all the sudden the deer and small game would alert and stampede out of the field. Moments later a starving dog would wander through the lush green field. The dog or dogs would scare all the deer and game away. BAM! The dog takes three running steps and then lands into a ball curling up in a fetal position. *Dead Dog.* Hunting season after hunting season, year after year, over and over again this scenario is repeated. Now the peaceful air is disturbed by the cussing of a grumpy old man who is banging down the ladder of his shooting house just to drag the stinking dog out of the field. After a few incidents they established a body dump or bone yard for the dogs because you couldn't just leave the corpses in the green field to rot and stink up the killing field. It was like deer repellant. This place wasn't a pet cemetery but was just an opening at the end of a dead end road that cut through some six year old pines.

I remember watching a Tarzan movie in which an old elephant is shot. He is intentionally wounded by "Bwana" the great white hunter who hopes to find a mythical elephant grave yard. Mortally wounded, the elephant heads to this secret valley, the poor beast limps on three legs while favoring the front leg. He is followed by the greedy ivory hunters. Finally after cresting the top of a hill the hunter and natives look down the valley at elephant grave yard. The hunter sees miles of bones and ivory tusks piled high and bleaching in the sun. That's the way the dog dump looked. The dog bone yard was just an old road covered in the skeletal remains as far as you could see. As I said, this went on for at least 10 years. After several telephone complaints in a busy deer season, we decided to setup our robot deer in a green field. Robo Deer was a beautiful little buck with a head that would spin around like that chick's head in the Exorcist, and a tail which would rise up and down. We used it to entice *road hunters*, to give them an opportunity to shoot and get arrested. *Road hunters* are folks who load up their vehicles with beer and ammo and ride the rural roads looking for deer standing in the open. The old hunters had complained to Montgomery that after about 4 p.m. that people would ride up and down the country road shooting deer as they crossed. To work this type detail in daylight, you had to have at least two posts. One post would stay and work the remote control on the deer, and when the time was right, call for a chase vehicle to come out and arrest the violators. The first-post-officer was supposed to make the deer seem like it was alive. Give a head turn toward the vehicle and finish the act with a wiggle of its behind in a dance of seduction. At the other post, or posts, is an officer in a chase vehicle who is hidden out of sight but close enough to get to the road and stop the road=hunting vehicle.

For this complaint, I left a wildlife biologist with the decoy deer. He was supposed to support the detail by recording the hunter with a video camera and keep the chase vehicle informed by working a radio. I had to move my police vehicle into a road that was some distance away but close enough to allow me to speed out and capture anyone hunting from a vehicle. I was the chase car. I had just returned into the hiding spot when I heard a loud, BANG.

The radio went crazy.... "He shot....He shot!"

I peeled out onto the paved road with my engine roaring, the tires squealing and smoking as I rounded the curve in the road. I first saw a brown F-150 Ford pickup truck come into view. I could just see a bald headed man with his face pressed down on the butt of the stock of this rifle. He was aiming out the window of his truck...*BANG*...smoke wafted around the vehicle. Cool, huh? I hit the blue light. After quickly exiting my vehicle I moved to the side of the truck and took the rifle from the shocked guy. He was so intent on blasting away that he hadn't even noticed that he was being arrested. It was old Joe. I knew old Joe. He was one of the club members.

"Joe. What are you doing shooting our deer?"

"What deer?" He asked. *He hadn't even seen the robot deer!*

I pointed to our pretty little buck out to him.

"I can't see nothing." he innocently replied.

"Wait." he said pulling a pair of glasses from their case on the dash of his dusty pickup. After putting them on he gave another look in the direction of the robot deer some 100 yards down the power line.

"Oh look at that" he said, reaching for his rifle.

I pulled the weapon back out of his reach.

"It's a fake Joe."

He was totally confused by now.

"Huh?"

"What were you shooting at Joe?" My biologist friend Joel had made it up to the vehicle.

"Are you going to arrest him?" This got his attention and cleared his head. Joe started insisting that he was innocent.

"I was shooting those damn dogs!"
I couldn't believe the odds of something like this happening, but I really didn't think this blind guy had seen the deer. I had a hunch that he had shot another deer in the edge of the road that Joel hadn't seen. After all, how many people will stop their truck in the road and blast a dog in cold blood. It seems an unlikely occurrence especially in an area over populated with prized deer.

"Show me." I demanded.

We followed old Joe a few hundred feet looking for blood or the dog. We found nothing. I still didn't feel right about writing the ticket, so I issued him a warning for discharge of a weapon from a public road. I asked him to move along. Joel began sporting a pout lipped expression and cocked his eyebrow at me before walking back toward his hiding place.

I jumped in the truck with an unsettled feeling in the pit of my stomach.

After a few minutes Joel called back.

"He is still here …the old fart is just walking around the woods in front of the robot deer."

"Dang." I said as I cranked up my truck and hauled ass back to the detail site.

As I pulled up, I could see old Joe dragging something out of the woods. At first I thought it was a coyote but closer inspection showed that it had a homemade collar and a leash made of clothesline. Without a word, Joe slung the dead bitch into the bed of his truck. He then in 'a show' forcefully slammed his tailgate up.

I heard running feet and it was Joel. He pulled his hat off and scratched his head.

"I'll be damned. Are you gonna arrest him?"

"Naw."

"Well he killed a dog! And he shot from the public road." Joel, like many of biologists, loves animals. These biologists tend to be regular guys, sensitive and probably not crazy about the whole gun fighting police thing. He bit his lip, and gave me the "stink eye"

"Look," I said, "I will fill you in on this club later. Let's get rid of him and continue the detail." I turned to walk away.

"And move that damn robot deer closer to the road so that violators can see it"
"How close?"

"Close enough so an asshole with cataracts can see it! I don't want this to happen again."

My biologist friend was a severe puppy lover. He was pissed off and disgusted with the old bastard.
There I was standing on the side of the asphalt road while watching an old bastard walking to his truck and mumbling like a drunken sailor the whole way.

"I will shoot a goddamn dog on my own hunting land if I want to."

"I thought this was America. I must be lost...this must be Goddamn Russia!" he mumbled pausing only long enough to look back and give me the stink eye. *Geez enough with the stink eye!*

On my other side a thoroughly pissed off biologist was stomping his way back into the woods all the while muttering about sick bastard shooting a puppy.

"Piece of shit bastard…Who shoots a puppy? She wasn't doing anything. Asshole….fucking asshole..." he said while turning briefly back and making a rude hand signal at the departing truck.

I stood there for a moment taking it all in…*what a fine mess*. I took a deep breath and let out a sigh. I waved at Joel after he got behind his tree. He ignored me, of course. And I then gave a final look at old Joe who was now pulling off. The old bastard is probably legally blind driving along the road scanning for more dogs…armed with a high power rifle and bullets that will drop an elephant three miles away. Probably taking a swig of Jim Beam and continuing his deadly patrol as he is leaving a blood trail of crimson syrup dripping out of his truck bed from his trophy rabid mutt. *Welcome to ALABAMA!*

I would probably have to meet with my supervisor after the old guy laid into us. Joel probably wouldn't return my call for a week or two.

Joel was pissed, but he wasn't stupid.

Later, he finally got an appreciation for the whole picture, especially after I told him that he would have been in the Commissioner's office explaining how he had messed up his turkey hunting arrangement with old Joe. Reluctantly he forgave me.

Another dog for the bone yard! Well we didn't catch anyone that day but you can now appreciate these damn 'appearing dogs.' What are the odds that a police detail would be set up and this kind of thing would happen instead?

I had an ominous feeling that something bad was going to happen. I didn't know- but in early May it was all coming to a head.

In the summer, when my work would get slow, I would sometimes work with my friend, Pat Oliver. He was a Marine policeman; he worked for the same department but another division. He was a police officer so it was cool for him to ride in the vehicle.

He was a squat built guy who wore a crew cut. His uniform was a snow white shirt and blue pants. He was a tenacious individual and that had earned him the nickname 'bulldog.' Believe me he earned the rep. I would work with him in the summer as we both would end up patrolling the same waterway. It was easy for me to hop into his boat and make rounds. A lot easier than me fueling and launching my boat which honestly wasn't a big deal, but when its 101 degrees in Alabama, you simply must take every opportunity to be lazy. And hell, it got damn boring without someone to talk to during the long, hot summer.

My duties required me to patrol the public streams and river landings to check fishing licenses and fishermen's catch limits. In retrospect, it seems that Pat and I always would get into some of the most epic adventures including foot chases, high speed vehicle chases and gun fights. We were either lucky or cursed, depending on your point of view.

Our opinion on these events varied and only depended on whether we had eaten a big lunch. Well, I stopped at his local hang out which was the marina motel. More accurately, the coffee pot at the office there. The marina where his police boat was located also operated a motel. Pat must have informally assumed the security position and I guarantee that was the safest coffee pot in Alabama. Pat would usually hang out in the lobby until about 10, or he might leave earlier if they were out of coffee.

On this May morning, I had eaten a big breakfast and in lieu of launching my boat, I had decided to make license checks at the numerous boat landings. I could probably catch some people fishing without a license and by checking the parking lots I would be able to see how many people where actually fishing on the lake. This is a sweet patrol which consisted of driving in the air conditioned truck. Most of the time, I could pull right up beside the fishermen. One time I pulled up to a guy and didn't even get out of the vehicle to hand him his ticket for fishing without a license. To make matters worse, I even borrowed his pen to write him the ticket. In retrospect I probably should have given him a warning.

This was the perfect patrol for a bloated game warden. I convinced Pat that it was a harmless patrol so he agreed. We crossed over the river bridge and turned down the dirt road to Run Away Park. As we continued down the dirt road we had a pleasant conversation and enjoyed the hiss of the air conditioning. It was already smoking hot with the temperature over 95 degrees and the humidity at 80 percent. Glancing to our right we both caught the shine of sun glare off of what we assumed was a windshield. The truck was suspiciously parked a hundred yards off the road on the backside of a 'green field' and backed up to the woods. We both knew that nobody should have been in that area.

Remember it is burning hell hot if we get out of the vehicle so you have to understand how obvious it must have been to us. Only the curious game warden type would have even noticed. For us, cynical from life, it was definitely queer and something was up.

"Hey…what's up with that," I asked.

"Something's up." Pat replied.

"I think it's someone dumping trash!" he hissed.

"OH NO YOU DIDNT DUMP TRASH IN MY COUNTY!" he growled.

"Well it is slow and I would like nothing better than to write a littering ticket to some asshole dumping trash at the park." I agreed.

I went into 'game warden mode,' or 'sneaky son of a bitch mode' if you are from Walker County. I let the vehicle coast down the road with the engine at idle and rolled into a logging road as I cut the engine. The vehicle came to a stop while it was still in drive. We both quietly eased out of our seats taking extra care not to slam our doors. They closed with just a modest "click." We quietly walked back to the dirt road that we knew would take us to the hidden vehicle.

The cable gate was locked. Most people wouldn't think twice about that…but to us…it meant the person had a key and was probably authorized to be there. Probably someone we would know. Probably one of those ancient hunters who had nothing better to do but to raise a stink about me harassing them. Well, we weren't deterred and preceded to move toward the vehicle; sure enough it was a blue vehicle that looked familiar, but because of the way it was parked we couldn't see who it was. We quietly approached the vehicle. We could make out the bald head of a man who was standing at the rear of the truck bed. He was pulling his arms backward rapidly like he was plucking or pulling the feathers off something. Pat looked at me….

"He's plucking a turkey."

Now I have to tell you that we weren't really making any effort to be super stealthy, and Pat spoke in a normal speaking voice. But the guy was so busy that he didn't even notice the two large police officers walking across the open field. I mean we were almost five hundred pounds of meat stomping up to the guy. The sounds of our pounding boots and rattling of our gear didn't faze the guy. Well, we still didn't recognize the man or the vehicle, so Pat went to the right side of the vehicle and I went around to the left side of the vehicle. What we saw was very disturbing. We both knew the guy. He sat at the round table in the front of the door of the local country restaurant. We saw him nearly every day. You have seen this table at country diners. All the old locals sit there smoking camel cigarettes, drinking coffee and making idle comments to everyone who comes in the door. My wife, Jackie calls these people 'the greeters.' I just call them smart-asses that collect wherever they can find cheap or free coffee. *Oops! Mental note! I ought to rethink that opinion.* We had seen this guy hundreds of times, and Pat had rabbit hunted with the guy and they had walked many miles through the woods trailing after his prize beagles. To make things more bizarre the guy was a big shot deacon at the big church, or so he claimed by always adding it into his introduction. This guy was one of the loudest complainers and was constantly bitching about the pathetic game wardens. He had caused more than a few memos explaining our ineptness to our supervisor. He was a notorious asshole, but now he became an entirely new creature Well there he was standing behind his truck with the tailgate of his truck down, his pants down and his privates stuck in the backside of a worn out old bitch of a dog. He had it by its hind legs and he was pulling it straight back. Yep, he was punishing this poor mutt.

Pat said, "Good Morning."

The 70 year old guy looked up so fast his glasses tilted and almost fell of his head. He released the mutt, and bent over and moved to his right behind the side bed. I could tell he was zipping up. I remember too vividly he was walking toward me and he had those bright bleached white slip-on tennis shoes…you know, the kind with no laces, and he was stepping into the mud. The white 'slip on' tennis shoes must have been brand new. The mud sloshed on them looking like feces. He was headed my way and I had a sudden flashback to the old turkey hunter and quickly put my hands in my pocket! I turned around and started walking back the way we came.

I hollered at Pat. "Are you gonna talk all day? Or are we gonna get some work done. I yelled as if he was keeping from some important game warden stuff. "

I remember Pat looking at me. He was completely stunned. I am sure he was trying to fathom if he could arrest the guy for dog rape or something. Nothing else was said.

"Ugh huh?" Pat grunted.

Pat just fell in behind me. I looked up and saw the abused dog at the edge of the woods. She was rough looking. Half starved and her tits where nearly dragging the ground. I remember we made eye contact, and I am sure her expression was one of relief…she trotted into the woods probably wondering where her pups were. She was headed toward the other fields dragging a leash made of clothesline. She was headed to the hunting fields where I am sure one of the ancient hunters would be mad enough to put a bullet in her heart. *Out of the pan and into the fire. Some creatures just can't get a break.*

When we got back to my truck Pat stared blankly out of the windshield. I just looked back and forth. I would look out the window and then glance at Pat. I was confused. Hell, we had thought this guy was some kind of civic leader. Wasn't he someone to be trusted? We had respected him even if he was an asshole. I guess he was just all asshole. Like I say this was a long time ago. It was a simpler time or maybe we where simpler. We didn't know what to say, but I felt that we had to get the hell out of there. I knew that we definitely had seen too much. We knew too much. I thought that the guy had to kill us. I mean if I caught you doing this, you would want me dead right. For Christ sakes, I am a game warden you could shoot me and say you thought I was a deer! You could kill me and get away with it.

I was upset, but I could tell that it really upset Pat. He knew the guy a lot better. I was disturbed. I mean it just seems that there isn't anyone you can depend on. All my childhood heroes turned out to be alcoholic whoremongers. I tell you this because it really affected me. After almost 50 years I think that it is understandable that I am slightly cynical. To this day when a hero emerges, I can't help but wonder what his 'vice' is or who or what he is screwing. I am sure that he will disappoint me and everyone else.

Well the sad sick truth is that this old arrogant DEACON was a serial dog rapist. For years he had been picking up the stray dogs in Demopolis and carrying them to this hunting club which was two minutes away. He was raping them and then turning them loose in the woods of this hunting club. Meanwhile, his old hunting buddies couldn't have a peaceful hunt because all of these starving dogs were wandering around the green fields and shooting houses. BAM! BANG! *(Another dog corpse.)* He would sit right there at the front table guzzling free coffee or at the hunting club and he would bitch about the dogs with the rest of the old hunters

What a sick bastard! Pat and I were at a loss what to do. We actually got into a little argument.

As we drove off, we both stared straight out of the windshield…Pat tilted his head in confusion…and shook it back and forth. After a while I knew I had to do something to break the ice. This was sickening. At heart, being a kid and possessing the mental maturity of a nine year old, and seeing that tough old Pat really needed a shoulder to lean on and some counseling, I was having a hard time not vocalizing my feelings. I couldn't believe I was seeing Pat all weak and VULNERABLE! Being a sensitive guy myself, I decided to go in for the kill!

I said, "Pat, hey Pat….that's your buddy Muhahahha! Hey Pat …he had his peeper in that puppy! Hahahahhah."

I started to quit but then I saw Pat flinch and heard his teeth grinding.

Hey Pat…did you see your hunting buddy? Man that guy is a puppy lover! WHOOOHAA. Hey Pat…didn't you eat barbeque with that guy? Was the meat stringy? Hahaha. Hey Pat. Hey Pat…your friend their…Huh…How do you feel about dogs? Haha."

Pat just stared straight ahead. He was truly upset but, man oh man, I on the other hand was having a great time. I was starting to feel a lot better. He just stared straight ahead until he finally had heard enough.

After Pat pulled his gun, I decided that maybe I had to take a more serious tone. I decided to take a more serious tone.

"Hey Pat Don't kill me! Put your gun away!"

I looked down his barrel.

"Seriously put that gun away. I read that laughter can help traumatized individuals deal with disturbing events. See I am trying to help you…seriously. Trust me.

Geez! I never realized how large that nine millimeter barrel on that Glock pistol is…wow…that's a nice weapon."

"Quit goofing off Pat. This is serious. For Christ's sakes act your age! We need to brainstorm this thing. Hmmm. Don't worry about it…you can watch me brainstorm...ha-ha."

I was out of control. I couldn't stop myself!

"What should we do…buddy? We have to tell someone because we are gonna be working out here and…Geez…if we walked up on him …and he had the drop on us…hell… he really might shoot us. I mean he has to!"

Pat is undaunted. He doesn't think that I am being sincere.

"Look you need me as a witness…I can't help you if you kill me." I got his attention with this.

Using my counseling skills, that I had just developed, I managed to beg for my life. And for a few moments for just a split second, I had a misgiving maybe *I wasn't as funny as I thought.*

We finally agreed to write Memorandums of Record to our supervisors and leave it at that. You are probably thinking that we should have cuffed the bastard and taken him to jail. We actually talked for hours about what the crimes might be. Of course it is morally disgusting but for us the question is 'What was the Alabama code for dog rape.' I mean Alabama 220-2-345 or something else? What do you write on the ticket? We didn't have training for stuff like this. I was a

Geologist and Pat had a degree in Forestry. The law enforcement position only required a high school education and the modest 'on the job training' didn't provide any significant insight to handling the criminal aspect of this offense. We knew that it had to be illegal but we had neither heard about it nor knew of anyone who had written a ticket. Neither of us wanted to be part of the horror of our suspicions, or be a part of the shit-storm that would fall on this little town if aggressive action was taken.

Today in this 'internet world,' people wouldn't even look up about a serial dog rapist, but in those days it would have been shocking. We didn't want to be the cops famous for catching a prominent figure screwing a dog, and I know the town didn't want to be known as being lead by a dog lover.

I wish that was the end of the tale. After the incident Pat and I were still trying to make sense of the event and we drove down a road that ran perpendicular to the area where 'it' had happened. Up ahead we saw the old guy with his truck sideways in the road, he was calling the dog. *Damn!* I mean the guy just got caught and here he was in the same area looking for his date. *Unbelievable.* Years later, Pat and I could joke about it. Pat, trying to make sense of the act insisted that the old guy's wife was hideous. I am thankful that I never met her. I have heard about a woman so ugly that she turned you to stone…but crap…make you screw a dog? Lucky, the old bastard disappeared from the front table of the restaurant for about two years. He reappeared for a short time and thankfully dropped dead from a heart attack. I am glad he is dead.

You know, while writing this book I had dinner with a 'retired' Pat, and we were talking about old times when my teenage boys brought up the event trying to get a testimonial from another source. Pat got upset and ended up finishing everyone's drink at the table. He was really upset about the matter and I am sure he would insist that he has post- traumatic stress from the strange story.

Maybe he has ADD now…I wonder if he can get a 'crazy check' for it.

Bigfoot

I know Bigfoot exists. He is real. I have seen him with my own eyes and came within seconds of capturing him on my video camera. He lives on county road 57 just east of Dayton. Pat has seen him too.

Pat and I had many epic adventures but this tale is bitter-sweet. It was the last patrol that he would work with me. It just got too strange. Well, it was the next summer after the "dog lover" incident, and I again picked him up at the marina. He was leery about going on patrol with me, but the marina was out of coffee. So for the promise of a cup of Joe and a honey bun, he hopped in my pickup. *Never take candy from strangers or strange lonely wardens.* Since I work in the twilight zone somewhere in Alabama probably in the 1800s, I had to head to a rural area of the county to issue a coyote trapping permit. I had to issue a permit to some guy who was catching coyotes and selling them.

I apologize from departing from Bigfoot and this is a long story… but interesting and unbelievable… so please indulge me.

During the 1980s, many landowners became frustrated with the game laws of Alabama. You see, at the time you could shoot one buck a day, every day, during the season. What it meant was that most bucks were 'harvested before their third year.' In the first three years, bucks are struggling to put on body mass and under pressure to grow to adult size. This stress reduces the animal's ability to grow significant antler mass. Bucks are judged by their antlers, and there is an elaborate measuring system to judge these 'racks.' Studies show that the secret for growing trophy bucks was simply to let them "walk." Let them get older. Clubs began requiring members to shoot only deer with eight points or better antlers. This plan worked so well that most clubs couldn't stand it and were harvesting the bucks in the third year. Well the wealthy landowners and commercial hunters began fencing in their hunting lands with 12-foot high wire fences in an effort to protect these aging bucks. I am not kidding…miles and miles of fences. It worked. Huge deer were grown on land that no one thought could nutritionally support them.

If you remember that hunting season for deer is really only three months long, you can understand why these rich folks wanted to find other activities to fully utilize the recreational and commercial value of their property. Well, these aristocratic clubs began a resurgence of 'fox hunts' from horseback. I am not kidding. While the internet and cell phones were beginning to change life as we know it, you would never expect it but, in rural Alabama it was TALLYHOE and off to the races. The Alabama nobles mounted on quarter horses, thoroughbreds, and even mules would trot off behind a pack of hunting dogs. Yes even mules after all they were legitimate because Festus on *Gun Smoke* only rode mules. 'Fox hunting' became a popular and expensive distraction. The problem was that a fox has a valuable coat and has a strictly controlled hunting season. A season designed to insure that the species was protected from extinction or over-harvest. So this protection presented problems for the 'wanna be' fox hunters. Leave it to Alabama ingenuity…they substituted coyotes for foxes which didn't enjoy the luxury of game law protection. No shit. A haggard, mangy coyote would be set out and the beagles set after it. Off they would go on a 'fox hunt!' It was like a sick episode of the *Road Runner*. This new sport lead to the demand for live- caught coyotes. Someone had to supply the live game, and without fail this attracted those haggard 'layabouts' who populate mine and your communities. These guys, without fail, seemed to be lanky poorly kept males who couldn't keep a job. No. They wouldn't keep a job. Thin because they were too lazy to keep a 'real' job, and due to their only nutrition coming from alcohol, marijuana and crystal meth. The new sporting event was only seconds from becoming a popular distraction when these entrepreneurs began looking for short cuts. The 'character' of the suppliers coupled with the "big money" lead to the importation of coyotes from Texas.

If you have never seen a coyote, just imagine a miniature wolf suffering from anorexia and mange and smelling like a skunk. Rabies, a deadly disease for humans, started making dogs and people sick. Rabies is nothing to take lightly. It

21

is a terminal disease, and your organs are literally consumed from the inside out. Rabies makes cancer look like a cold. Well, that is why I had to provide the "crack head" trapper with a permit. The department was trying to monitor the participants in the business and get a handle on the epidemic of rabies.

I hope this was an interesting aside because we are talking about Bigfoot, not fox hunts. But in reality it is strange; I don't think any patrol which started on such a bizarre mission could end in anything less than weird.

This area of the county would be considered the hills or upland. It used to be farmland but now is covered in pine trees. It is sparsely populated and there are just a handful of people or "characters" out there. Well it was in this area that Pat and I were traveling. I was driving and Pat was just looking at the right of way. We weren't talking much because it was after lunch, and it was a 40 minute drive. Deep fried chicken with an order of French fries and fried okra and a fluffy biscuit dripping with honey tainted butter had set the mood. I drowsily steered the vehicle down the desolate country road. Pat made a comment about having some pears that the deer where eating on his farm. He thought the deer meat might have a special taste. That was Pat. He was either eating or talking about eating. I agreed, and volunteered that we should have gotten that piece of pecan pie we were offered and that we so proudly refused, like we were concerned with our diet.

I drove up a little rise and a figure caught my eye at the top of the hill. I slowed the vehicle. My eyes got wide…

"What the hell?" I said as we topped the hill.

Poor Pat…sitting there innocently thinking about little deer eating his pears…pondering recipes to prepare their sweet meat. With my outburst he turned and looked out the open window and was eyeball to crotch on old hairy naked Bigfoot. I took a deep breath and was about to bust with some crude comment when he paused, shook his head and then without emotion … emotionless …he turned to me and in a matter of fact voice said."Take me home."

I turned to him, "What?"

"Take me home. I want to go home."

"Why? What's wrong with you….I didn't do anything."

He was serious.

I replied quickly, "GOOOLLY did you see that Pat."

I was never without my video camera and grabbed it out of the door pocket with my left hand. I went to the next intersection about 200 yards from the sighting and spun the car around.

"Grab the wheel." I hollered. I tried to get the camera up and powered on.

"What are you doing?" he asked.

I was struggling to control the vehicle and hit the record button on my camera. I tried to hold the steering wheel with my knees but I couldn't find the power button.

"Hell what do you think? That is goddamn Bigfoot! I am going to video tape this creature. Take the wheel, Pat!"

Pat just shook his head and replied, "Here I am having a nervous breakdown and all you can think of is getting this on tape."

"Yep."

We came over the hill and I remember it vividly. Crazy old Max 'Pumpkin' Larkin, all five foot eleven inches, was standing butt- naked by his mail box. He had one hand and elbow on the box just like he was standing there in a tuxedo, all prissy and proper. He was hardly the male model type. Max was an old hippy with hair that ran down his back. He had a huge beard that went down over his chest, and he was a hairy rascal with hair covering his chest, back and legs. He was standing statuesque looking like a big hair covered ape-man, huge belly pointed to the road. The man creature was standing there proud as hell just giving the road the 'FULL MONTY' with a bush that looked like he had fur underwear on. In his mind he must have thought that he was a Calvin Klein underwear model. He calmly turned and started up the hill to his house, which was a one person camper shell. He turned and looked back at us. His arms were swinging by his side as he leaned forward and strolled up the hill.

Now I know that you have all seen the guy that jumps off the horse and video tapes that Bigfoot creature, the camera wobbles and then a black, hairy gorilla comes to focus in the frame. Bigfoot glances back and with its arms swinging as it strolls away. I swear that is what I saw. He looked just like that video except that instead of black hair, my creature had grey-brown hair.

Unfortunately, I didn't get it on tape because my partner refused to hold the steering wheel. The thoughtless bastard decided to have a nervous breakdown. *Some friend... insensitive jerk! I could have made a million bucks selling the video.* Honestly, I was only bold enough to drive slowly by the horrid creature. I definitely wasn't going to stop.

I am sure the nasty bastard would have run down the hill and wanted to talk or God forbid SHAKE MY HAND!

This creepy story was bittersweet because this was the last time Pat would work with me. Truth is that something had snapped in him. Enough is enough, and his vomit level was breached. He was done with the adventure. Personally, he was eyeing retirement and had already seen too much! He was also tired of writing memos to our supervisors. Truthfully, he was a professional and he really took his job seriously. And I, in contrast, was just a kid playing hide and seek and who thought he was *Batman*. Can't say I blame him. For him it was just another depressing footnote in the frailty of the human species, and he had already had enough of disappointments.

But for a cartoon hero like me it was just another bizarre day at the office...Mr. Freeze, the Joker...and BIGFOOT.

Rendezvous

You tend to become good buddies with the game wardens operating in the neighboring counties. The poor bastard is also hopelessly trying to patrol a 100 square miles just like you. A hopeless lonely game of hide and seek which is ninety-nine percent nature hike and one percent sheer unadulterated terror. Sometimes he is just a voice on the radio, other times he is the only one who is wondering if he needs to start heading in your direction to save your ass. They are a reassuring voice in the lonely darkness like a radio talk show host at 3 a.m. To this day there are wardens that I have talked with in those early morning moments that I have never met. It's 2 a.m. and you are out working night hunting complaints and there is no one around but you and maybe a deer sitting on the side of the road silently feeding on the winter rye grass. The deer is your bait for a passing drunken or high night hunter. Lo and behold there is another voice in the dark. It is your buddy game warden. It's comforting to know that there is someone else sharing your mission just 30 or 40 miles away.

Mike McNeil was my neighboring game warden in Sumter County. He could be one or two miles away as the crow flies, but an hour or more away by road because our counties where separated by the Tombigbee River. In the heat of summer, we would look out for each other. On his side of the river there was a boat landing that had washed away, and on my side there was a boat landing that was covered by a sand bar. Both landings attracted bank fishermen and drug dealers because it was a real journey to reach the site, and then a good walk down a steep bank to the river. I would drive 25 minutes on paved county roads and then drive nine miles down a rotten dirt road to get to the site. The remoteness of the site was attractive to outlaws. Mike's patrol was just as difficult and basically mirrored my journey. To make things simpler we would take turns traveling to the site. One day I would go to my park and check it. While there I would use the binoculars and "glass" his side. If anyone was there I would let him know that it was worth the drive. Honestly, if someone was fishing in this remote area you could bet they didn't have a license or were carrying drugs. They just knew that no one would check them at this remote site. Well, it was my turn, and there wasn't anyone on my side of the river but there were a couple folks fishing on the other side. I figured there were at least three fishing license violations in these guilty looking suspects. I went to the truck and radioed to Mike. He said he was already headed that way and would be there in a few minutes. I didn't have anything to do so I just hung around to watch the show. There wasn't anything I could do to help him without swimming across the river, but I could call for help if he got in trouble or simply be a witness. I saw the dust from Mike's truck and all hell broke loose. There were people running around at the top of the grassy park area. I did a quiet growl and began pacing around the truck and struggled to see what the commotion was about. The people along the shore of the river heard the commotion and looked up the bank but continued fishing. Mike, now breathless, came over the radio on the 'car to car'

I asked, "What's happening?"

"Pat …I drove into the park and two blondes where naked on a blanket! Serious now, I immediately asked "Mike do you need any backup."

"No." He replied. "They were thespians!"

"What? I asked. "Are they putting on a Shakespearean play or something at the park?" My mind is now thinking *naked actresses*. "I love art."

"No…not that kind…the kind that does girl on girl action."

I looked at the muddy water in the river and it suddenly didn't look that far across. *What? I was just really concerned about Mike's safety!*
Sadly when they jumped up it turned out that one of the hot chicks was a dude in a blonde wig. Now even though Mike was a city boy, I could tell even he was taken aback by the strange couple.

Okay …now I was over it and after catching my breath, "Mike, I said, there are four people below you on the rocks."

I watched Mike as he climbed down the rocky hill he looked across at me and grinned and gave me thumbs up signal. As soon as he started down the hill one of the guys dropped his fishing pole, took his cap off, scratched his head, and then started walking up the hill. His reaction was like he had suddenly awakened to find a fishing pole in his hand. "What...what the hell is this? He pretended he wasn't fishing throwing it down like it was a poisonous snake.
Too late. Mike had seen him! Sure enough he did not have a license.

"Oh I am just holding this for a friend."

"Yes sir...I see that…but in Alabama we call that fishing."Mike said with classic game warden empathy.

You know you might dismiss a story like this, but Mike is just not that kind of guy. After dog lover and Bigfoot, old masturbators, and countless standard sex acts that I have stumbled on in the woods, I believe him! I just called Mike to get the details and he said that I was correct. I think the thing that startled him the most was what they did after getting caught bare-assed and busy. When he went by again leaving the park, instead of hauling ass out of the area like most people would do, the two lovers instead just sat together on the blanket eating sandwiches and waving as he went by. *People have nerve.*

I use to tell everyone that if they felt like they needed a weapon while in the woods then they should stay at home. I want to publicly apologize to all of you.

I was so wrong! At the very least take a gun, video camera, and keep your dog on a leash …a short leash!

Chapter Two:Poachers

By far, the most rewarding law enforcement involved tracking humans. Now that might sound creepy, but I mean it in the best and most innocent of terms. To me, it was like grown up hide and seeks with the off chance that someone might shoot you! (and hopefully miss!) Wow…exciting! I would tell folks that asked about employment qualifications that we had to take a 'big test' to become game wardens. Those who took the test and passed where not offered the job. I make light of it, but truth is that most of the wardens that I hired on with were pretty dang smart. Obviously, for most folks, this is not a job for people with good sense or a strong sense of self-preservation. Okay after writing this I realize this sounds stupid! I need to give you a little background on poaching. I feel that if I don't explain my motivation for loving this type of work then you will dismiss me as 'A Complete NUT!'

Poaching, for the most part, consisted of hunting out of season, and for this chapter simply hunting on lands belonging to others without written permission. In Alabama, most of the land is privately owned. Hunting is still one of the most popular sports, and people travel to our rural state to participate in our generous bag limits. 'Bag limits' refer to the number of a hunted species a hunter may legally kill per day, or even per season. In most states you are limited to 1 or 2 deer a season, and that is all for the year. In others states, you must participate in a lottery to even get a tag to take a single deer. In Alabama, overpopulated with deer, you can kill a buck a day. Later you could shoot two does and 1 buck a day. That's 200 pounds of deer meat per day! Lots of deer and lots of hunters created a system where lands would generate thousands of dollars from annual "strictly" private hunting leases. A fair hunting lease might cost $1,500 a season. A couple of hunting clubs required a $25,000 membership plus monthly dues. While this might not seem like a staggering amount of money, you have to realize that it was basically for about 3 months of the year and primarily for deer hunting season. It became, and is, a billion dollar industry. Almost every inch of the state is leased out to hunters hoping to harvest whitetail deer.

Now, the facts are that Alabama is one of the poorest states in the country, with an average income below the national poverty level; this leaves most of the citizens unable to afford a hunting lease. This disenfranchisement of the average Joe is a phenomenon that has developed in the last 25 years, and even in my lifetime I have seen the change. When I was a boy there were no private leases, and the community got together to hunt deer usually running tens of dogs in what is called a "deer drive". In my late teens the method of hunting changed from stalking deer and organized deer drives to planting green fields and ambushing the feeding deer. The average guy cannot come up with $5,000 or $25,000 to hunt a dream property for three months. Poaching was on the rise. The fine for hunting without permission from the landowner was and is only $250 plus court costs of another $120. So for a possible $370 fine you could hunt priceless deer preserves. With a tiny bit of planning and coordination, many of these determined hunters never get caught and end up hunting for free. Ninety percent of the time they are caught by the owner who will accept the excuse that "I am sorry, I am lost" and "I promise not to come back on your property." Many of these landowners are simply unwilling to prosecute the trespassers for fear that the aggravated criminals will burn down their trees. And there were instances where large paper companies who had previously let citizens hunt for free suffered from the arson committed by displaced and disgruntled hunters.

We label these illegal hunters as 'poachers.' While most of these trespassing hunters are just opportunistic hunters, others travel hundreds of miles and use elaborate systems of drop off vehicles, radios, and support personnel. For me, enforcing most of the game law was a thankless job, but working poaching complaints was very different. Here, I feel I have to give you more insight because after writing all this down …it seems like the utter cliff of insanity to pursue these premeditated violators into the dense undergrowth and woods.

I know you are familiar with the cop shows and the typical scene where the supervisor is hollering at the hero cop.

"You are off the case. You keep stirring shit up. Damn it! I have the mayor and the commissioner breathing down my neck!"

Well, you probably just think that is typical banter for movies. Trust me; this is a scenario that is played out daily. It is just the nature of the business, and sadly over time most of the supervisors get promoted by not making waves. This is good, but they tend to place them in confrontation with aggressive officers. I mean the supervisors soon learn how to play the lip service to integrity, and in reality rarely perform well when you have just cited a state senator, or a large insurance corporation's annual dove hunt, or thrown the mayor's nephew in the county jail.

In law enforcement, the supervisors walk this line by delving out a special treatment or discipline using a different type of psychology. In the military they call it negative reinforcement. The supervisors can't say "don't write the mayor a ticket," or "stay off that hunting property where the senator is hunting"

So instead they say, "Pat …you were on the senator's hunting lease. Please write me a full written report."

Here is where a game warden does a mental Charlie Brown...*AAWWWGGHHH!*

What …a written report? A lot of paperwork and phone calls later, and you begin to get the message. Paperwork is dreaded by anyone with a game warden-type personality. Remember *Dracula* hissing at the cross and staggering backward in pain. This is the way that paperwork affects heroes like *Batman*.

Oh you can treat the rich like everyone else, but you are going to have to write a lot of paperwork and attend a lot of uncomfortable interviews every time. While you are young and fresh it is totally worth it, but as you get older and get 'whipped' you realize that I am going to get paid for a 40 hour week. How do you want to spend the week? Do I want to spend all day on a typewriter or go running through the forests? It goes right to the top, and any officer who makes a supervisor get up and take their feet off the desk becomes a nuisance. An assertive officer making a lot of cases will stumble on the 'big insurance company' dove hunt and arrest all the big shots from out of state. The big shots will tell him to his face, "You are going to regret this."

"No hunting licenses," pretty straight forward that's what the young officer thinks. No problem. You get a sickening feeling when you check on the tickets at the court house and find out that they have already been dismissed.

"Well, shouldn't I go ahead and file them before you dismiss them."

"Of course," the Judge replies. "I really can't dismiss them until you do!" You mentally hear the addition of idiot at the end of his statement.

Everyone involved will have to write a memorandum explaining what happened. All big shots will file complaints.

Well, I promise you that I wrote all kinds of memorandums explaining my arrests, and I am proud to say that I was such a 'bother' to my supervisor. Well the point is that when I was enforcing these laws I was self-motivated and stood alone. It was a thankless job.

I am not trying to make a point about tickets, and or integrity, but rather trying to justify why I really enjoyed chasing the poachers.

I totally get that it's insane to track after dangerous and desperate folks. After dealing with all kinds of violations and tickets, I realized that by catching the poachers I would get a 'thank you' from the landowner and any of the legitimate hunters. The reason that I have gone into such detail to justify my enjoyment is that chasing poacher is so damn dangerous!

At least the victims were thankful; they really appreciated it. And when the poacher filed complaints I could call the victims and they could talk with my supervisors. Then the supervisors would stand by me. It became very rewarding. For a 'pat on the back' or a heartfelt 'thank you,' I developed some techniques that helped me catch some of the legendary poaching clans. If they read this, they will cuss out loud and no doubt change some of their methods. Wait, did I say they would read? Never mind- they will never know. I do feel like I might be giving some trade secrets away but with the advent of video games like Xbox and Madden NFL, I don't think the poaching is as prevalent as it was in those days.

The Remarkable Parsons

The Parsons and the Lawsons are clans from Walker County in North Alabama. A rural county that is famous for missing the civil war due to the hills and rugged terrain, nobody wanted to go up in there to fight or try to find them. The area is also famous for the coal mining industry, and the land is hilly and almost mountainous when compared to south Alabama. The country is rugged and hard to travel. The people are fiercely independent and are known for bootleg whiskey, pot, and now crystal meth. Because of the near vertical terrain there is little hunt able land. These same folks are known for driving 160 miles just to road hunt or night hunt in Marengo County.

One night I had a Dodge Colt pull up, and illuminate the robot deer with its headlights. The silence of the night air was shattered as round after round of a 12-gauge shotgun began blasting my decoy deer. The lady and man had driven down from Jasper just to night hunt from a vehicle. He explained it in a very straight forward manner.

"We have been doing it since I was a little boy."

It was what they did. Unfortunately for me, on this lovely evening I was working with a lunatic game warden "rookie" who I will tell you only lasted about 6 months. The divorced game warden had been whining all night about being lonely and now thought the charming night hunting couple was a special freaking 'Hallmark card' moment and got all choked up.

"Gosh," he muttered. "What a great wife. To drive him around all night long while he gets drunk and shoots deer on the roadside.
Why can't I find someone special like that?" He sniffled.

Foregoing a firm slap, I instead replied. "Shut up, put your big girl panties on and write the lovely couple a thousand dollars worth of tickets!"

"Do you think you can write it out before your mascara runs and gets all in your eyes?" I thoughtfully added.

He gave me a hurt look, an indignant grunt and then whipped out his ticket book.

Training rookies was fun, and I was getting better… don't you think?

Back to the poachers. When I was first hired with the state I quickly heard the name of this bunch, the Parson Clan. Their season usually began by leasing a small house on a 3 or 4 acre home site, which they called their hunting camp.

This site is the center of operations in case anyone asks them questions about what they were up to. For the record, this is where they hunt. I mean you are talking about a lot that is a couple of hundred feet wide with a couple of shooting houses scattered around it. It looked ridiculous. I mean they could have shot anything from there shack of a camp. It must have made them feel legitimate, pulling their vehicles up to their shack with a small circle of green winter grass just behind it. A couple of feet from the trucks and shack was/is a small hunting box where they claim they hunt. I guess we could just call this 'the club.' After setting up the hunting club, they would proceed to walk right off the property and onto the adjacent property. After a couple of days of slaughter they would expand their operation by using drop off vehicles. They would drive a couple of miles away, or farther as needed, to find more hunting land. They should stop the vehicle and let a hunter out to wander the new territory. After dark, the vehicle would cruise to a predetermined pickup spot. Most average poachers will be captured when they return to the vehicle, but without a vehicle a poacher is nearly impossible to catch. I mean even if seen by a landowner, or even the local warden, most sensible people simply are not going to have a game of chase with an armed suspect. He is running and scared, so just how hard are you going to chase him into the dark, scary woods. A typical episode begins as the poacher gets dropped off. A game warden that had been notified would set up surveillance on the area in hopes of watching for the pickup vehicle. Well, the pickup vehicle would come back at night, and even if the warden was lucky enough to stop them they would not have the gun or a deer. The warden really couldn't make the hunting case. A trespass case required a formal notice before prosecution. It's a lot of trouble for a misdemeanor case. Truthfully, the crime lab couldn't care less about evidence for a Class C misdemeanor. Later after the 'coast is clear,' the team would pick up the deer or weapons but never with all the evidence together making it practically impossible to put together a case. And hell, the poor warden can't testify to what they were doing because it was dark. Well now you probably have a million ideas about how to proceed with prosecution, but you must understand that the hunting season is only 90 days or so and thousands of people are hunting. During this surveillance time there are literally dozens of calls coming in for the warden. With one guy covering ninety- eight square miles, it is just about hopeless without someone specializing in pursuit of the groups. I had watched my previous warden's struggle with this balancing act, and I came up with a strategy that was bold and hadn't been tried before. I told one of the troubled landowners, Rex, who was particularly troubled by this bunch about my plan and he agreed to assist me. I mean this landowner would guide his paying hunters out, and the Parsons would be seen in the fields and even seen sitting in Rex's shooting houses. It was very frustrating for him and affecting his mental health to the point that he was contemplating taking law into his own hands. He was willing to help me regardless of the cost.

The one weakness of these poaching clans was that they would shoot everything. They were hunting on the run. A deer was a deer…doe…spotted fawn. It simply didn't matter for them. Hell, they were already hunting illegally and taking no small risk to do it. (Every year we had shoot outs and murders regarding these type incidents).

I told Rex, "Look I want you to call me when these guys get into their camp. I don't care if it is lunch time. I want you to call me right then. And then and this is most important, I want you to leave them alone! When I get your call, I want you to meet me at your house. Then I want you to drop me off at their camp while they are running the roads." That was the plan. I would just watch them until they broke the law.

During the summer I went to the old shack on the side of the road where they were camping and got a pretty good feel for the place. I intended to hide out close enough to watch, or even hear, what they were doing and talking about.

It was the first day of deer season at lunchtime.

Rex hollered into his phone, "Pat, the sons of bitches are here…I am going to whoop their asses."

"Just give me a chance Rex," I replied trying to calm him. "I will be at your house in 30 minutes. Can you pick me up?"

He reluctantly agreed, so I drove like a maniac to his house before he changed his mind and went 'postal' on the hunters.

I hid my truck at Rex's house and climbed into his truck. He drove me by the shack and no one was there. He said that they had a small truck, and they were already running the roads. As he dropped me off, I told him not to worry about me, and that I would let him know how it turned out.

"Rex…I need you to get lost. Don't follow them. Let them hunt. I want them to bring an illegal kill here."

Rex grimaced. He just couldn't stand the thought of them killing even one deer from the road. He agreed to leave them alone and leave me alone to deal with the clan. I made him promise. It was a hard thing for him, and I saw him staring in his rearview mirror as he drove off.

I had come prepared with warm clothes and I was prepared to wait them out. Almost from the beginning my plan changed but for the better! I planned to hide in an old shed beside the house, but when I stepped into the dark shed I tripped over a large, furry body. Yep, it was a dead deer. As my eyes adjusted to the darkness, I could make out that it was a buck. Damn, a legal deer. Wait a minute. Underneath it was a tiny doe deer! An illegal deer killed out of season! Just possessing the carcass of the doe was against the law. I could charge everyone at the camp. It was a ticket and a "sure thing." Problem was I couldn't hide here because it was the butcher shop. I wanted to hear their conversations and observe their behavior around the deer. If I could catch them handling or watching the processing of the illegal deer, then I could charge them all with confidence. I could convince the judge that they were all complicit in the crime. I walked around to the back side of the old shack. It was a big shack but half of the roof had collapsed, falling into most of the rooms. Although a hunting camp, I didn't feel comfortable entering it without probable cause or backup.

I walked around the back side and noticed that the wood covering the crawlspace was missing. After looking around I quietly slid into the opening. Underneath it was dirt but other than some old cobwebs, it was clear of debris. I slithered on my belly over to the side of the house. I peeked through the boards so that I could see the butcher room. I couldn't let them get rid of the illegal deer, and I had to see them with it to make the case. I had just gotten into my damp little hiding spot when I heard the revving of a small engine. A small blue Nissan pickup truck slid into the gravel drive between the shack and shed. Almost immediately I heard the tail gate drop, a dull thud and then dragging sounds that I hoped indicated the arrival of another illegal deer. I watched them and listened to their conversation. They were happy and chattering about the shot they had made. They dragged the buck and the doe out of the shed and started making the cuts needed for field dressing. I didn't want them to destroy the evidence so even though I wanted to wait for others I just decided to make my move. I quietly backed away from the crawl space boards where I was peeking through and softly slithered to the opposite side of the house. I walked around to the opposite side so that they would think that I had just walked up the road. I quietly walked around the side of the building. They were bent over the dead deer, busy skinning. I just kept easing up until I was just a few steps behind them. I patiently watched and listened to them.

"I am gonna get this buck ground up into hamburger, one of the guys said as he worked the blade of his knife down the hind leg of the deer.."

"Might as well," the other confidently said. I have a feeling that this is gonna be our best year ever!"

"Yep."

And suddenly they stopped talking and started to straighten their backs. They knew I was there. I watched the big fellow tighten his grip around his knife and take a step toward the back side of the shed. I had my gun out.

"Don't even think about it. I am Pat Reid, the game warden. And you are under arrest."

They paused…backs stiffening.

"Don't even think about it fellows"

They both let out their breaths in a sigh and their shoulders dropped. "I want you to slowly drop your knives and take one step backwards." They dropped their knives and turned. They looked at me and groaned. I guess they were hoping it was some landowner or one of their buddies playing a joke. Luckily for me they both had wallets, and I asked them to take out their licenses and toss them to me. I picked up my radio and made a big show about reading the names to the dispatcher. When I say big show I mean I wanted them to be surrounded and totally defeated. You know I usually just faked talking to the dispatcher, but I honestly could reach the county jail by radio. It was a miracle. Even God wanted these two to go to jail. It wouldn't do to let them know that I was all alone in Bigfoot country without even a ride home. I made the dispatcher repeat the information. You should have seen their shoulder sag when they heard their names read back over the radio. I advised the dispatcher that I had the two under arrest and would be delivering them to jail. I holstered my weapon. I got the big one in cuffs and put them into their truck. I walked over to the skinning shed

"Bless my heart and hallelujah!" I hollered. The new deer was a 20 pound spotted fawn, a small deer but a large fine up to $1,000. I grabbed the little deer and threw it into their small truck. As I walked back to the little truck I carried the little deer with my index finger and thumb. I made quite a show of dropping the critter in the bed of the truck like it was as heavy as a napkin.

As I slid into the truck by the sour-faced two I groaned, "Gee I think I pulled my back out with that deer. Hehehe."

I thought it was funny as hell but they didn't seem to appreciate my sense of humor. I made the small guy drive us to the jail. It was a 20 minute drive and the guy's truck was on empty.   He looked at me cockily and said, "I am out of gas."

"Well you better stop in Thomaston and get some."

"I don't have any money," he replied. It was obvious that the smart ass was dunning me for gas money. Are you kidding me?

"I tell you what, if you would rather we can park it in Thomaston and I can call a deputy to pick us up. That might be best anyway. We can put some handcuffs on you too, and then my deputy friend can put you in the back. You know in the cage."

"Oh… wait… I think my fuel gauge is broken." The small guy remembered as his smile evaporated.

"No." I coldly said, "we better be careful and get you in the cage."

"I am sure we can make it." He insisted.

"Well, if you're sure it's no trouble. That's too bad. Riding in the cage is an experience that most people won't forget. You never get that smell off your clothes!"

We completed the journey to the jail in silence and without incident.

I had purposely left the other doe deer and buck in the skinning shed because I strongly suspected and hoped that there were others in their club. I could use the other doe as evidence to make a 'possession of illegal game in closed season' case on any returning hunters. After briefing the jailer, I asked a trooper at the jail if he could drop me back at the shack and he agreed. After waiting until 8pm, I was convinced but quite disappointed that there were not any more of the clan in town. I didn't think that I had spooked the rest of the hunters because my arrest of the first two had taken less than five minutes. I guess their statements that they were alone were true. They had assured me that they were the only hunters, but I just wanted to be thorough. I radioed the jail and had them call Rex and tell him to pick me up where he had dropped me off. When he got there I could tell he was disappointed…

"Did they get away? I didn't answer his question but instead replied.

"Rex lets load these two deer." When we got into Rex's truck, I took the drivers' licenses out and read him the names of the two poachers who were waiting in jail.

"Rex they are in jail," I calmly told him.

I explained about the spotted fawn and all the charges. I watched as the tension in his face melted away. He got all choked up and I really thought that he was going to cry tears of joy and relief.

"Pat, thank you so much. If I can ever do anything for you just let me know," he joyfully said.

I felt great about it. His relief and attitude were a stark contrast to the two skin heads that I had left at the jail.

When I got back to the jail I found my two prisoners were a total wreck. They had been in a holding cell separate from the population but not out of sight or range of cat calls. The other prisoners and trustees, mostly poor blacks had been complaining that the white boys were getting special treatment. To make matters worse, my prisoners had crew cut haircuts and looked like skin heads who at the time where violently aggressive to minorities. They should be put into the cells with the rest of the prisoners, the inmates demanded. My prisoners were transformed and broken. The arrogant cocky attitude was gone. They were terrified of spending the night in a real jail.

"Put them white boys in with the rest of the nee…gars." Louis hollered from the kitchen.

"Whew…look at that…it's the other white meat!" someone screamed from upstairs.

I filled out the bond paperwork. I charged them both with taking a doe deer in closed season and with possession of a spotted fawn. They were wide-eyed and shaking during the booking. After they signed the documents, I told them they could leave. They thanked me vigorously. They were so very relieved not to be going into the jail population. After they left the jail, the jailer confessed to having the trustees taunt them with promises of passionate night in jail.

As the two white boys walked to the little truck, they received cat calls through the bared windows on the second floor.

"There goes my sweetie?

"I love you, baby!"

"Come back sugar britches…I love you."

The prisoners had had a lot of fun at their expense. At the time there was only one tiny TV with one local channel in the hallway that joined the cells for these prisoners. This was just good fun to these jailhouse regulars. Honestly, I was glad that I had let those two sign bond and leave. It was just a misdemeanor charge, and it would be a crime for the idiots to get abused in jail. Whatever the taunting these two received, they would never return and no one else would use that particular campsite. The inmates should have received Scared Straight accommodations. In my years as a warden I only put two people in jail for game violations. I mean a fine is fair for a game law violation, but even I didn't think it was worth a sexual assault in the jail.

People joke about jail and getting thrown in jail. The old game wardens would joke, "Yes that bastard might beat the ticket but he won't beat that ride to the jail."

Jail is a horrible place. Now conditions have improved at our jail after some Federal Intervention but I can't imagine that the character of the resident is any better. I remember my first day as a Game Warden we had gone to the jail for lunch and to eat with the deputies. The food was great, but it was prepared by the trustees who are inmates who are allowed out of their cells to wash police cars, clean, and cook. I only ate there a few times because I couldn't stand the thought of what the inmates might put into the food. I asked one of the deputies about it and he said,

"Pat, we feed the food to the rest of the prisoners. While we couldn't really do anything about it, if they did something to the food then the inmates would eat it too. The culprits would be murdered or beaten to death by the others." I accepted his explanation for trusting the food handlers but I didn't tell him that I thought his logic was flawed. It depended on the handlers having good sense. That same day I came inside and one of the inmates was beaten and bloody.

What the hell happened to that guy?" I asked the jailer.

"Oh him…he kept running around naked shaking his weenie in the other prisoner's faces, trying to get them to fuck him"

"Big Joe, his cell mate, got tired of it and beat him to a pulp."

"Big Joe is in for murder, right?" I questioned.

"Oh yes…Big Joe will kill you but he ain't no queer!"

The jailer pointed at a doctor's prescription for Louie our amorous assault victim. It said, "For rectal bleeding, tell Louis to stop sticking things in his rectum!" I swear that's what I read! Even though our jail was a rotten stinking concrete bunker, it was the occupants that really made it the pit of hell.

So I couldn't justify locking anyone up for hunting or fishing violations. No one should be assaulted for a $20.00 fine. This was my opinion, but I am sure Rex would have preferred that the two skin heads meet their new husbands in jail. There is no doubt that their dance cards would have been full.

After my success with this bold style of surveillance, I was sure that I could nail any poaching campsite using this method. I was aware of another campsite that was used by these determined poachers and their kin.

It got silly because I would check the old shack religiously. I would ease into the little settlement looking for any sign that anyone was camping at the site. *Nothing.* No hunters showed up for several years. During this period, I had the opportunity to train a couple of officers and told them all the same thing,

"If those guys ever come back then I will stake them out." I would promise.

The officers would reply, "We have heard it before…yeah…yeah whatever."

It became the myth of the poaching clan. And of course it would be when I was alone that I would have to do it again. There would be utterly no audience to admire my skill at thwarting the determined masterminds of poaching. It was almost two years later when a club called and told me about some hunters that they thought were poaching. At last I would make short work of these shifty poachers and surely capture the masterminds behind the ring. Sure enough it was the Parson Camp. I was delighted, but when I checked the camp that same evening, they were gone. *Dang.* I called the president of the club that had reported the activity at the Parson Camp.

"How do you know it was from the Parson Camp? They are pretty smart." I inquired.

After pausing he replied, "Well, Junior came walking by our trailer in long red flannel underwear and boots with his 30.06 rifle over his shoulder. My wife saw him first and screamed, so I ran outside to see what the problem was."

"Take me home right now! Take me home!" she hollered and ran inside and started packing. Can you believe that she was acting like a little bitch…geez…she had a gun right by the door. You ever dealt with anything like that?

I thought back to Bigfoot and my friend Pat. I softly replied, "I feel your pain."

"I ain't taking her all the way back to Mobile cause she got shook up!"

He continued, "I walked to the road and had a conversation with Junior. Swear to God that's what he said his name was. The first thing I asked him was where he thought he was going hunting."

He laughed and said, "Depends on where ya'll are going. Ha-ha. Just kidding. Hahaha. We hunt Preacher Smith's old home place"

"I asked him how much land they had leased, and he said it was "a 40 acre block," but I know for a fact it is only 6 acres of pasture and a small stand of trees."

I thanked the president for his time and promised to give him a call if I had any luck. I presume that there was more to the meeting and that some threats had been issued because Junior and his gray-headed father left that same day. If they had intended to poach the adjacent club's land then it made perfect sense for them to hightail it out of the area.

The incident had occurred on the weekend, and I think that was the problem. Junior and Daddy had no interest in hunting when this club was going to be sitting on the main road watching them access their little lease. And it would make it nearly impossible to poach their property while they were there.

About a week later during the regular week, I made the long drive out to check on another complaint, and when I went by the camp I saw coolers on the porch and fresh truck tracks. I immediately turned around and left the little village.

This shack was surrounded on three sides by poor country folk who would sound the alarm and warn the hunters if they saw me. I drove home and got tooled up for the mission by putting on warm coveralls, gloves, and gathered equipment including my flashlight, radio, and ticket book. I waited till after 3:30 p.m. before I made my move. I parked about two miles away and cut through the woods. I guess if you're interested in the game warden's job then I will add here that it helps to have a good sense of direction. Of course it is something that gets better with practice. Back to the story, I parked on the northeast side of the property in an area where it was so thick that I didn't expect to find anyone hunting. It turned out that I was wrong and thankfully not dead wrong. After fighting through the briars I entered a little scratched out green field with a metal tripod stand. Evidently someone with limited funds and ambition had scattered the pathetic little fields in the direct path that was between me and the hunting shack. It was too late to change my plan, so I stalked quietly through the areas hoping that I wouldn't run into the two suspects. After a few minutes the woods opened and I could make out the backs of houses and single wide trailers that made up the little village where the Parsons had set up shop. I shadowed the yards and trailers until I was behind the shack. Just like the other hunting camp, this one was about 2 foot off the ground creating a large crawlspace. I watched for about 15 minutes…and listened. Finally when I was sure no one was watching or hanging around the camp, I calmly walked to the edge of the back porch and slid underneath the old house.

The house sat on pillars of cinder blocks and was about two and a half feet above the ground. I was afraid that someone would see my shape underneath, so I crawled to the center of the crawl space and leaned against an old brick chimney. It was a good choice because as it got dark the floor boards around the fireplace had gaps which let light stream through from the room above. I would soon find out that voices would also travel through these gaps.

I sat there cross-legged, calmly pulling cobwebs from my hair and listening to the sound of my breathing. I hadn't been there but for about 30 minutes when I heard the sounds of a cough and the thuds from footsteps of a walker who was getting closer. It was a hunter, and from the description it had to be Junior. He walked up the road in blue jeans and an olive drab old army field jacket. He had a rifle strapped over his shoulder. He walked briskly straight at me and leaped onto the porch. He went inside and turned on some lights, and when he walked above me dust fell through the cracks in between boards. Of course I was a little disappointed that he didn't have a deer, but I was determined to stay there all-night if necessary. They would probably go night hunting, and if I was lucky I could catch them with an illegal kill such as a doe deer.

About 5 p.m., dusk, I saw the gray-haired man approach, and I correctly assumed that this was 'Senior' who I will now call Daddy. He also went right in the shack.

Now I was really close to the guys. I was outside but the only thing separating me from them was ¾ inch pine floor boards which had many gaps. I was only inches from their feet. As they walked and stomped around over my head dust would shower into my eyes. I sat there in the complete darkness of the old chimney and listened. I thought that I was hearing things when the old guy starts.

"I tell you what; we got to put some more corn out!"

"Yes!" Junior replied. "It's all gone."

(I was giggling inside. Somebody pinch me. I would definitely return to check them for corn tomorrow). And then Junior said something that really got my attention.

He whispered hoarsely, "Keep a lookout."

He went out the front door letting the screen door slam shut. He jumped onto the ground, and now wearing tennis shoes he was quickly out of sight at a full run. A few minutes later I heard a rustling and then saw his legs march by and behind him stretched a thin white rope. Bless my heart he was dragging two tiny little spotted fawns. Two protected illegal to kill, and even illegal to possess spotted fawns. Two fawns that looked just like the one that Judge Ken Snow had taken care of. Judge Snow was the judge who heard my cases and he loved animals. *GOTCHA! OH. I GOTCHA!* How did I feel? I felt like a genius…I mean I had only been here an hour or so. Heck, it wasn't even dark yet. I watch Junior's legs march around the perimeter of the building. I leaned and stretched to keep eye contact on the deer. Well Junior had a surprise for me. Rather than hang the deer on a skinning rack out back, he instead stopped at the side door. I heard it creak open. He tossed the little deer inside and then walked to the electric well and pulled a water hose into the house and closed the side door. These bastards had built a cleaning shed inside the house. The butcher shop was completely hidden and out of sight.

Really a pretty good plan, especially with the search and seizure laws of Alabama. If this had been a home I probably would have needed a search warrant. I felt pretty confident that I could prove that this was a hunting camp, which wardens can enter and search. Even better I had seen the illegal game go directly into the door, so in a sense I was in pursuit. But it makes you think, and you really had to consider these things before acting. I patiently listened to them talk and get settled into their work. Finally, when I thought that they were busy skinning and away from their rifles I slid out from under the house. I cautiously eased up to the door. It was a wood frame with roofing tin covering it. A homemade door, it had a one inch sized crack where the hose entered the room. I peaked in and the Parsons were facing the opposite direction. I made a quick check to make sure that I didn't have any dirt on my uniform. I pulled at my hair trying to get the cobwebs out. They didn't need to know that I had been under the house. I gently opened the big door and they just went on chatting and cleaning. I mean I just stood there and watched and listened.

Finally, I announced trying to hide all my excitement, "Pat Reid, State Game Warden, and you are under arrest."

They slowly turned to look down the barrel of my Berretta. As they made eye contact, I looked to my side and toward the front of the building.

"Wesley, you watch that side of the house and the front door in case anyone else is coming," I spoke to my fictional side kick.

"Put the knives down."

I made Junior back up to the door and put his hands behind his back. I smoothly snapped the cuffs on him. The old gray-headed guy, Daddy put his hand to his chest and started breathing hard… grabbing at his right arm.

I looked him straight in the eye and cocked my eyebrow. "Don't even think about pulling that crap on me." I shouted.

Must have been something in my tone, because he went, "Oh…okay." And started breathing normally

I leaped up into the room and asked for their identification. The old man presented his driver license. I then followed him to the living room where he retrieved Junior's identification. They had driver licenses, but no hunting licenses. *How delightful! It just keeps getting better for me.* I asked them whose truck it was. It was the old guy's, who I address here as Daddy. I told him to get the keys and we went out the front door. Suddenly Junior started moaning.

"Oh my back," he moaned.

"What's your problem?" I growled.

"I am disabled!" You are killing me…aaargh!"

"Let me get this straight. You can hop off a porch, drag 2 deer out of the woods, and you can toss them into an elevated skinning shed. And then hop flat footed into the shed. But now you can't sit in the middle of the padded bench seat of this truck without back pain."

"That's right." he moaned "…and I have A.D.D."

"What the hell is A.D.D.?" I asked.

"I ain't sure but I get an extra $300 a month for it. It is serious, and that's why I can't keep a job or make good grades?"

"Please…give me a break! First your dad tries to act like he is having a heart attack and now you have a backache. You two are getting on my last nerve."
Junior stopped moaning and looked at Daddy, "You had a heart attack?"

Daddy nodded. "Yea…I did."

"Oh I didn't see you do that!" Junior said.

Junior stopped moaning, but I could see the little mouse of his brain on its wheel running just trying to come up with a scam.

"The handcuffs are starting to cut into my wrists and damage my joints and stuff." Junior added struggling to come up with some leverage to beat the ticket.

"Well you are already disabled so how much damage could they do? They are already paying you more than your worth," I coldly added.

His eyes lit up with that joy. I could hear his thoughts. "Oh I am telling…you can't talk to me like that Oooh...you are in big trouble."

Shaking my head and realizing that I needed to head the little mouse off at the pass, I said, "Listen up you two. You are now under arrest for several offenses. We are driving to the county jail. I know you guys have had speeding tickets before and obviously know that a trooper has to let you go if you sign the yellow paper."

I paused letting them catch up, or at least Daddy. I paused and looked at Junior trying to make sure that I hadn't lost his attention!

I glared at the both of them and stated, "I AM NOT A STATE TROOPER. I DON'T HAVE TO LET YOU GO WITH A SIGNATURE. I can put you in the jail and leave you there until the Judge comes in on Monday morning. That's right, the whole weekend in the Marengo County jail. A fabulous all expense paid weekend at our lovely jail fondly called the HOTEL HELL. Just you two arrogant north Alabama hunters and 48 pissed off angry brothers with no hobbies, and no TV. That's right- just sitting around staring at each other and sticking things up each other's rectums." I again paused as their expressions changed from arrogance to utter horror.

"While all that crap about being disabled might work in the neighborhood and not make anyone call you a lazy piece of work, I don't think the cell 'bull' will be interested in your doctor's excuse saying that your backside hurts. I am pretty damn sure that everyone's backside is quite sore in the jail."

Daddy started huffing and breathing hard and Junior started to shake so I added quickly.

"My plan is to sit down in the office and let you two sign a bail bond, and then you can leave on your own recognizance. But if you are going to need medical attention for heart problems, back problems, and A.D.D. then I am going to have to check you into a cell at our friendly little hotel. It's standard procedure! IT'S MANADATORY!"

They both looked at each other and Daddy blurted out,

"We are fine!

Junior bounced up and down in his seat.   "Yea look my back is fine. Hey look the pain is gone. It must have stretched out."

"Well I am not a doctor. I don't know," I said feigning heartfelt concern. "What about that A.D.D. disease stuff? I wouldn't want you to have some kind of mental episode."

"Trust me," Junior reassured by looking me straight in the eye …and winking.

"It ain't no problem."

Surprise, Surprise. What a change in attitude. They went from foul smelling, gut covered criminals, to foul smelling gut covered boy scouts. It was all "Yes Sir. Right away, sir."

An Academy Award, that's the very least that I deserve. I totally made this tale of horror up for these customers. If it had been two black guys, then the jail would have been full of angry skin heads. On the off chance that a rookie game warden or anyone is reading this, let me add this little caveat. THESE WERE SOME SCARY DUDES! DON'T EVER TRY THIS ALONE. IT WOULD BE SUICIDE. While they didn't give me any trouble after my performance, I had laid a whole lot of bull out there to confuse and disorient the two poachers. Remember me talking to a fictional Wesley. I also, without shame, twisted the squelch button on my 'walkie-talkie' and pretended to call in the two's identities. Although I couldn't reach anybody, and no one heard my radio transmissions, mentally the suspects went from unknown strangers who could 'bushwhack' a lone game warden, cut him up and dump him into a stump hole to the last subjects whom had seen the missing game warden. If they had known the truth, I would have expected a completely different attitude from the jokers. I would expect polite cooperation with many glances for an opportunity to hit me in the back of the head. It's pretty terrifying to watch people moving and making knowing looks at each other. A silent conversation between two criminals and the subject is YOU. An unspoken agreement starts hanging in the air like a puff of cigarette smoke. "Watch him…one mistake…kill him!" Will they be simple folk who got a hunting violation ticket? Or will my actions pull them across the line into something more serious?

Quickest way I know to paper train puppies like this is to keep them guessing. After I faked the radio call the old guy, Daddy, got quiet like he was thinking about it. Something wasn't right. Junior cut his eyes toward Daddy trying to make eye contact.

"Is there something you want to tell me?"

"Yes sir, There are some pistols stashed in the door panel and under the seat," Daddy confided.

I thanked him and located the weapons. I noticed that he seemed relieved as I took possession of the two revolvers. Junior was clearly disappointed. Maybe he expected Daddy to shoot me in the head?

I mentally sighed and looked at the vehicle. Hoping that there were no more hidden weapons, I loaded Junior into the middle of the bench truck seat and made Daddy drive. I had him back the truck up to the side door of the shack. I took the keys from him and told him not to move. I jumped into the house and hurled the two spotted fawns into the back of the truck. The hunters jumped when the dead deer thudded in to the truck bed. I climbed into the cab by Junior, and we were off to the jail. I didn't make any small talk on the way into town because I didn't want to give the two any information. After signing the bonds and photographing the evidence, I gave them their stuff and let them go.

It was a slow day for news, so I wasn't surprised when a reporter from the paper showed up. Pat Oliver, my little buddy, showed up and we both stood there with our "smart ass grins." Side by side we stood…each holding a tiny deer that could have been stunt doubles for Bambi. They looked like big rabbits.

I had a pretty good idea that the judge was going to take interest in the arrest because he had rescued and raised a spotted fawn.

It went just like I thought. The judge tore them a new one,' and they each paid almost $2.000.

But hold on, this story isn't over yet. The two jokers had to go by the jail to complete some paperwork and while there they had a cocky conversation with some of the staff. I probably would have left it alone, but Junior told the trustees at the jail that if he ever saw me again that he would kill me. *Oh! No he didn't!* Clearly, I was pretty proud of my sneakiness and cunning in the arrests but talking smack like that is just asking for trouble. As far as the "kill me" comments from Junior, all I thought was "Get in line Mother Fucker!" I wouldn't have pursued them except for one little fact. Remember the comments that Daddy had made about needing to put out more corn. Truth is that I hadn't even checked them in the woods hunting. So no, I wasn't done with them. But I wasn't a fool either, so I called Pat Oliver and asked him to go with me. Please understand that I use the term 'fool' based on my relative perception, not anyone else's perception or idea of a fool. Pat was more than happy to help me with some 'badass' violators. I had let the hunters keep their weapons, and so I hoped they would come back. And bless my heart, THEY DID!

The place they hunted was only about 8 acres, so I felt that if I went in behind them that I could catch them crossing onto private property. I also expected to catch them sitting or standing in a pile of corn. Pat Oliver rode out to their camp with me and a wildlife biologist named Chris that had been tricked into thinking that this was a quick trip for a snack. I offered him some coffee and doughnuts, and then after getting him back into the vehicle I told him that I needed to run an errand. Never take candy from strangers or strange wardens! We parked a few hundred yards from the property where I suspected the two hunters would be hunting and walked into the little area where they hunted. We spread apart over a distance of about 30 yards and walked forward through the fairly clear pine woods. We got to within about10 yards of each other when I glanced back and noticed someone. Dang there was Daddy. He had an orange hat on top of a green hunting cap. The orange hat was balancing on top and had a large crease where it had been folded in his pocket. Pat came over as we looked at Daddy's new hunting license.

I pulled Pat to the side and said, "No way we missed that hat....he must have pulled it on after we walked past."

"Yeah…I am sure that he did, but I didn't see it." Pat replied. Sadly, we didn't see any corn.

I asked the old guy where Junior was and he pointed to the west. We continued our foot patrol, more slowly, because I wasn't going to walk past Junior who wouldn't be wearing the required hunter orange. Sure enough as I approached the end of the property, I could make out a barb wire fence and a green field. I looked around and there was Junior. He was sitting on a 5 gallon plastic paint bucket among three trees. He was slumped over his rifle snoring like a bear. He was DEAD asleep. I turned my video camera on. I wanted to capture this image of Junior because he wasn't wearing his hunter orange. I looked to my right, and saw Pat Oliver walking up. I started making big arm movements trying to get his attention. He glanced up and I gave him a big wave. He cocked his head confused and I pointed to Junior who was still snoring and asleep in the trees. He looked in that direction, bending over and bobbing his head trying to see what I was motioning about. Then he saw snoring Junior. He looked at me and grinned and gave me a big okay hand signal. I then videotaped Pat stalking up to Junior. I was biting my tongue and snickering. It's funny because it was fall and the leaves where dry. It was impossible to be quiet, but Pat kept getting closer with each crunching step. Finally, Pat was standing right behind him. He gently tapped Junior's shoulder. Junior let out a high pitched squeal and nearly fell off the bucket and dropped his rifle. I was recording all this on tape trying not to laugh and then in horror I watched Junior's face change. It changed to rage! He had remembered he was going to kill me. He grabbed at his rifle and started to push it toward Pat. Pat brushed it aside by extending both hands and arms which pressed the rifle back onto the guy's chest. Pat calmly told him to "hold it, buddy." I hollered in a booming voice "HEY!" Junior froze as I walked up to him. He was embarrassed and pissed. I asked to see his hunting license and he proudly and confidently produced it. *Damn*. He looked confused when I kept the license and I pulled out my ticket book.

"Hunter orange?" He reached into his Jacket and pulled it out of his pocket relieved.

"That's great" I said. "But you are required to wear it. Please put it on your head now."

I wrote him his new ticket. Later there was a newspaper story about the big fines that he and Daddy paid. Sadly, that was the last of them. They never came back.

I called Rex. "I think I got the rest of your bunch Rex." I told him the name and he gave me their descriptions and I said, "Yep that's them."

During my time as a game warden that was the last trouble we had from that bunch and the last time that Rex would need me for a poaching incident. I would still help him with some other issues but nothing as serious as this clan.

THE BLUFF

I have to tell you that the old school game wardens were a persistent and patient lot. They would set out Friday morning and be out all weekend during hunting season. They would run wide open working one complaint after another. Wandering around, listening, and being nosey at the peak of activity would result in many arrests. In contrast with these old school wardens I did not have the patience, but what I lacked in that department I more than made up for with persistence and a long memory. I would camp on a detail as a last resort but if I could figure out some method to prevent these lonely wasted hours then I wanted to try it.

It was during Turkey season when I would get an opportunity to try a 'special method' or short cut. Right at dark, I got a call from a rookie game warden Michael Jackson. He was new to the game warden racket but had been a professional cop for 12 years for a large city police department. His call explained that he was working a mysterious vehicle that had been found on the Jones' farm. The owner had found the half ton truck that was locked up and left behind a large oak tree at the edge of a field. Michael had backed off and watched the truck for several hours. At dark a young fellow named Ralphy May Bullock came strolling to the vehicle from the paved road. He was wearing full camouflage but did not have a weapon. He had some lame story about the vehicle running hot and he was taking a walk while it cooled. He had to hide it because he thought someone would mess with it. He had gone for a walk, "a nature walk." Yeah right! Give me a break. Mike was frustrated because without a weapon he couldn't charge the guy with hunting without permission (poaching). The weak trespass law of Alabama wouldn't stick either so he simply let the guy drive off. Michael just stood there and watched the son of a bitch drive away. From his voice I could tell that he was pissed about the cocky jerk beating the ticket. It was dark now, but he felt that the gun had to be nearby, perhaps in the ditch near the road.

We both knew the guy had probably placed it close to the road and someplace where he could come back tonight and easily pick it up.

"What do you want to do?" I asked.

"Pat, will you come over and help me look for it."

"Sure." I replied.

I arrived at the farm a few minutes later, but it was already 'pitch black' dark. We went on to conduct a search tripping and stumbling around the fields. I thought I had a bearing on my direction until I walked into the backside of my truck. Damn this was impossible. The area was open fields with trees along the fence rows and the ditch that bordered the paved road.

It sounds like it would be easy, and we both believed that if it was light out we could find the weapon. I knew Ralphy May, and there was no doubt to what he was up to, but we needed proof. We gave up the foot search in the dark, but neither wanted to wait on the roadside for the guy to try to retrieve the weapon.

We both were happily married with small children and sitting by the road all night to prevent the guy from retrieving his weapon would be miserable and lonely detail. We just gave up. On the way home I sorely considered the cocky poacher getting the best of us. Yep…Ralphy was a prepared and cautious violator who had 'done the math' figuring it would be cheaper to buy a new shotgun than to have to pay the fines which would be over 350 bucks. He was cautious and might wait for hours or days to recover the weapon. Cautious…hmmm…I thought about it and realized that I needed a scare crow to keep him away from the area until daylight. I called a retired game warden, Chester Pugh and told him about the situation.

"What do you want to do Pat? You want to perform a stake- out? I could watch it for you."

"No Chet that is just too much effort. Naw," I continued, "I was thinking about taking my Bronco and parking it down the logging road …just far enough so that when a car is slowly creeping along the driver will just make out the headlight. Maybe they will assume that I found the weapon and that I am waiting for them to try to pick it up."

"Are you sure you want to leave your police vehicle unattended?"

"Well, I was thinking that I could take all of my equipment out of the vehicle so that there would not be anything to steal. I think most people will 'shit' when they figure out that it's a game warden truck and probably think that I am around it somewhere. You know 'fixing to pounce on them'! I figure that Ralphy May will think that I can't even hide my vehicle out of sight because of my incompetence.

"Okay I'll help.' he insisted.

I could tell that he wasn't sure about the plan and probably thought that I was lazy. But he was willing to give it a try. By the time I had unloaded the valuable items from my Bronco, Chester had arrived. He followed me about 15 miles to the remote area. I backed the Bronco about 15 yards down a logging road. If you were moving at legal speed, your head lights would not hit the Bronco's headlights or cause a reflection from the glass of the windshield. You wouldn't even be able to tell that there was a vehicle hidden down this road. We drove by again but this time more slowly. Now when we passed the road, you could just get that sparkle from the headlights and windshield. You could tell that there was a mysterious vehicle hidden down this road. Now, if you were an innocent citizen you wouldn't think anything about it. Heck, there might even be a house down that road. But if you were a sneaky poacher trying to retrieve your weapon, you would see a more threatening explanation. After all you had just walked that road and there weren't any houses or any legitimate reason for a vehicle to be waiting there. Ralphy and I had run into each other before and he truly figured himself for an 'outlaw.' If you are thinking that I am prejudiced or something .I knew his self-image 'cause his favorite shirt was a Hank Williams concert T-shirt. It was black and had OUTLAW in bold across the chest. Ralphy was a proud outlaw, and in just a few minutes anyone could tell that he had a pretty high opinion of his intellectual prowess. He clearly had contempt for game wardens which was aggravated by the fact that he failed the employment test for the job. He was a real piece of work and I always had a sick stomach after dealing with him.

I figured that a hunting buddy would drive Ralphy by the area where he ditched the weapon a couple of times just to make sure the coast was clear. After a couple of passes, if it looked clear, he would turn into each of the roads to see if a vehicle was hidden. He would be pretending to turn around. If he was stopped he would be all, "What's wrong officer I can't turn around on this road?"

Once he was satisfied that no one was around. He would then drop Ralphy off near where he had left the weapon. Ralphy would wait and listen as his buddy drove off. After a few minutes, he would snap on his flashlight and go pick up his weapon. He would then hide in the ditch until his buddy came slowly back. His buddy would probably flash his headlights to signal that it was his truck coming down the dark road. With this signal, Ralphy would know it was safe to come out of the ditch and stand on the road side. Once in the vehicle if they were stopped they could say the weapon had always been in the vehicle. In the dark there wouldn't be any witness to say it wasn't so.

I know that seems like a lot of effort but it really is simpler than it sounds especially when the poachers have their little support group. This technique makes it extremely difficult to make a solid case. I think it really adds to the excitement for these determined poachers. It definitely makes a better story at the bar, where they drunkenly brag about "beating the game warden." I know this is true because in another story we got statements from the players and actually used the flashlight of one of the suspects that we arrested to signal and catch the pickup vehicle. I'll tell you about that story later, but for now suffice it to say, these idiots do go to all this trouble.

I felt we had set the bluff, and as we came back by the vehicle Chester was impressed.

"You know, that looks good…real good….I can almost see you lying back in the driver's seat…asleep…hahahha!

"Yeah me too." I agreed, just happy to have all the help.

I went home with a really good feeling about the setup. I could just imagine Ralphy May and his buddy easing along in that little pickup. They would be checking things out and they would be really suspicious of every little shadow. They would catch a glimpse of the empty vehicle and continue straight on, slowly accelerating down the road. Ralphy's friend would say. "Dude, I am glad we didn't drop you off...he's waiting for you."

"Yeah, let's go back to the camp...we can get it tomorrow. We will let the game warden stay up all night and freeze his sneaky ass off...ha-ha."

Well the game warden was snuggled up to his skinny wife under a warm down comforter. I was giggling and dreaming that this might work. I had called Michael Jackson and he said that he would be there at first light to look for the hidden weapon. He arrived at the scene before me and waited for my arrival. I got there early too, while it was still dark No use just sitting at the house, I couldn't sleep. It was like Santa was coming tonight. I was just too excited! Mike and I drank a thermos of steaming black coffee as we watched the sun come up. He showed me where Ralphy had come up the paved road from his 'nature walk'. Mike began to walk ahead along the tree line that ran between the road and the huge green pasture. He hadn't walked 50 yards, and there it was a camouflage-painted Remington 870 and a backpack. There was a belt in the back pack that had a name on it...A big old redneck belt with a name monogrammed on it. Yep it read "RALPHY MAY BULLOCK," the bastard's full Christian name. What a proud mother fucker!

My plan had worked because the gun was only eight feet from the edge of the road. It was beside a large prominent oak tree. It would have taken 10 seconds to stop and pick it up. I mean, you could have almost leaned out of the vehicle and picked it up. The 'bluff' had worked, and my bandits had believed that I was waiting for them through the night. Mike, Chester, and I had all been asleep at home while the old game warden truck watched over the crime scene. I had a big head for awhile, and I had to keep reminding Mike and Chester that it was true that I was lazy but I was a freaking GENIUS. Well in this line of work never get cocky because you will get put in your place. But for today the *Batman* won.

Average Poachers

I have broken these next accounts away from the truly aggressive and planned poachers because most poachers are just neighboring hunters who begin to trespass on adjacent properties. 'Hunting without a permit' is the second most common complaint during hunting season. Our county, because of the excellent deer hunting, is a Mecca for illegal hunting and the resulting paranoia. I really enjoyed working this type of complaint because it was exciting and most satisfying. I was taught by the old game wardens to assure landowners that we would keep an eye on their place and they told me this with an air of it's too difficult. For me it was just easier to catch the guy crossing the property line. The patronizing promise to keep watching the place just wasted my time. I mean, I wanted to catch poachers and to do this I needed actual poachers.

I have mentioned the paranoia of large landowners and it seemed that no matter who they are they would have sycophants hanging around them who wanted to hunt their land for free…you know, to help keep an eye on the place for them. To do this they had to keep stuff stirred up all the time. I don't know how many times that I would get a call from one of these irate landowners.

"THEY are tearing me up and killing all of my deer! You guys aren't helping me."

After chewing me out, they would call the home office in Montgomery and complain. And then my supervisor would call and ask me what the hell was going on. After a while I felt that I had nothing to lose, so I took a hard line with the 'paranoid landowner,' and in the end I honestly became a counselor for many of these guys. I guarantee you that I deeply helped many of them. Here is an example of a call.

"Hello."

"I am Bob Johnson. I have called you before about this poaching problem…I have to have some help."

"Okay Mr. Johnson, please start at the beginning," I would say trying to slow down his thought process.

"Well I was talking to Ronnie, the guy who looks after the place for me, and that bunch in the camp on county road 15 is night hunting by foot. They have killed twelve buck deer on my place this year!"

"Mr. Johnson, can you give me a description of the suspect?" I would innocently ask.

"No." he would pause, and then say "I haven't actually seen anyone on my place. Ronnie heard about it at the restaurant."

"Mr. Johnson…have you ever killed a deer?"

"Well YES I HAVE!" He would insist.

"Was there any blood or hair…where you killed the deer?" I would question.

"Yes…a lot of blood, and handfuls of hair. Even bone fragments." he explained.

"When was the last time you were on your place Mr. Johnson?"

"Well, I go in the middle of the week and hunt every weekend."

"Mr. Johnson isn't your place almost two miles wide and the roads are made of post oak mud and red dirt."

"Yes, it is hell getting in there this time of year."

"Have you seen any tracks…4 wheeler tracks, drag tracks, gut piles, foot tracks or have you actually seen any humans on your place?"

(He is getting calmer now…he is a country boy and understands where I am going with these questions).

"Mr. Johnson, would you try to imagine the amount of dragging, riding, gut piles and blood associated with a group of people killing this amount of deer. Can you imagine the mess and litter associated with a bunch of drunks stumbling and riding around in the dark trying to night hunt your place? You haven't even seen one track."

After a pause he is much calmer.

"Well, Ronnie says I got a problem?"

"Mr. Johnson," I explained, "I like catching poachers…it is my favorite thing in the world to do…but to do this I have got to locate a track. I want you to understand that I am not a security guard who is going to go down there and sit on your place without some evidence of a poacher. If you can put me on his track…I will catch him."

"Well, I will have to catch up with Ronnie and see if we can find you that track. I will have Ronnie call you."

Guess what? Ole Ronnie would never call.

As a special message to all landowners, "What is the name of your douche bag that keeps an eye on your place and never misses an opportunity to yank your chain???" No answer needed or required; it's a rhetorical question.

Most of these landowners did have some limited problems. Hell, if you have a decent place to hunt eventually you are going to have an incident. Usually a neighbor would cross the property line and walk their roads looking for game. Other times, like during the Christmas Holidays, dog hunters might make a deer drive across their property. With the cooperation of the landowner, and patterning of these seasonal events, I would usually catch them too. They were simple and predictable. Many times, the landowner would know exactly the guy who was poaching. Know his name and where he worked. The landowner had probably even caught him a few times, getting madder every time but not wishing to sign a warrant on the guy.

The Bus Driver Who Shot Me

I got a call from the president of a hunting club who was out of Louisiana, and agreed to meet with one pissed off Cajun. His name was Louis and he was in construction. He would lease large blocks from landowners, and he made a good living entertaining influential clients of construction projects. At first he had the same kind of attitude as the landowners regarding poaching and how to use the game wardens. After I walked him through the mental exercise, he calmed down and realized that he didn't have the scope of the problem that his buddies where ranting about. He was able to focus and he got some very effective help from this game warden. After discussing his huge problem, we were able to narrow it down to a specific individual and field. The incident began when he called me, and I drove to his hunting lease near Saltwell. At first, he drove all over the huge block of leased hunting land, but the problem was I didn't see any tracks.

I said, "You have got to show me something, Louis …some evidence of poaching."

"Well there is one field on the north side, by a small subdivision, where the son of a bitch has torn the door off the shooting house.

"Show me." I insisted

We drove to the field and parked under the shooting house. Sure enough the door to the brand new shooting box was broken. The door was hanging by one hinge and there were cigarettes butts on the floor of the small box house. A lot of cigarette butts, and CAJUNS would never smoke in a shooting house because of the scent. Hell, they pee in jars so that the deer won't pick up the human scent.

There was no doubt that an idiot was poaching and he was a bold mother fucker. I walked north through the field. The field was 150 yards long and the mint winter grass was lush and knee deep. Evidently well fertilized and for the record this indicated that the Cajun had tilled the land, fertilized it and planted premium seed. This field had several hundreds of dollars and a lot of sweat invested into it. At the end of the field there was a stand of 6 year old pines about 7 feet tall with green briars woven through the trees…it was a thicket. It made an excellent obstacle to anyone trying to hunt the field from across the fence, which was about 40 feet behind the thicket. That being said…there was a beautiful little trail cut through the mess, it looked like a cow trail worn to the dirt with big boot tracks. I followed the tracks to a three strand barb wire fence. The top two strands had been twisted together to make it low enough to be stepped over. There was even some thread caught on the barb of the fence. This wasn't some animal trail. This was a trail cut for a big lazy "bold mother fucker." I walked back and talked with Louis.

"Louis you got a big, bold fellow here. And you have a legitimate problem."

Louis had his hammer out and was intent upon repairing the broken door to the shooting house, but I convinced him not to mess with it. I wanted it left alone. I wanted it to look like no one cared about it or had even visited this field.

Let's get out of here."

When we got back to camp I told him that I would work the property. He was delighted but I could tell that he didn't believe me.

"Louis, who is the guy?" I asked. He gave me a strange look, "What?"

"Who is the guy?"

He shrugged his shoulders like he was puzzled.

"Look, Louis, you hire all these locals to work on your fields and build shooting houses. Your problem field is located a few hundred feet from the property line and the guy is having to park and walk across an open field. If your workers haven't told you who he is then I know you well enough, and know enough about 'Cajuns,' to expect that you would have stormed up to that house and demanded the information." I stared at him and waited.

After kicking the ground and searching for birds in the sky he said, "It's Ben, the bus driver for the high school."

I started to laugh but caught myself, "So he makes his run between 2 pm and 4 pm, and then slips across the property line to hunt your field?"

"I think so," he said.

"Why haven't you said something to the guy?"

"Well I didn't know for sure…"

"You didn't notice the big yellow bus parking in the pasture over there?"

"Well, I did think that was suspicious!" Louis, you give Cajuns a bad name. I have a good mind to confiscate your man card!" I jokingly added.

He laughed, "Yeah, I guess so but I didn't want no trouble. I figured he worked for the county and would be connected."

"Well, I can understand you thinking that since he has a connection to get a powerful position like …bus driver!" I continued with a raised eyebrow and with a mildly sarcastic tone.

You can't really blame a Cajun for thinking this way. From what I have learned about the culture and the lifestyles of the people of his home parish, I know for a fact that a good hunting club is more important to him than a fancy restaurant or a bottle of champagne. I had just arrested the sheriff for Chalmette Parish, so I had a new appreciation for the south Louisiana politics.

Louis had been promised by other wardens that they would keep an eye on his property. I had promised, in contrast, that I wouldn't keep an eye on the place but would work this specific field and this particular subject. I thanked him for his information. By grilling Louis, I now had a clear understanding of the suspect and his work schedule

Now you have to understand that a poacher like this one has a schedule. He will be on your place as soon as you leave and just as soon as his work schedule will allow. LIKE CLOCKWORK. It is the weak link in his method that narrowed the job of catching him from a random 24 hour and 7 day-a-week surveillance, to a specific day and hour. One of the traits that a bus driver must have is the ability to keep a schedule. It was a Monday, and this was important because Louis' hunters were all back home in Louisiana. I knew that was true. But more importantly all the locals knew this. No one would be hunting on Monday, and our poacher would know it.

Louis wasn't going to hunt, and he, himself was packing his gear to head back to Baton Rouge. He had only stayed to give me the tour of his place. I promised him that I would work the complaint. It was already two o'clock, so I figured that our bus driver would be at work picking up the kids. I drove right into the area…right by his house. No one was home and more importantly NO BIG YELLOW BUS. I hid my vehicle south of the field where it wouldn't be bumped into or seen by a nervous stumbling poacher. I then crossed the field and used the little goat trail to access the fence that the poacher used. I moved west, and lay down in the thicket. From this vantage point, all I had to do was raise up like I was doing a pushup to see the crossing point in the barbed wire fence. I checked my watch and it was after three in the afternoon. I lay down and enjoyed the cool fall breeze. I fantasized that I heard the faint ringing of the school bell and the pounding of little feet running for the big, yellow bus. I laughed out loud and prepared to catch my big bad bus driver. I was totally relaxed when at four o'clock I heard a metallic squeak. I looked at the portion of the wire fence that I could see and watched the wire on the fence vibrate and bend down. I just smiled and silently giggled. I rose up and saw a large black man in blue jeans and blue sport jacket. He had a 30.06 bolt action rifle on his shoulder but was carrying a 12-

gauge pump shotgun. I remember the shotgun had gray duct tape holding the forearm wood stock on the barrel. I was only ten feet away. I was so close that if he had turned he would have seen me plain as day. He was gazing intently toward the shooting house. He was trying to make out if anyone was hunting. He was staring at the black rectangular hole which was the window in the wooden structure. He appeared mesmerized, and was straining intently. I probably could have walked up to him and poked him with a stick. He would have probably screamed and looked at me like I had teleported to the spot. I decided to wait, so I just slowly sank down into the tall grass and weeds which filled the gaps between the small pine trees. I needed him to finish looking and cross over that fence completely. I concentrated on breathing quietly and not moving a muscle. I focused on his sounds. He had to commit to the act. Then I would pounce on him, and with a big grin proudly give him a citation like it was a major award. I heard him let out a breath…I guess he had been holding it too. After a few minutes I heard a grunt and the thud of his footsteps as he crossed the fence. I heard him move into the thicket, his every step crushing dry fall leaves and dead briars. I listened like a little kid trying not to giggle as the sound of his footfalls put him farther across the property line. Finally, I felt that I had a good case for arrest and that he would have little chance of beating in a foot race back to his side of the property line. I eased up and quietly moved to the crossing point at the barbed wire fence. I started toward the shooting house, but he wasn't straight ahead. He should have been half way across the field and out in the open. He wasn't! For some reason, I looked to my right. There he was! He had taken a side trail and was creeping further to the right trying to skirt around the side the field. He wasn't sure if anyone was in HIS shooting house.

It is an eerie feeling to enter a 'green field' and walk straight on toward a hopefully empty shooting house. If it's not empty then you have just entered the field of fire…the killing field of a now totally pissed off hunter. I followed him and entered the side trail which was pointed due west right into the now sitting sun.   To his right and front was a thicket. To his left was a field with a possible hunter. Behind him on the trail was a uniformed policeman. Me. I felt he was trapped. The guy looked to be in his late 50s. He was at least 6 '2, and over 250 pounds. I was surprised when he bolted.

Glancing behind him he uttered a loud,   "SHIT!" and then he leaped into the thicket. *Damn!* I thought.

I hollered not 10 steps behind him.

"State Game Warden, you are under arrest."

He turned eyes wide and then charged headfirst further into the thicket. He quickly disappeared into the thicket, but I was right behind him.

Damn. DAMN!

To keep up, I had to listen to him crashing through the briars, and I could hear the ripping of his clothes as the green briars clutched at him hindering his escape.

Shit! I was playing cat and mouse with an armed violator. To make matters worse we were headed into the setting sun. I had to keep my head low to try to see into the weeds and briars, my vision was now a blue smear from the sun's glare. Not to be beaten, I hollered in a booming voice.

STALKING THE WARDEN

"Wesley, he is headed right for you!" Thinking quickly I added, "Don't shoot him."

As you know there was no Wesley, it was just my typical psychological warfare intended to mentally defeat him.

Right on cue, I heard a grunt and stumble followed by heavy breathing. I took a step forward but I couldn't see him because he was in the shadow of a pine that was covered with honeysuckle vine…he was essentially hidden. My vision was that blue smear that occurs when you look into the sun. I couldn't see shit. I knew that he was sitting down in the pocket of darkness, and before I could lean down to get my head into the shadow, before my vision could clear I heard it.

"CLICK."

It was the unmistakable sound of a firing pin falling on an empty chamber. *Are you kidding me?* I thought. *Damn dude, you are taking this way too seriously."*

My gun was suddenly in my hand, and I was aiming into the shadow at the base of the tree. Staring at the dark blue nothing, I heard the slide of the bolt of the rifle and the chamber as the extractor lifted a cartridge from a magazine.

I screamed "Don't do it! It isn't worth it!"

As time stopped, it became quiet, and not even the birds where chirping. After several milliseconds, I heard his breathing increase to panting. I leaned down into the shadow, and there he was, breathing hard with rifle across his lap and right hand on the rifle bolt. I looked at him, unable to see his blue, blurred face...

"It isn't worth it…it is just a ticket."

"Wesley, I hollered in the direction behind him. I got him. Everything is okay. Just wait there."

I made him set his weapons aside and retrieve his driver's license. He started panting hard and trying to grab his chest.

"Don't even think about it," I said with authority.

He immediately started breathing normally.

I must be a great healer. I can stop a heart attack by pointing a Berretta .40 at you and telling you to 'stop it!' I made a big deal about getting his name and information to the dispatcher. Again as always, he just withered away as Dan, the dispatcher repeated his information. *There is nothing like hearing your name on the police radio to make you feel small.* He lost a couple of inches and pounds as he gained tons of humiliation. Now he wasn't an unknown, but instead he was once again Ben, the bus driver about to get a ticket. It was over. He stared at me. He was a broken wreck, and I could tell that he was waiting to see if I was going to arrest him for the attempted murder. Without a word about the incident, I confiscated his weapons and gave him a receipt and a ticket. I escorted him to the property line and watched him cross the fence and walk home, which was only a couple of hundred yards. I could see the yellow school bus parked in front of his trailer. I couldn't help but wonder how his life would have changed if he had remembered to chamber a round in his rifle or simply use the shotgun that he had at ready.

I tried to make sense of it and kept mulling the whole incident over in my mind. I wonder if he figured that the shotgun wouldn't have penetrated my protective vest. I hope he hadn't thought about that. I hope he was just panicked and that he really wasn't a killer. I wrote him a ticket for hunting without a permit and failure to wear hunter orange. I didn't write him one for the attempted murder because it would have been difficult to prove, but I bet when it's quiet and he is alone he wonders how close he came to having a very different life. I know that I think about mine. Lucky for both of us he was incompetent cop killer, and I was one lucky cop.

As an aside, game wardens have been killed and prosecution of their cases weakened as the juries allowed and accepted that the warden had startled the hunter. The hunter had no premeditation or some other legalese that I don't care to understand. It would have been a tough case to prosecute with my blinded vision and his silence anyway. He knows, and I guess more importantly I know. And in this particular life my opinion is the only one that matters. He was a typical poacher, and some things that I can point out here might help in later stories.

Poachers don't like to wear hunter orange. Hunter orange is that same orange that construction workers wear on the highways. It is rated to be visible at three miles and is sometimes called three mile cloth. While humans can see it, deer are colored blind and don't respond to the color. More importantly, for a hunter like Ben the bright color ruins the sneaky part. They simply can't hide. I never met a poacher who was wearing his orange.

In Alabama, hunters are required to wear the bright color during the open gun deer season as a safety precaution. This law was adopted because of the high percentage of hunters being shot because they were mistaken for game animals.

Why did Ben, the big hunter have two powerful weapons, a shotgun and a high power rifle? Poachers have to sneak through thick brush and quite often jump game. This is a rapid instinct type shooting. Thus they carry the shotgun, which fires a handful of pellets which spread out and are devastatingly powerful at close range. 'Pellet' is probably not the proper term for the projectiles; they are lead marble-sized projectiles. As the white tail deer jumps up from tall grass or brush, it will raise its white tail as it accelerates in speed. The desperate hunter will fire at the flag and mostly miss, but sometimes he can track the rear end of the deer and hit it. The 9 marble- sized pellets will impact the entire buttocks of the deer, breaking the hips, destroying the muscles, severing the tendons, and shattering the leg bones. It is usually not a quick kill, but it usually cripples the animal which will slowly struggle to get up and hobble off. The hunter will pursue and try to finish the deer. So that is why they carry the shotgun which is basically a short- range weapon. As poachers like Ben enter field areas or open bottoms, they use the rifle with a scope to glass the open areas and wood lines. The rifle lets them shoot game at very long distance of up to 300 yards or further. At these distances, the deer won't even respond to their presence.

No hunter orange. Shotgun and rifle…it's a pretty typical poaching configuration. It seems odd to most, but to the game warden it is pretty informative and indicative of the method of hunting. More importantly, you won't be getting a warning ticket!

Chapter Three: Robot Deer

I guess this information might seem shocking to people who are unfamiliar with hunting but some hunters load their rifles into their vehicles; they put beer on ice and ride up and down the roads during the day and night looking for deer standing on the road side or in open fields. From the comfort of their heated vehicle, they cruise around the rural areas looking for an unsuspecting deer. Once sighted, they quietly roll the window down, stick out the rifle and BLAM. They shoot the critter. If no one is around they will scurry out and drag it to the vehicle and take off. It's bad enough during the daylight, but with nightfall they will move into the suburban communities or even the city park.

As darkness falls they will hold large spotlights out the vehicle's window and scan or 'shine' the roadside. Later, they will drive to the high school football field, and then to the city park shining the light around the swing sets and seesaws looking for any deer who thinks "I have got it made here." These hunters will even shoot the deer in the front yard of your house. Yep…you will be sitting down at the dining table and headlights will light up the window. BOOM, the little doe standing under the only oak tree in your yard drops to the ground. Seconds before the little deer was just innocently munching on the acorns and now it tumbles down into the brown crackling leaves. You watch, horrified, as pellets knock out a window and listen to the slugs bouncing against the siding of the house. You are stunned and reach for the phone and dial 911.

"Yes. Hello, there are some people here and they have just shot a deer in my yard."

"One second sir," the dispatcher puts you on hold.

Before momma and the kids can crawl out from under the table, you watch as the assholes back their truck into your perfect lawn and knocking over the fake flamingo by the mail box. You finally get your nerve up, and run out on the stoop and holler just as a big fellow jumps out of the passenger side of the truck and grabs the little deer and flings it over the tail gate.

The dispatcher returns, "How can I help you sir?"

You sadly reply, "Never mind, they are already gone. Could you have the game warden call me?"

Alcohol, guns and vehicles is a sport of its own and is a chronic problem. Well, in years past, the old game wardens would work the problem with utmost patience. They would sneak into an area where there had been night hunting complaints. They would try to find a wide area in the road and some deer feeding in the ditch. This is easier than you think, especially in our over populated county. Once a spot is located, the wardens would drive around and try to find a 'hidey hole', which is a hiding spot for their police vehicle. Hopefully the 'hidey' hole is close enough where they could get to the shooter and the shooter's vehicle. Finally satisfied, the wardens would roll their windows down, and cover up with a blanket and patiently listen. They would stay like this freezing their asses off, waiting for the loud boom of gunfire. They would wait all freaking night if necessary. When someone shoots, they would then peel out onto the asphalt road and try to catch the hunters red-handed. Patience and persistence would eventually pay off. The problem is that by the time you get set up, you have probably scared off the deer. And furthermore, the deer are what they call rudiments, meaning they gobble up mouthfuls of grass and then retreat to the woods to chew the cud. They would lie down and regurgitate the grass from a special chamber in their stomach and chew it again. You could never be sure if the deer where even in the ditch feeding while you waited. After enough patience, you would eventually catch some idiot who would pull up and blast the old doe.

Oddly enough, many times a buck would be seen at a particular spot feeding on acorns. Word would get out. Sure enough, if you could go find him, sooner or later someone would crack and try to take him at night. This practice really works but you had to invest a lot of time. There had to be a better way. At the time our department had thought about using fake deer but had come up with a two page guideline for using it. The old school game wardens just didn't feel there was any way to use a decoy within the parameters of the rules.

Well, I have to tell you that when I first started working during gun season, right after dark the phone would start ringing...

"They have shot a doe in my front yard can you come...No, wait they are loading it...they are leaving."

I would get 5 or 6 of these calls right at dark and then all night long. I would drive to the area but I had the hardest time trying to find deer to "sit on." The old school wardens would just stay up all night and sleep in their car. They would answer routine calls all day and then return to their stake out at dark. They would do this Friday till Monday morning. Needless to say the divorce rate was very high for game wardens.

I had a beautiful, sexy wife and two twin little boys, and I swear they would get on your nerves, but after about 15 minutes away from home I would be whimpering like a puppy missing his mother. If I was going to work these crazy hours, then I was going to catch these assholes. I mean these assholes had absolutely no regard for the law or the safety of people. I wasn't about to let a two page guideline keep me from trying something new.

I had a high school buddy who had also become a game warden and he was working in the next county. I had mentioned that I would like to try a stuffed deer. He said they had a full body deer that they used as an educational tool, but none of the wardens in his district wanted to risk getting in trouble using it because of all the rules of use.

I had made my mind up that I was going to try to use it. Come hell or high water I figured that it was worth a reprimand to attempt a detail with the fake deer. I told Wesley who was my partner that we should try it. He was doubtful and wanted to tell the supervisor, but I asked him to just play it cool. He had been in the military, and we had a saying that it is "easier to seek forgiveness than to get permission." Of course, he was just as frustrated as I was about our severe night hunting problem, so this helped me convince him to give it a try. After discussion, we both agreed that our fallback position was that if there was any protest or someone raised hell about the fake deer then we would just have the cases dismissed. After all, it was county court. We saw the district attorney and the Judge all the time, and for the most part they were good sports. Wesley was Mr. Personality, and they thought the world of him.

I finally got the deer from Allen and it was a medium size buck with spikes that you could remove. He was skeptical about using it saying,

"You are never gonna find a place to sit up a detail that will meet the guidelines for using it."

Taking a lesson from my father-in-law, I just agreed with him and moved on.

"Yes, you are right but I have a presentation to make at my kid's first grade class; they will get a kick out of the stuffed deer. You know, take a picture with it, and pretend to feed it. You know how the little ones will like it."

"Oh if you are gonna use it for education why don't you just plan on keeping it. I know where to find you if the boss wants it"

"Great. And thanks, buddy."

It was just as well that I sort of lied to him. I trusted him, but heck it was assigned to him. This way he would have some deniability if I screwed up.

He could say with conviction, "I had no idea what crazy Pat Reid was gonna try."

I had my deer but that was just part of the plan. Finding the right site is tough, and remember you are about to bait someone into firing a rifle bullet that could travel three miles. This bullet will pass through brick and probably come out the other side of a home. You had to try to anticipate every direction that a bullet would fly. Safety was paramount, and there was no excuse for getting someone hurt!

I picked a curve in the road with a deep ditch. I figured that if they shot from the road, the angle would put the bullet in the dirt right behind the stuffed deer. Wesley was going to provide the chase vehicle, and I was going to sit on the road side with the radio and tell him what was going on. Wesley, now a senior warden, had a 4-door sedan with a spotlight mounted on the driver side of the car. During set up he would drive by, and I would move the fake deer around until it was just enticing enough to attract a serious hunter.

Well, this first night, Wesley kept coming by with his light on, and I would have to move it again and again. I had moved it a couple times, and I was getting a little pissed. He came by, stopped, and shined it.

On car to car radio frequency he said, "Ain't nobody gonna shoot that fake son of a bitch. "

He abruptly pulled off.

Well, I was lying behind some trees in the ditch when he drove by again with his spotlight on the driver side of the vehicle focused on the decoy deer. I jumped up.

I was tired of his bullshit. I started stomping up to the passenger side of his car.

Now when someone is holding a 1 million lumen spotlight across the hood of a vehicle, it messes up your night vision and puts the whole vehicle in a black hole. You can see everything in front of the light, but right behind the light is utter darkness. I was walking up to the passenger window which I could tell was open. *Open so that Wesley could bark some more orders at me.* From my view, the passenger side window was a black hole. I was standing at the backseat door and was leaning into the passenger window to tell Wesley something.

"Listen hear you son of..."

BOOM, right in my face, a huge fire ball erupted out of the window. I thought I was blind as a blue smudge covered my eyes. It wasn't Wesley at all. It was two guys who where night hunting. The driver was working the spotlight out the driver's side window. It looked just like Wesley's spotlight because the driver was holding the spotlight out the driver's side, which is where Wesley's police spotlight is mounted. For a split second I just stood there blind and dumbfounded. It worked. *Oh God it worked!*

I stumbled and ran away to the rear of the car. I wasn't sure if I had been shot. Once I realized what had happened, I grabbed my radio and started hollering.

"Wesley they shot it..."

"Who shot it?"

"They shot it... they are here right now."

BOOM.

They fired again. *Are you kidding me?*

Wesley even heard it through the radio. They must have heard my high pitched yell because the car burnt rubber and hauled ass. They zoomed by Wesley and he made a power turn and fell right in behind them. They pulled over when they saw the blue light. He wrote them up as I hid the decoy deer.

I walked down the dark road and found my truck. I loaded the fake deer and then went to the jail. Wesley processed the two guys who hadn't even realized that it was a fake deer.

Remember this was the first time we had, and as far as we knew, that anyone had used it in Alabama. Wesley told me later that the guys kept asking questions.

"Did we kill the deer?"

Wesley said at first he didn't know what to say.

"Is it going to cost more if we killed the buck?"

"I called my partner, and he said that the deer got away," Wesley said trying to play along.

"Lucky for you," He added, thoroughly stunned that they could not tell that it was a fake.

I went in the jail and the dispatcher was surrounded by deputies. They were all grinning and talking to themselves. Something was up!

"Hey Pat"...He paused for effect cutting his eyes at the roomful of deputies and trustees. "Hey Pat...Did they shoot the shit out of that son of a bitch…Hahahaha." The whole jail just erupted with laughter, even the damn trustees were laughing at me. The pot-bellied dispatcher was holding his stomach and wheezing with laughter. I thought he was going to have a heart attack. I watched with gritted teeth, thinking I *have a cure for heart attacks*. He finally calmed down and lit a cigarette. He would take a puff and then burst out laughing and then start coughing and wheezing. I swear I have never seen a happier human. *Laugh it up asshole.*

It seems that I had yelled that statement enthusiastically into the radio as I was running up the road. I cringed and could only imagine what would happen if my boss heard about it. Lucky for me nobody mentioned it to my supervisor. I faked a grin and retrieved a cup of coffee from the kitchen. I pulled up a chair in the radio room. As the laughter started to subside and all eyes were on me in anticipation of my response, I put my feet on the desk top.

"Yes they did," I said matter of fact. "They did shoot the shit out of that son of a bitch!"

The jail erupted with laughter again. When Wesley got through with the tickets, he came to the radio room.

"Let's do it again!"

"Alright, let's go."

The night was young and we really hadn't planned on catching anyone this early. We both agreed to head to the south end of the county. There would be less traffic and less witnesses if we screwed up the fake deer detail. In the lower part of the county, it would be highly unlikely to catch someone who knew the previous two idiots. They wouldn't be able to share information about our new weapon or stumble around and mess up our new detail.

As we left the jail, the two fellows who had just signed their tickets were standing by the bed of my truck. We walked over to the vehicle anticipating a showdown over the fake deer.

"That is a nice deer"

"I wonder where you hit it.' The other said

I watched in horror as the shooter reached out and touched the stuffed deer on the shoulder.

"I was aiming at the shoulder."

Wesley and I looked back and forth at each other.

"Can I have the antlers?" The shooter asked.

"No, sorry." I answered as I climbed into the truck. I gunned the engine and nearly backed over the two. I speed south on the highway stunned about fooling the two.

Wesley chimed over the radio, "Can you believe that?"

We left the jail with a lot of optimism, but this quickly changed when we got to the dark southern part of the county because we had to find another place to put the decoy deer out. Remember all the rules! We had all the rules and safety concerns plus we needed some traffic. The location had to be a spot that hunters would be searching. And then we had to find a place to hide the vehicles. We drove around for hours. None of the spots met the criteria. Finally I found a spot on a long stretch of asphalt road where the roadway widened by a field. The only problem with this place was that we couldn't find a place to hide the vehicles. There was one logging road that was exactly across from the spot. It was a narrow road cut through a red dirt hill side that ran up hill. So steep in fact that after backing up about 30 feet, the banks where higher than the side of the vehicle. I spun my tires as I backed up the steep road. After stopping I started sliding forward until I put the parking brake on. I opened the door and squeezed out the narrow space between the door and the red dirt bank. Pressing my face against the sheet metal of the truck I climbed over the side bed of the truck. I picked up the little decoy deer and looked left and right trying to figure out a path to get the deer around the truck. Impatient, I pushed the decoy over the cab of the truck and let it tumble over the windshield and slide across the hood. The truck was already six years old and covered in dents and scratches; a couple more scratches wouldn't hurt. I followed Bo Duke style and slid down right behind the decoy. I made a quick look left and right making sure that no headlights were headed in my direction. I ran across the asphalt road with the deer on my shoulder. I decided to stick the deer on the hillside on the opposite side of the road. I was too tired to do any fancy camouflaging and for all intents and purpose it looked like a stuffed deer standing on the side of the road.

Wesley came by in his sedan and stopped with his interior light on and I could see he was scowling. It was late now, and we both were tired, so he pulled off and went west to find a hiding place. We sat there for about two hours and nothing happened I would gaze out of the windshield every time a vehicle came by and watch as the headlights lit up the fake deer. The cars and trucks never even slowed and I began to wonder if they could even see it.

A car came from the west slowly and then when it was about 50 yards east of the decoy it made a u-turn and came back slowly. The radio cackled. It was Wesley.

"Nobody is going to shoot at that fake deer!"

I grunted into the radio feeling down about it too.

"I see some headlights coming!" Wesley said as he gunned his engine and took off back westward to his hiding spot.

I waited but the headlight didn't get there.

I wrongfully assumed that the vehicle must have turned off on a side road.

After a few minutes in the absolute dark, I began filling out my weekly report. I was doing a rough draft with a pencil and planned to type it up Monday. The paperwork was illuminated by a pen light that I had clenched in my teeth. I was deep in thought when I glanced up at the fake deer. It was glowing! Now when you are staring into the darkness the light can play tricks on your eyes. Sometimes the whole sky seems to get lighter, and I don't know whether it is a cloud moving off of a full moon or if it is night sky glowing from stars. I knew this so I didn't react to the strange phenomena. *Enough!* I thought and decided to wrap up the detail. I put my report in my brief case and cranked the truck. As I started to roll down the steep hill I pulled the headlight switch on sending a bright light across the road which really lit up the decoy deer. As soon as I rolled down and cleared the high bank on the side of the truck I could see the headlights of a pickup on the road also angled to the deer. I immediately cut my lights and turned off the engine.

BLAM!

BLAM...BLAM!

A pause in the shooting and then the old truck spun it wheels headed west toward Wesley.

I hollered into the radio.

"Wesley, they shot the decoy...Wesley" I repeated.

A single reply came back, "Bullshit!"

"Wesley I swear there is a truck hauling ass straight toward you."

I pulled on the road and turned west toward the fleeing pickup just in time to see Wesley's sedan pull out from a side road and blue light the truck. Lucky for us, the occupants assumed that it was a major operation and surrendered without trouble. I also continued to the stop site and was now shining my spotlight on the occupants and making sure that my blue light was seen. This was more of my psychological warfare but it turned out that it was unnecessary. I saw that a sheriff's deputy in a marked county car had also stopped to help Wesley.

Pickup and meet me at the jail." Wesley called on the radio.

That tickled me because I hated doing the paperwork. I pulled off the road and quickly loaded the decoy deer and, once back into the vehicle, poured myself some black coffee. I slowly drank it as I drove north to the county jail, and all the time I was just grinning to myself. The feeling about the events is like the feeling when you pull a prank. It is very satisfying.

I waited at the jail for Wesley's return. He got there just a few minutes after me, and he had brought the suspects to jail. Two men and a woman were marched into the booking room. Wesley put them in jail. It took about an hour for Wesley to finish, but he never complained. I drank coffee and waited patiently in the kitchen. While drinking black coffee and munching on a honey bun I finished my weekly report. All my paperwork was done! Wesley came in and got a cup of coffee from the pot and sat down. Jesse, a deputy, sat down with him

"Wesley, why did you put those three in jail?" I asked.

Wesley stirred some sugar into his coffee and said, "Pat, we just caught the Barton and Brasher bunch."

"Who are they?"

"We have been trying to catch these two guys for years. Everyone from Sweetwater to Dixon Mills hates these two cocky bastards."

"Wow." I said.

"They openly brag and taunt me when I run into them at a quick stop or convenience store. They act like they are just kidding, but everyone knows they are the biggest night hunters in two counties."

"Yep they are some good ones Pat," Jesse agreed.

"In fact, their kin in Clark County were arrested in one of the largest commercial deer harvesting busts ever conducted."
I admitted that I was stunned.

"Me too" he agreed.

Although Wesley was stunned, he was sold! We worked the little deer for another two weeks, and we made 20 night hunting arrests.

One of the rituals was to call in cases on Sunday. On Sunday after lunch the supervisor would go on the radio and ask for a verbal report of hunting arrests during the weekend. The supervisor would total the arrests and then call them into the Montgomery headquarters where they were compiled into a report that was delivered to the department chief and commissioner on Monday morning. We, the game wardens, would all be at home or roaming the roads, but we would also be waiting for the supervisor to come on the radio. It was kind of like the score board report for the previous week. The others would call in with reports:

"This is GF 525 (Mike in Sumter county) one each hunting license and one hunting over bait, total 2 cases. 4 other counties would call in pretty much the same." Then Wesley or I would call in …"This is 515 …8 night hunting, 2 casting a light, 8 hunting from a public road, 8 hunting without a permit, 1 hunting without a license, 1 failure to wear hunter orange…total 28 cases" The radio would get quiet.

The lieutenant would ask "I am sorry could you repeat those cases."
Again we would repeat the cases, being extra slow and speaking very clearly.

"Wesley are you calling in cases for other counties or just Marengo."

"Just Marengo," Wesley replied grinning from ear to ear.

"Sounds like y'all had a big weekend."

"No big deal. Ya'll finally got me some decent help." Wesley added.

I could have cried. I was so proud. After all Wesley was my hero.

You have to understand that this was going out over the repeater towers. And it could be heard by a lot of concerned wardens, and trust me they would feel lower than whale shit. They would feel like they had been owned. I know this because I had called in on other occasions with a couple of cases only to hear other wardens call in 10 or 12 duck hunting cases. I would feel incompetent and like I had wasted the whole week. Delighted, I knew that the other wardens would be super pissed. Meanwhile Wesley and I would be high-fiving each other and grinning like mental patients. This went on for several weekends, and we became celebrities, in our own minds anyway.

Well you can imagine that once word got out then, it became ROBO DEER mania. After the other game wardens realized that we weren't going to get fired for working the damn device, the chicken shit bastards decided that they would adopt our little gimmick.

This backfired on me because Allen in Choctaw County called up and said "Hey I need to get that deer back." I said okay and agreed to meet him at the county line. When he got there, I hauled what was left of the deer out of the back of the truck.

What the hell happened to it? Oh my God this is fucked up!" he exclaimed. He was overly dramatic, but I could tell that he was getting excited.

I looked him dead in the face, "Well Allen. They shot the shit out of that son of a bitch."

He cracked up because he knew the whole story about my excited radio transmissions.

He picked it up and shook the deer.

"What the..." he commented as it rattled. "Is that buckshot bouncing around in this damn thing?"

"Yep."

He shook it again with a confused look, "I can't believe that anyone would shoot this fake son of a bitch"

I smiled thoughtfully, "Gee that's exactly what Wesley said."

Well, the race was on to catch every last night hunter in the state, but unfortunately it was near the end of the season. Pretty much everyone working began to look for a stuffed deer. I was in a panic because although it was a tough detail to work, it was fun as hell. I was always startled and surprised when someone would stop and shoot the damn thing.

I mean, we had really been getting our asses handed to us by the night hunters with 10 or 15 complaints a night. All of the sudden we were tearing them up. It was like that practical joke show *Punked!*

Unfortunately, Wesley and I didn't really have any big shots who would buy us a decoy deer, and they cost about 600 bucks. We were both too broke to buy one. Wesley had two ex-wives, and was working on his 3rd, and I had a wife, twins and a brand new mortgage. Oh my God...it was so painful to work without the decoy. I was so spoiled that I didn't have any patience trying to find a live deer to sit up on.

In Hale County there were two old timer wardens who had totally owned the arrest records, and they hadn't taken lightly to us embarrassing them on the Sunday scoreboard. These guys were legends and catching night hunters was their special skill. One of them was even a third generation warden, and he was connected. He had a decoy that next weekend, and it was painful to hear them chasing and catching night hunters with it. I just sat there in agony that first weekend listening to the radio traffic as our buddies were arresting night hunters left and right. I was determined to get a new decoy by the following weekend.

Wesley and I went down to the local taxidermist Don Capps and he had a huge full body mount without a head. I mean if it had been a real deer, it would have weighed almost 300 pounds...freaking huge. Now one of the rules was that the rack or antlers on the buck had to be a 4 point or less. The department heads didn't want any monster racks. I really think they were afraid of who would have been caught probably a lot of on-duty deputies working the graveyard shift. So it was just as well because the body of the deer didn't have a head at all. I mean it was just a shell laying in the attic shop storage of the taxidermist. Don did have a small head from a yearling buck. It was a small little 6 point that someone hadn't picked up. I took a hack saw and cut off two of the points making it an even 4 point rack. For about150 bucks we had a decoy deer with no motors or any electronics. It was just a stuffed body of a "pony" sized deer with a tiny little head. The head looked as if it had been shrunk by a voodoo witch doctor!

When we worked with the decoy, we were encouraged to put it where it was not visible from the road and innocent traffic. We endeavored to keep it off the road but sometimes the roads were so narrow it was almost impossible. One time when Wesley was checking my positioning of the fake deer on the road side, he drove by really slowly. Knowing that I was watching him from the ditch, he made a big deal about putting a turn signal on and then he weaved into the other lane acting like it was in the road. *Haha. Very funny,* I thought.

 Well he again said, "Nobody will shoot that fake son of a bitch."

He pulled off using his turn signal and returned to a logging road down the roadway several hundred yards. He hid his vehicle and got ready for a chase that he didn't think would happen. Smart Ass! I swear he could be so critical as long as I was the dumb sap running around in the dark repositioning the damn deer. No sooner had he got in position he called. "This is a crappy set up…it looks so fake. BOOM. What was that?"

"Well Wesley, a large jacked up 4-wheel drive just pulled up and shot the leg off the decoy! Please come arrest these guys…"

"YOU'RE KIDDING!"

"Wesley they are getting away."

After he chased the drunken guy down we both just laughed. After putting the drunk in jail, I told him that from now on I always wanted him to tell me how lame the set up was. You know a ritual or christening of the detail like when an actor tells another actor to 'Break a leg' before a performance. For us I guess it would be 'Get a leg shot off with a 300 Winchester magnum.'

Well, baby we were back, but I have to admit my $150, ROBO DEER was turning into confetti. I probably shouldn't tell you this but what the hell. Anyway, it was late and deer season had been out for a week, but we still had some areas, really rural areas, where we were getting some complaints. In these areas seasons didn't really apply; truthfully there never is a night time hunting season for deer, so I guess if you are going to hunt illegally, what did it matter. For us, the rut is the time when a mature buck starts going crazy and chasing any fertile doe, and it will occur as late as February. So one Sunday evening, I sat up a detail east of Thomaston. You might remember this area as Bigfoot land. The land of a lot of strange stuff and very little traffic but also known for big deer. Large bucks with wide spread antlers would stand the roadsides for two weeks or more in early spring. Seeing as I had the big deer, actually a small horse, I thought that it would be a great set up. I was determined to catch some of my more trophy oriented night hunters. I got out of the truck and tried to set up the *Hulk.* That was the name of our three-legged stuffed pony because he was huge. I worked on the set up for some time, but I never got the reflective tape right on his eyes. I wanted it positioned so that when you shined your headlight on him he had a green glow.

This particular night, his head kept falling over and this messed up the reflective tape on his glass eyes.

I would watch cars go by with absolutely no reaction. No break light. No speed change. *Nothing.* I would check on the set up, and the whole deer would have fallen over or the head would have fallen off. I finally picked up a small oak tree limb and used duck tape to splint it to his stump of a leg. *(I bet this is one use of duck tape that you never imagined!)* I tied the freakishly small head with a piece of radio wire. In an effort to compensate for the shabby look, I upgraded the eyes with some of that red reflective plastic from a broken tail-light cover I found on the road. I was still disappointed because with the taped leg and the crazy angle it was standing, I hadn't gotten the head in a position where the eyes would meet light from the road. I was trying to make the eyes light up as some vehicles came down the roadway.

Frustrated, I left it at that because a vehicle was slowly approaching, and I was simply tired of messing with the scene. I dove across the road and lay in the ditch. Whoever it was, in my opinion, was definitely looking for deer. The vehicle stopped as soon as it got alongside the decoy. It was a van. A Dodge minivan just like the soccer moms uses to ferry the team to games. *This should be interesting*, I thought to myself. I waited and then I heard the large sliding door quietly slide open. I waited for the bang. I held my breath and tried not to giggle. Instead I heard voices of children talking,   "Oh...aw...look at the deer."

I heard a little girl's voice, "Look he has a hurt leg."

My duck tape must have blown off, and I imagined the big buck tittering balancing on three legs. As I got up to run the family off, a gust of wind nearly blew me down and I grabbed my cap before it sailed off my head.. The quiet of the night was broken with the sound of little screaming voices. I heard the van door slam shut. I could still hear the screams as the minivan laid rubber getting out of there. I ran across the road and what I saw was creepy...creepy as hell. The wind had blown the head off the decoy and it was swinging in the breeze. And, oh yeah, now the eyes were glowing blood red. Finally, they were glowing just like an evil demon which reminded me of that house in Amityville Horror. I quickly grabbed the large creepy decoy and ran back across the road and put it in the back of my truck. I laid some of my own rubber getting out of the area, just in case the family came back with witnesses, and truthfully, I have to admit I got a 'creeped-out' feeling too. I doubt that the family ever went looking for deer at night again. I did get wind about a devil deer some years later, but I hope none of the kids needed therapy. I was only too glad to call it a night and happily wrap the detail.

Part of the law enforcement effort is to prevent the acts and educate the public in order to deter night hunting. I laughed to myself as I drove home, I would call the detail a success. Successful and weird!

Tow Truck for a Tow Truck

You can't imagine the queer shit that is going to happen when seriously tricky wardens continue to pull these little stunts for drunken redneck night hunters. I mean we have drunken rednecks shooting high-powered rifles into our willing and available target and then hauling ass in 'wobbly' high speed chases. We have the most 'over the top' enforcement details which placed us on a collision course with some of the most drunk, most redneck, and most ignorant characters imaginable.

Some of the most ridiculous stuff happened when I worked with a buddy named Kevin McKinstry. It seemed that every time he got in the vehicle we got into some ridiculous stuff. Now, writing this down, I realize that in these work details Pat, Wesley, Joel and now Kevin all ran into some silly and strange stuff while working with me. I think that I am about to have an…epiphany. *Maybe it was me? Naw.*

One of the first times Kevin and I worked together we sat up a detail south of Putnam, just off of highway 69. (For the record a 'detail' would be a fancy word for any mission that we attempted.) Kevin and I sat the deer in a clearing near the major road. Wesley and Deputy Mason would be in a sedan just north of us and would be the primary chase vehicle. They were in a sedan and could easily outrun most vehicles. We would follow in my slower 4-wheel drive pickup as back up, just in case the fleeing subject went into the woods or off-road. We backed the pickup into our little 'hidey hole' and could see the traffic on the road by watching the headlights and tail-lights as they passed along the road which was separated from us by a thin curtain of pines. We had just poured a steaming cup of coffee and were going to get into some powerful bullshit when we heard a large vehicle slow down. We couldn't make it out but from the sound we imagined that it was a large commercial truck or '18 wheeler.' Sure enough, we could tell by the choking engine that it had seen the three legged deer (this time head firmly attached with Velcro and eyes reflecting an innocent light green). When they came by the opening, we couldn't tell what kind of vehicle it was, but it had at least 20 little yellow lights behind the cab, just dotting along the side for 40 feet or more. For heaven's sake, it looked from the lights like it was a big RV, mobile home or a trailer. For a split second I had a horrific premonition of someone's brand new single-wide trailer not being delivered because some dumbass of a driver jack knifed it in the middle of the road at 1a.m. I shuddered to think of the multiple car pileups that would occur and could see Kevin and me talking to ABC News about my opinion of the multiple car pileups.

"Pilot error I think," I would say while staring innocently and blankly into the camera. Then I would quietly side step out of the area as the drunken driver began to recount the "demon deer that he shot five times with buckshot but just wouldn't die! Fortunately the large vehicle continued on down the road.

"He probably just thought the deer was going to run out in front of his truck." I said to Kevin, while exhaling a deep breath of relief.

"He probably thought it was going to hop out in the road on its three legs and tear up his grill!" offered Kevin.

Smart ass. I thought. Ignoring my assistant's attempt at humor, I was truly relieved that the huge rig had a competent driver who didn't night hunt!

Well, three minutes later we see lights coming from the opposite direction. The vehicle was coming slow. Very slow. It was definitely too damn slow to be innocent. The lights began to light up the road directly in front of us and as the cab passes we see the long familiar line of yellow side lamps. Kevin looks at me with his jaw dropped.

I look at Kevin with my jaw a-gape, and we say simultaneously, "NO WAY!" We both continue mumbling.

Kevin is saying, "No way...No way…No way."
I join the babble repeating,

"Shit...shit…shit…oh… shit," as my vision of the terrible 50 car pileup returns.

I listened in horror to the sound of vehicle rolling to a stop.

"Shit, shit…shit."

We both held our breath. BLAM...BLAM…BLAM…and BLAM. The determined driver shot until he must have been out of ammo. The stupid son of a bitch had obviously been gone for three minutes trying to find a place to turn the big rig around.

I hollered to Wesley on the radio. "Come get him Wesley"

"WHO?" Wesley asked.

"A semi-truck just pulled over and shot the decoy." I continued advising Wesley as we peeled out onto the black top to pursue the huge vehicle.

"Yea right!" Wesley replied always assuming that I was pulling his leg.

I handed the mike to Kevin. "Wesley, he ain't kidding. A freaking '18 wheeler' and trailer just shot the decoy."

Wesley, who hadn't even put the window down, who hadn't even heard the shot, and who was totally confused, pulled out and attempted to block both of the traffic lanes. Poor Wesley, he pulled out like a drunk stumbling into traffic. He later told me he thought when he saw the lights that he was going to get run over by a transfer truck.

Kevin and I watched in horror as the truck tried to ram Wesley. Wesley dodged by backing up. His tires were screaming and churning up steam and smoke. The big truck missed and ran off the road. Well. The driver or 'pilot' of the truck was determined not to get caught and flew into the ditch. He wasn't about to give up and he continued by racing in the ditch alongside the road. Wesley punched the accelerator, and then he made a powerful, dramatic U-turn. It was surreal watching the big truck fishtailing in the ditch and plowing through mail boxes. Wesley kept his sedan right alongside, preventing the guy from getting back up on the asphalt. It was like that race scene in *Grease* where the guy was trying to ram John Travolta's car in the big race.

In our vehicle the babble had changed from   "Oh shit" to "oh my God. I can't believe this is happening."

I pulled off the road beside the decoy and opened the door hard, knocking the decoy over. I couldn't leave the fake deer standing without police protection…there might be more insane truck drivers. Punching the accelerator to the floor I joined the mad chase following behind the two vehicles. Now with my headlights illuminating the racing vehicles we finally got a look at the violators. The 'pilot' was driving one of those tow trucks that you see in a beach towns or that the repo men use. It has a large cab just a little smaller than a semi truck's cab and just behind there is a large flat bed that can be inclined to the ground. Once the flat bed is inclined, a large winch pulls your vehicle onto the back. Unloaded it looks like a 30 foot long flatbed. What was really weird is that at the time the fine for night hunting was around 250 dollars, but this truck was worth 80,000 dollars. You can really appreciate mental competency of the idiot driving it if you could see it bouncing in the ditch and plowing over mailboxes and their posts.

Obviously desperate, the fool turns hard to the left trying to get onto the road whatever the cost. Avoiding a near collision Wesley pulled away and surrendered the road. The chase continued north on the asphalt road. We followed Wesley as he chased the hunter at speeds just under 100 miles per hour. I heard a click and noticed Kevin unhooking his seatbelt.

"Dude you need to put that back on." I suggested.

Kevin never looked up as he grabbed his bullet proof vest and pulled it over his head.

"This guy is crazy…this is different."

I laughed, "I am pretty sure he is out of bullets."

"Mmmphf." He grunted as he located his 18 inch black metal flashlight, which was also useful as a club. He struck it in the palm of his hand. Satisfied that he was ready for battle he clipped his seat belt back on.

In an effort to escape from Wesley's four- door car, the tow truck turned onto a narrow dirt road. Wesley followed closely but soon became covered in orange road dust. We were far enough back to get a full view of the chase as the big rig began fishtailing across the road. The road dirt and dust bellowed behind the truck, and Wesley's green car was totally obscured in the cloud. Like most unimproved roads, this dirt road twisted and turned as the makers looked for the sturdiest path to cut the road. The flatbed of the truck would fishtail across both lanes as the driver took the curves too fast for the loose gravel to hold. I again had a vision of death, imagining that a family coming home from church would enter the curve from the opposite direction. They would meet the flatbed of the truck moving at 70 mph like a lawnmower blade. I was sure that if it was a small car, the flatbed would shear off the top of the unfortunate vehicle.

It was horrible. I grabbed the mike to try to make Wesley back off the idiot, but Wesley called first. "Stay back Pat, this guy is crazy."
I double clicked my mike which was our code for 'roger.'

The chase seemed endless, but the whole distance covered was only about 9 miles. It ended at a Y intersection when the driver was forced to pick left or right. It proved to be too much of an intellectual challenge, and we watched as the huge truck split the difference. The truck smashed through a stop sign like it was made of card board; the vehicle traveled 20 feet into the air and landed with a loud thud, and the front wheels splayed outward like the axle was broken. I drove past the wreck and made a U turn, placing the light from my headlights on the east side of the accident scene. It was a tremendous wreck and the occupants should have been thrown through the windshield. Instead I was impressed when the driver and the passenger jumped out and started running into the bushes. Both doors opened on the wrecked truck and an avalanche of beer cans preempted the exit of the occupants.

The driver ran head first into Wesley, who must have played football because he placed his forehead into the chest of the big guy. It was the prettiest tackle I have ever seen. If you have played football then you have seen guys who get hit hard and lose their breath. They panic and start howling...uuuugghhhh!

This guy was struggling to get air.

I bet Wesley's high school coach would have been proud. Naw, a true southern coach would say..." Yea Knapp if you had hit like that when you played...we would have won state!"

Wesley was busy rolling the howler over to put handcuffs on him. And Kevin chased after Deputy Mason, who was tracking the passenger who had headed to the woods. It was funny because the skinny guy hit a patch of kudzu and got all hung up. He would run a few steps and then get pulled back by the vines, and he looked like a running dog on a short leash. Bill pounced on the guy, but the guy was still determined and tried to get up, only to be swatted back down with a forearm to the forehead. It was clear that these cops had really benefited from football because I am sure that I didn't have a class at the academy using a three-point tackle or forearm swipe. I guess this is what the old guys mean when they say   "We don't go by the book."
Obviously they go by the book, but it is the high school coach's secret play book!

Kevin was assisting Bill, and I went to the cabin of the truck to turn off its engine which was still revving and smoking. I looked in the cab.

"Wesley there is a little kid in the truck," I hollered.

Sure enough, there was an eight year old kid in the middle of the bench seat. His hair was greased down and combed perfect. He just sat there, bravely smoking a cigarette. I took a step back and scratched my head. You have to understand that although this takes a couple of hundred words to explain, in reality the whole ridiculous episode probably lasted a handful of minutes. I just starred at the kid, waiting for the old timers to get through packaging the two adults into the back seat of the sedan.

Bill came by with a passenger who was a 28 year-old skinny guy with unkempt hair. He smelled like shit. I first thought that he had soiled himself, but after we got him back to jail it was clear that he hadn't bathed in weeks. We later found out that he was homeless. I hate to say it but he looked like a typical homeless half-starved crystal meth addict. Kevin came up and saw the kid.

"What are we going to do with this guy?" I asked.

"I don't know," Kevin replied, obviously disappointed.

After all he had put on his vest and flashlight, but there wasn't any gunfire and he didn't even get to hit anyone with his new flashlight.

"I wonder what they were running so hard and desperately for," I asked Kevin. Kevin opened his mouth to reply but was interrupted by *Fonzy* junior. The kid blew a huge breath of smoke out.

"The chicken shits didn't want you to find their dope in the glove box." I leaned in and opened the glove box, and sure enough there was a bag of marijuana.

"Slim there is on parole for drugs and doesn't want to go back to jail," the kid informed us while making a fist and punching it forward, which for the record is the universal sign for "getting ass raped in jail."

"Bob," he continued by motioning to the driver, "has his driver's license revoked for Driving under the influence. And he don't want to go back to jail,"

Again he made the same sign with his fist.

Kevin laughed, "Yeah, I guess I can't blame em' for running so hard!"

Wesley, who had finished with the two adults, came over to the car. He took one look at the kid and snatched the cigarette out of his mouth. He grabbed the boy and lifted him out of the cab.

"Boy, I ought to whoop your ass."

You have to understand that Wesley was the only person in our gang who had teenage kids. You would have thought that the kid was his own boy.

It is truly amazing how people's attitudes will change after getting handcuffed. Some folks get very polite, while others start talking shit. Our driver Bob decided he was a shit talker.

He insisted that he had to stay with the wrecked truck and make sure nothing was stolen off the vehicle. Wesley assured him that he couldn't stay because he was going to jail. He began threatening lawsuits if anything happened to the rig.

"You want to wait for the tow truck, Pat?" Wesley asked.

"Hell no." I replied.

I heard the guy behind Wesley saying, "That's an $80,000 tow truck, and if anything happens to it y'all are responsible."

I looked at the crushed front end with steam from the busted radiator coming out, and the cartoonish looking wheels splayed outward from a broken axle.

"Tell your passenger that it use to be an $80,000 vehicle."

After a few minutes, Wesley called back. "That shut him up."

On the ride to jail, Kevin and I joked and debated about what the idiot would say happened tonight. We couldn't imagine what he would tell his boss in Tuscaloosa on Monday morning.

"Where's the truck, boy."

"What truck? "

"My $80,000 truck."

"Huh?"

"My truck…Where is my truck?" The boss demands menacingly.

"Well boss, the truck got arrested for night hunting…"

I wonder what he would have told his mother.

"Where's your little brother?" Mom asks very concerned.

"What brother?" Bob asks looking innocently confused.

Mother glares at him. "Little Timmy."

"Well mom…little Timmy is a night hunter..." Bob would say with an indignant voice.

As I tell this story I can hear that healthy V-8 roar. Wow that was unbelievably fun. This was one of those game warden adventures that we are famous for and that ended without loss of life or injury. Looking back, I admit that we were damn lucky no one was killed.

The homeless/meth addict/passenger showed up for court, but the judge dismissed all charges against him including the drug charges. I swear he was wearing the same soiled Lynyrd Skynyrd t-shirt, and was dirty as ever. Of course we didn't even charge little *Fonzi* because he was supervised by these two idiots. Noble Bob stepped up and plead guilty to night hunting and the marijuana, and his fines were about $1,100. That's right, after the incredible risk of loss of life, after resisting arrest and totaling an $80,000 tow truck, he was fined $1,100. He didn't even lose his job. You are sitting there thinking that I made this up and that I am kidding. You are wrong. I think you will agree that old Bob got a good deal. Even with the break, the son of a bitch didn't pay his fine. That's right, he stepped up because he knew he had no intention of paying the fine, but meanwhile got the charges dropped on his drug buddy.

In early summer I got a warrant because he hadn't paid anything. I know for a fact that he didn't lose his job because I called the owner of the tow truck asking to speak with Bob.

"He is on a run, and he will be back in a minute," the owner replied. "Can I take a message?"

"Tell 'ole Bob that this is Officer Reid from Marengo County, and I am on my way to arrest him for not paying his fine." I said.

"How much is the fine?"

"It is $1,100 dollars or 110 days in jail," I informed the owner. "You can also tell him that he will be sleeping in the jail tonight and that his dance card will be filled!"

"What..?" the owner asked.

"I will be there in an hour!"

I wasn't lying, but when I got to the auto dealers place of business on McFarland Blvd, the owner told me that Bob had driven to the courthouse to pay the fine.

I called the circuit clerk and she confirmed that the bill was paid, and that the subject was terrified that he was going to have to go to jail. I guess the owner had heard my little threat.

I went to Piccadilly restaurant and had a nice lunch without having to worry about transporting the cocky loser to jail in Linden.   This incident really made me question, *what am I doing*? It was a miracle no one died. We still did $80,000 worth of damage that I guess the insurance company paid. For the first time I blinked. I wasn't sure that the work I was doing was important. As a young officer, I had strong desire to protect the wildlife and that I was on an important mission, a 'jihad' for nature. Looking at the results, I really had my doubts that anyone cared. The results definitely didn't merit the risks or the liability. Disheartened, I did what any policeman would do; I ordered a piece of pecan pie and a large coffee. Not as healthy as spinach, but Popeye never had to deal with little *Fonzi!*

Dr. Doolittle?

I would soon begin to think that Kevin and I were cursed because of the queer stuff that happened when we worked together. I can't make this stuff up. Okay, I admit that I have an active imagination, but damn, this stuff was weird. The next fall we sat up a detail near the big paper mill out near the Black Warrior River. We sat the deer on some Gulf States Paper Company land, on a power line, in an area that had several recent episodes of bold night hunters. It was hard to see our deer but there was good traffic, so we considered it a promising mission. This area was covered in cotton and soybean fields, and according to the "locals" it was also covered in night hunters. There wasn't much cover, but we managed to back so far into one of the fields that we were out of any beams from headlights; we had an excellent view of the decoy and the road.

If you ever look closely at the game warden's vehicle, you might notice that someone has taken some flat black spray paint and painted all the shiny chrome. We do this so the moonlight and stray light beams don't create a shine that would give our position away to suspects. My vehicle, of course, was painted like this and you couldn't see it unless you pointed your spotlight or headlights right at the truck. It was very effective night camouflage, and it looked cool. I know *Batman* would have approved. My supervisor just grunted and looked away when he saw it.

Kevin and I had just parked in the 'hidey hole' when a *Ford Escort* pulled by the fake deer. We could tell immediately that the driver had seen the deer because it turned around and came back. The car pulled off the road with the headlights glaring at the 'peg legged' deer. We waited and waited for that shot, but nothing happened. Suddenly the door on the passenger side opens, and a white male steps out and he puts his hands out like he is greeting a space alien. I mentally hear him saying *take me to your leader*. He then slowly took steps toward the decoy.

We were disappointed, pissed and confused by the bizarre behavior. We finally decided to go ask the idiot to leave before he could put his greasy hands on the decoy deer. We pulled up, and when he saw us he trotted back to the car. His name was Michael Reilly and he was from Bellamy, which was just across the river. He was 19, and his car was being driven by his 14 year- old girlfriend. She gave us a big, toothless grin.

"What are you doing?" I asked.

"Momma says if you keep the light on them that you can touch...or grab em."

Kevin, always the serious one, jumped all over this feigning interest.

"Is yo momma Dr. Doolittle?" He asked quickly, cutting his eyes in my direction and grinning.

I grimaced at Kevin and shined my light on the guy's face.

I couldn't tell if he was drunk or just thick headed.

"Look...sir. I know that you are trying to catch this deer...but it is fake...it is stuffed...please leave."

He cocked his head confused.

"It is not a real deer, sir! Please leave so we can catch some night hunters. I think you should go back across the river. These Marengo county deer are mean, and if you try to molest one it might hurt you."

He finally got the drift of what I was saying, and we let his 14 year-old girlfriend drive him away. I could have arrested her, but damn I didn't want to drive them both to jail.

Now this was pretty weird, but I am just getting started. I have to depart here to tell you this story.

The next year I was teaching a hunter safety education class, and there was a guy accompanied by a young girl. They were at the class because her birth date fell after the legal cutoff, so she was required to take the class to get a hunting license. Everyone born after August 1, 1977, had to take the class. I thought they looked familiar but didn't say anything. My portion of the class was hunting laws, and I brought a sexy little robot deer to the class. By then we had a 'sho nuff' amazing decoy. I told everyone about the decoys and told them that we had many different sizes, so that if they saw a good buck on the road then they could bet that it was a trap.

"It is a trap! Don't shoot it! You will go to jail!" I emphasized.

I saw the guy look at the young girl and they exchanged a knowing nod. Later I was going into Wal-Mart after class and ran into the couple.

"Excuse me, sir. Have you ever worked the decoy out near the mill?"

"Sure. I have worked there and everywhere else." Then it clicked. "Were you the guy who was trying to pet my fake deer?"

"Yes Sir," he laughed. He began to explain about taking the class so his very young girlfriend, who was now his wife, could hunt. I told Mr. Reilly goodnight and left it at that.

Now you know what's going to happen don't you. What do you think he is going to do? He will probably mess up a detail. Right?

In the fall of the same year we had decided to work a long stretch of this road out by the mill, and we would use two decoys.   Well, it turned out that we just had too many helpers. That's the reason we decided on this plan. David Nelson and his two subordinate biologists, as well as two vehicles wanted to help. Actually, their boss was riding there asses about making some arrests and doing some enforcement time. I had to bring the big three-legged pony out of retirement. I put Nelson and Martin on a side road across from a freshly picked bean field. I sat the decoy up because it only had three legs and with my experience I could get it to stand up. I had to push the one front leg into the mud…I mean really deep. Nelson came by and shined it with his spotlight.

"Looks like a rabbit with its ass way up in the air." He said.

"It will be okay." I assured him. As I got out of my truck at my 'hidey hole' north of the new super robot deer, I heard him say

"It looks like a big jack rabbit. Ain't nobody dumb enough to shoot it."

"BOOM. BOOM." Somebody had shot the new robot deer.

I jumped into my truck and pulled out to make the stop. I got their weapons and identification. While I was standing by the stopped vehicle I noticed a small *Ford Escort* creeping slowly by. I didn't pay much attention to it. Please understand that we nearly had the road blocked. Two game warden vehicles where pinning a night hunter vehicle against the ditch, and all these things were happening while our blue lights illuminated 40 acres. Three big fellows were bent over the trunk of the car being searched. You honestly couldn't miss us. We were noticeable and interesting. We were not being sneaky. No way. My God we could be seen from outer space!

When we finally had all of the suspect's identification and weapons, we convoyed south toward the jail and would be passing by Nelson's detail. Nelson had called and had a question about writing the tickets. I said if anyone is stupid enough to shoot the 'jack rabbit' then just pick up the deer and bring the night hunters to jail. I hadn't realized that he had caught anyone, and I thought that he was just being a smart ass because I had left him and his team to guard the 'jack rabbit decoy.' I mean dang; we were illuminating miles of highway with blue lights. This all happened within ten minutes. Nelson got to jail just minutes behind us, and would you like to guess who he had? Yep. It was Michael Reilly and his young bride. Unbelievable! We weren't 2 miles from where he had tried to pet the decoy years before. He had attended a class and been instructed and warned about the decoys. He had passed by while I was arresting some night hunters. Nelson informed us that Reilly's sixteen year- old bride was driving the little car. Reilly was the shooter and he had been drinking a Sterling Big Mouth beer. (This is beer that was sold in quart jar style bottle). Reilly had leaned out the window and shot the three legged, pony size, fake deer with the freakishly small head. He had done this even after going to a hunter safety class where I had told him about how we worked this area with the decoys. Oh my God. You can't make this stuff up.

Kevin looked at me, Ain't that Dr. Doolittle?"

"Yep." I replied.

"That Sterling beer must be strong beer...crazy strong." Kevin laughed.

"I hope so Kevin. I hope so." I offered not wanting to believe that anyone operating a vehicle or for that matter walking around with a gun was that damn stupid.

The Complaint

Time out: I have to insert this here, right here in this story. Remember I had told everyone at that hunter education class about the decoy deer and about how tricky I was. You will be shocked to know that the day after the deer season came out my supervisor called and he was pissed off.

"Pat where did you put that decoy last night...you know the rules."

"Captain, I didn't work the decoy last night. Heck, I went hunting on the last day. It's all in my report. I was off duty."

"Are you sure?" He added suspiciously.

"What's up?"

"Jacob Ester called and complained that you put the decoy in his green field last evening. He said he knew it was a fake because when it jumped over the fence it moved…" the captain paused.

"Huh? My deer doesn't jump. Hell it only has three legs." I quickly added during the Captain's pause.

"Yes, hmmm, never mind Pat. The quack said that he knew it was a fake because it moved like a robot. That's impossible." the captain concluded realizing the total absurdity of the complaint.

I told the captain that I would call the guy and see what he was talking about. I got the number from the captain and called the paranoid idiot right away.

I called him up.

"Hey Jacob, this is Pat Reid, the game warden. The boss called and said that someone set you up with a decoy yesterday. I want you to know that I am going to help you find and prosecute the idiot for impersonating a police decoy deer. Can you please tell me what happened?"

He bought it and explained. "I was sitting in my shooting house and it was getting dark. I was hoping that a big buck would show up before hunting season ended that day. About 30 minutes before dark I looked up and there at the end of my field was a 12 point buck standing like a statue. I watched him through my scope for 20 minutes. I realized it was a fake immediately. I wasn't going to fall for the trap."

"Wow, Jacob!" I said feigning concern.

"Someone has some sophisticated equipment. I want to assure you that if they pull a stunt on you again that you have permission to shoot the decoy. Don't think twice about it. It's your property for heaven's sake, and it is not illegal for you to shoot a deer or for that matter a fake deer."

"Oh really?" he asked.

"That's right, Jacob you would not be guilty of any crime. If someone fooled you into shooting a fake deer, then it's not your fault they fooled you. I can't imagine why any police officer would do that because it isn't a crime if you shoot the thing.

"Oh." he said sounding down.

"That's right…hmmm. Did you walk down and look at the fake decoy?"

"Naw," he said slowly, "I just watched it walk slowly to the barbed wire fence. It jumped over the fence and chased a little doe into the woods."

"That's odd Jacob. I have never known a stuffed deer to mount a female deer. Usually they don't pay attention to does. You know because they are stuffed, dead.

Quiet.

"That's some amazing technology, Jacob." I continued pouring salt into the wound, and during this uncomfortable pause I asked him,   "Jacob…Are you still there?"

"I have to go," he said solemnly.

"What is the matter, Jacob? You sound a little depressed," I quickly added.

CLICK

I promise you that this was real. The paranoid idiot had let a trophy deer walk around his green field on the last day of hunting season. He didn't shoot it because he was afraid that it was me working a robotic deer. A trophy deer walked into his green field and posed for a picture and then slowly walked out! I can't make this stuff up.

This idiot would later walk to a wreck where a damaged vehicle had rolled over his property line. While the trapped passenger was still in the vehicle, the idiot walked up behind a first responder and hit him across the head with a flashlight for trespassing. I guess he had been watching *The Andy Griffith Show*, and decided to make a Gomer Pyle Style 'citizen's arrest' on the ambulance driver for trespassing. Genius!

I had to insert this story here because he had attended the same class as Irvine and wife. I just had to lump him in here because of this chapter seems to be collecting stupid people. Later that same year, I caught two more graduates from the class while they were hunting from a vehicle near Faunsdale.

I must be an inarticulate instructor. Truly, I must be one lousy teacher.

Well let's go back to the first night where my student wanted to pet the deer. This was the very first night when Reilly aka *Dr. Doolittle* tried to molest the decoy. After we had run Mr. Reilly off, Kevin pulled out some dripping sticky caramel cake.

Homemade caramel cake is delicious moist cake covered in caramel syrup.

Oh. It was so good but it was dripping with delicious caramel. It is so messy to eat and it is only surpassed by barbecue ribs. Kevin's new girl friend, and soon to be wife, had made it. I poured some coffee and Kevin got the cake out. We both agreed that once we got into the mess that someone would pull up and blast the decoy. I mean, we were sure of this. We both laughed it off. I took a bite, and the caramel just dripped through my fingers. I moaned like I was making a porn movie and smacked my lips.

"Oh my God it's so good." I moaned.

Kevin was chewing but looking intently out the window. I looked up, and a car pulled slowly by the decoy but kept going.

WHEW that was close! I thought.

I would have said it out loud but my mouth was stuck together with caramel. I can't imagine how we could have chased him while eating this messy cake. The car turned around, and we looked at each other and then at the messy cake in our hands. The car's headlights illuminated the fake deer and it rolled to a stop. *BLAM...BLAM...BLAM...BLAM.* The driver just laid into the stuffed deer with what sounded like a small caliber rifle. It was probably a .22 rifle. I just dropped my full coffee cup on the floor and tried to shove the whole piece of cake into my mouth. Of course it was a 'game warden size piece of cake,' which means it would have made 4 regular slices for 'normal' people. Before the cup hit the floor I grabbed for the gear shift, but my hand slipped off because of all the goo. The second try I grabbed it with the edge of my cuff and slammed it into drive. I smashed the gas pedal and the truck leap forward. Poor Kevin's coffee splashed onto his shirt and bulletproof vest. He cut me a look. I tried to apologize with my mouth full of the cake;

"IMLjuffflsortyt." It just came out muffled.

My hands were covered with caramel sauce, and I could barely hold the stirring wheel. It kept slipping out of my greasy hands. When we tried to climb up onto the asphalt road, I couldn't turn and we shot straight across into the ditch on the other side. I slammed on the breaks. I grimaced and wiped my hand on my freshly starched uniform shirt. I quickly got enough goo off so that I could safely grip the steering wheel. I managed to get straightened up on the asphalt road as the hunter pulled off. The violator pulled off slow, just like most of the hunters did. They were usually confused about why the deer didn't run or die. They were probably wondering if they were shooting blanks...or just missing. Some would blast away and then pause like they were looking at their guns, and then open up again. When I got behind him he saw the blue light from my police truck and he punched it. It being a 1973 blue Eldorado Cadillac, which I am sure, could run in its heyday, but now it was a 20 year- old classic. I felt like I was covered in coffee, and had caramel dripping off my uniform, when I noticed that the windshield was being covered by black material. No it wasn't a James Bond device, but rather the old Cadillac was blowing oil out of the tail pipe. Enough, in fact, that when I hit the wipers it just smeared across the windshield. I was blind. I had to stick my head out of the side window to see as we raced after the old car. I could feel moisture from the oil and bugs hitting me as I chased after the night hunter. We finally got him stopped and it turned out that our night hunter was just an old black guy. He explained that he was trying to run the deer off the road.

"You know to keep it from running out in front of a car," the old fellow insisted.

Kevin thought that was hilarious and of course had to comment on the matter.

"Who hired you to do this?" Kevin asked feigning interest. "How much does it pay? Does your job fall under the department of public safety? How did you get that job? Who appointed you? Did you have to fill out an application?" Kevin was having a blast.

The old guy didn't appreciated Kevin's humor but signed his tickets. It was no simple matter preparing the bail bonds because the paper kept sticking to my caramel coated fingers. And to make matters worse, the ticket book was soaked in coffee which made my cheap Wal-Mart pen quit marking. I had to write a letter and then take the pen and rub it on the card board ticket book cover until it started marking again. It was like one of those glue skits on the Lucy show. The paper kept sticking to my hands. I had to put my forearm sleeve down on the paper to hold it still. I finally shook it off and released the old fellow to continue his illegal patrol. He took the ticket and noticed the slimy brown coating. He held it between his index finger and thumb. He cautiously held it up to the light and then sniffed it. Then he gave me a funny look and left in a confused huff. I looked at my shirt and I had bugs on my tie. When I had stuck my head out of the window the bugs got trapped in all the caramel just like a glue trap.

By now I had a little knowledge about the decoy and how to work it properly. In later years, rookies would come over and ask to work the decoy. One of the real facts is that having the deer decoy 'out on the side of the road' wasn't enough to catch the night hunters. You had to time it so that these opportunistic hunters had the means. It was only effective during the gun deer season because most of these types had their weapons in the vehicle but not after the season. During the closed season, they might see the deer and shine it. They would be curious, but they didn't have the gun to 'close the deal' with a gunshot. It would turn into a big waste of time. More often than not they would ride by and blow their horns, or sometimes they would get out on the side of the road to see if it was a fake. Or on some magical nights the idiots would try to catch it with their hands like Reilly.

I had asked Reilly, "What were you gonna do if you had grabbed the deer?"

He stared at me blankly and shrugged his shoulders. It was clear that he hadn't thought that far ahead. Soon after, Wesley began getting calls from a lady asking if her son had been arrested for night hunting, and would he be able to be a game warden.

Wesley immediately knew who the woman was and said, "No Mrs. Reilly, getting a night hunting ticket won't keep Michael from being a game warden, but being a dumbass will."

She never called back again. From what I had seen, his mom was probably very young and probably first cousin to his daddy. This winner didn't even make all of his fine payments, and later a warrant were issued for his arrest. I searched for about a year but didn't find him, so I returned the warrant. It was only for 40 dollars, so it wasn't a big deal. Later that summer, I was taking my twins to the Boys Scout Jamboree where I was going to drop them off with their friends. They joined their tribe, and I walked around to all the little class sites that were set up like outdoor classrooms.

I walked by one of the sites where they were teaching the kids how to build a fire by rubbing sticks together. I noticed a familiar looking guy. It was Reilly. He was wearing and eagle scout uniform and those silly khaki short pants that they like to wear. He was decked out in all kind of badges and must have been a general or something.

Damn. I thought. *I will have to get my kids out of here.* He looked up and his face went white as all the blood drained out of it. He was on the other side of a group of adults and children. I wasn't going to arrest him, but he didn't know that. He squatted down behind the people in front of him and duck walked away from the group. Curious, I walked around the crowd just in time to see him running across the parking lot. I was relieved to see him leave. Run Forest Run!

Robot Deer Attacks the Florist

In the central area of Marengo County there is an intersection of a major paved road and a well kept railroad track. As you come off the hill from the north on the paved road, you get the sensation that you have entered a large, green valley. The road is widened in this valley and there is a large parking area. To either side of the road the railroad runs straight as an arrow off in to the distance. The 100 foot-tall pines and oaks come right up to the road, and the forest is split only by the man-made valley for the railroad. At this intersection, you are in a 20 mile circle of forest and mostly timber farms with only a speckling of homes near the edges where the woods meet the road. Hunters would park in this bottom, unload their four wheeled all terrain vehicles, and then use the railroad to access the many different land holdings. Some days this isolated spot would look like a Wal-Mart parking lot. During the peak of 'rut' it was very busy. On many occasions, the wardens would wait at the parked vehicles and check hunters returning from their leases. They would be checking for hunting licenses and waiting to see what the hunters had killed. I was no exception and sometimes patiently waited out these hunters if I wasn't called away on a complaint in another location.

Invariably, as darkness fell, there would be empty vehicles indicating that some of the hunters didn't return. Of course, they could be camping or trailing a wounded deer. I would often listen to their ATV engines as they drove around the large isolated woods. There was always one or two who would be moving around as late as nine p.m. Were they raccoon hunting? But I never heard the coon dogs? Maybe they were lost? Or were they riding around using the light on the 4 wheeler to scan the hundreds of green fields scattered in this large expanse of forest? I always felt like these guys where beating me. Sure I could borrow an all terrain vehicle and try to locate these guys. Stop and listen and then try to move toward them. I had tried this before and I got lost in the maze of hundreds of trails and locked gates. When I finally got close to the hunters, they simply shut off their engines and turned off the lights and disappeared into the night. I am a good tracker, but the road already had the tracks from a couple of dozen ATVs that had returned earlier making it nearly impossible to figure out which set of tracks are the freshest. There was simply no way to cover the distances and not give away the fact that I was hunting them. Now, there are electric vehicles and that might have been useful in those days but only if I could have gotten through all the locked gates. So you can imagine that this bugged me. It worried me. Ate at me! I made an oath that if I could catch someone still in the woods after eight in the evening, and if I had the time, then I would hide the truck and grab the decoy deer and run into the woods. Once in the woods, I would pick one of the trails and sit up the robotic deer and just see what would happen if one of my late night hunters saw it.

This plan would require a lot of details to go right, but the game warden has time.

It wasn't the first year or second, but more like 5 or 6 years later while I was training a rookie game warden from Hale County when opportunity would knock. He was a young guy and was ex-military. Now, even though we had a lot of variables that had to go right, I had been thinking about this for years…several years. There was a large block of property on the hill above the tracks which was owned by Gulf States Paper Company, and the owner had signed a release. This was a permission slip for us to deploy the decoy deer. Yep, we had to have landowner permission. One of the variables met. It was a quiet Sunday evening and I wasn't working any complaints. The rookie was the new Hale County warden and wanted to work night hunting; He had no idea what he was getting into. Yes, it seems that Brian was no exception to the fact that whenever I worked with him some weird shit happened. He hadn't even been to the Police Academy yet, and that is one reason the supervisor had sent him to Marengo County. He was in for a real treat. I picked him up in Linden and for some reason; we ended up in the remote area. As we came off the hill my headlights illuminated the front chrome grill of a brand new Suburban with Louisiana tags. Cajun tags! Cajuns are fun. A small one vehicle trailer had off-loaded an all terrain vehicle. At least that is what I figured from the vehicle and foot prints in the mud, but truth was that it was a 'best guess.' I could tell that he, the owner of the ATV, had gone under the Gulf States cable and used their road to enter the forest area. We sat down there by the railroad and listened to the engine of the subject's 4 wheeler. He would start and stop. After a few minutes, it became obvious that he was wandering around and didn't seem to be concerned with the fact that it was nighttime. We listened for about an hour, and there was no indication that the guy was in any hurry or panicky lost. BOOM, came the faint sound of a gunshot.

I smiled and said, "Oh No He Didn't."

"What?" Asked Brian, the new warden.

"The son of a bitch just shot?"

"Do you want to try to find him?"

"Naw, I got another plan. Get in the truck."

I drove to the top of the hill and turned off the road on the opposite side from the hunter tracks. There was a gate blocking the drive, but the genius who had hung it put both hinges pointing up. So even though one side was chained up, the hinge side could be lifted straight up. I walked to the panel gate and lifted it up and swung it around to the other side. Oops. I should not have told you about that, now every hunter is going to have to re-hang his gate. I hopped into the vehicle and pulled down the road so that it could not be seen by casual traffic.

"Grab your light and your ticket book," I barked at Brian.

I grabbed the decoy deer, which thankfully was a tiny little thing. It was one of the new ones, and it even had a servo from a remote control car so that you could rotate its head and raise its tail.

(High tech, it was but it still wouldn't chase a doe.)

"Where are we going to position the decoy?" Brian asked.

"We are going to run into the woods…we are going to pick a trail and hope the asshole comes back on it! I want to see what he is up too. I don't care if he figures out it's a fake. I, by God, am going to check out his intentions."

"But… Can we do that? Is it allowed?"

"Look if we make an ass of it then we will just tell him to have a nice night and haul ass out of here. He is already three and a half hours beyond legal hunting hours."

I took off across the road, and Brian decided to play along and followed me. Either that or he just had to keep up because I had the only flashlight.

This all sounds easy but it wasn't. Marengo County has the worst soil in the world for walking. It has a high level of clay in it and if it's just rained then it will stick like glue to your shoes. After a short distance your boots look like muddy Bigfoot feet about the size of those old fashioned snow shoes. Huge and heavy from the clay, it quickly becomes sheer drudgery to try to walk. We struggled through this mess while following the fresh tire tracks of the hunter's ATV. Luckily he had turned off the logging road and into the woods onto a pine straw covered trail. We circled down the trail and crossed a small creek. We paused to kick some mud off our boots, and left foot long clay molds in the pine straw. As we were doing this we heard the ATV.

"DAMN! It is right on top of us!" I whispered while stamping my feet.

I shined the light up the hill and saw a clearing in the curve of the trail; I ran back to the clearing and stabbed the deer into the soft ground. The hunters light would sweep through this clearing if he chose the trail. He would see the decoy. But it was pretty close, so it was highly possible that we might get laughed at and be made to look like jackasses. This wasn't a detail that a rookie should take on but by this time I had enough credibility. I figured that the worst I would get was a thorough ass chewing from my supervisor. That's probably the most that would happen, unless I got the rookie killed or maimed. After a split second, I decided that it was worth it. As soon as I sat the deer in position, the light from the ATV swept through the woods. We both panicked and dove down the hill where we ended up sprawled face down behind a holly bush. Now one thing you have to keep in mind is that if this guy is hunting and he is heading our way, then what's going to happen if there is a real deer between us and his rifle. If he takes a shot, the bullet can travel up to three miles. Hell we could get hit or killed by accident.... The rookie was mindful of this, and turns out that he was no fool.

What if he shoots at another deer…in this direction?"

"Get behind that pine tree, keep low and think small."

"Huh?"

"Just kidding… get down."

Keeping this in mind, we pressed down into the pine straw and tried to think 'small' behind the trunks of some tiny trees. I held my breath as the motor revved and the headlights flashed over the top of the hill. He was almost upon us. Then as quickly as he had come, he left. We heard the engine and it started to get more distant. When it started to fade we stood up.

"What do you want to do?" Brian asked.

"Look, this guy is definitely hunting, and he is not headed to the truck so he still might head back on this trail. Do you think we could wait a little while longer?

"Sure."

(Ex military…gung ho…rookie…God loves em.)

We had some time to work on the set up of the deer, so I would walk up the trail with the flashlight centered in front of me. I held it at the same height as ATV's headlights. After a couple of tries, we had a brilliant setup. And there was no way you would miss seeing the deer. We had a small limb set up so you couldn't see the neck seam. We even got the electronics working. When you approached, you would see the deer looking off in the distance. Just like in a senior's portrait in the high school annual. He was staring off into the horizon and looked to be pondering something spiritual. As you came around the curve you would see his body, and then Brian would turn the head to look straight at you, his glowing green eyes would reflect the light from the headlights.

It was a spectacular night, crisp and cold but no wind to speak of. The sky was clear, almost blue- black, and the stars where like perfect clear white Christmas lights. *Neat.*

Well, I had begun apologizing to Brian for the wasted effort when he stopped me.

"Pat I hear that ATV."

I listened and we both gave each other a sinister grin. Shit the guy had come from a completely different direction. We trotted back to our hiding spot and giggled as the engine came closer and closer. I looked at Brian.

"Dude if he stops with the light on us don't jump up…and holler…he might mistake the shine from some of the metal on our clothes as the deer eyes…instead wave the light at him."

I had one of those moments. You know, a game warden moment. I can't believe that I am getting paid to do this shit. Well, maybe not exactly this. Yes. I am pretty sure that this strange patrol has never been mentioned in my job description.

What happened next is surreal. As we hunkered in the pine straw, the 4 wheeled motorcycle came over the hill. The headlight swung around, sending lights throughout the trees and over our heads. The driver stopped midway up the hill. We were behind the hunter now and covered in the darkness. I could see that he had indeed seen the decoy and appreciated the view. He had his shotgun across his lap. He aimed the Remington 1100, and without turning off the ATV started shooting.

BOOM…BOOM…BOOM….BOOM…   BOOM.

He shot the decoy until his gun was empty. Hair and straw flew, but the deer just turned his head and glared at the hunter with green, glowing eyes. We were on our feet as soon as he stopped firing. A quick ten steps and we were on him. He was frozen, staring at the decoy, and that's when I noticed a buzzing sound above the engine noise. The hunter turned to us with his mouth wide open and his eyes stretched open. He was crazy looking, with the whites of his eyes shining while he was screaming. Screaming in a high pitch. Screaming like a little girl.

I turned my light onto my uniform and in a booming voice hollered "GAME WARDEN." He continued to scream.

I put my hand on his shoulder and said, "I am the Game warden please stop yelling." I patted him on the shoulder and said "You are okay. Please give me the shotgun."

He surrendered the weapon which was still smoking and empty. I turned off the four wheeler and the lights went out.

Brian, without a word, eased around and took off with the decoy. I continued to calm him down and asked for his identification. He effeminately handed me his driver license. I ain't saying he was gay, but he acted like a sissy regardless of the screaming. It turns out that he was a florist from New Orleans and had joined the big club that leased land from a prominent landowner.

"What were you screaming at?" I asked.

"Ghost…Ghost deer!" he sputtered.

I shined my light up the hill

"It was there…I swear…"

I never let on that we had the decoy. Brian had removed it so quickly that we had pulled it off like a magic trick.

I advised the florist that he was on Gulf States property without a permit, no hunting license, hunting at night, and hunting from a motor vehicle. I told him that if he settled the ticket next week that I would only prosecute the night hunting ticket. He thanked me for the break.

Honestly, he was so scared of the ghost demon deer that he was relieved to see a uniformed officer. Okay, I felt a little sorry for the guy because the sweet little fellow was definitely out of his element. Probably, the only way he was going to kill a deer was to shine it with his headlight. Heck he had enough perfume on to run off all the game in the valley. Brian emerged from the woods and I made a big show about getting his permission to just prosecute the night hunting case. What a pal I was huh?

We escorted him back to his truck and helped him load the ATV. He thanked us for our help and prissed off. After he drove off, we eased back and loaded the fake deer. The fake deer now had forty-five new buckshot holes in it. Back in the truck we had a great big laugh and kept replaying the event.

"What just happened?" Brian asked.

"He was screaming."

"Yes. I thought so…screaming at the top of his lungs!"

"I thought the guy was going to hyperventilate!" I said expressing relief.

"Is every patrol as exciting as this one?"

I thought for a moment, "I guess it just depends on who you are working with, but the guys I work with always get me into a mess. They are some real characters!"

We decided to unwind and call it a night, so we went into town and got coffee and no, not a doughnut. That's what you were thinking. I got a honey bun and it's not really a doughnut. We were both pleased with the strange arrest. After years of waiting, I finally got to check this cancerous little haven for night hunters and the happy rookie got to report his first night hunting arrest on the Sunday radio report.

You know looking back I had some pretty amazing luck while training rookies. In an epilogue I must tell you that the fellow paid his ticket the next week, and I never told the landowner about the incident. Later, when I ran into him at Wal-Mart, I did ask him about the hunters.

He said, "The guys from New Orleans packed up their camp and left suddenly… and never came back."

"Wow…that's odd," I added.

Poison Man

I wish that Reilly was the only idiot that continued to get arrested. He seemed to be begging for attention.

At times I would tell the rookies that "some people are determined to get put in jail."

It is nearly impossible to get locked up for a misdemeanor, but some people are just persistent as hell. Honestly, if you ask the deputies they can tell you who will end up in the county jail on any given night. It seems that 90 percent of the crimes, mischief, and disturbances are caused by the same 'regulars.' This also reminds me of an epic tale with a fellow down near Miller.

The story starts with a call from a professional coon hunter. *Professional Coon Hunter?* Yea, I know it sounds like a joke, or that maybe I am making this up. But no! While the sport has become quiet now, 20 years ago you could make a living raising hunting dogs that would sniff out raccoons. It all began in the 1970s when fur prices for raccoons, foxes, beavers, and bobcat where incredibly high. It was after the Cold War and Eastern Europe wanted fur hats and coats. When I was only twelve years old I got paid twenty bucks for one raccoon hide. It was a big one, but you could average ten to twenty dollars a pelt. Everybody my age had a trap line. Now twenty dollars doesn't seem like much money, but in those days it was three tanks of gas for the skin of a little critter. Now trapping wasn't for everyone because running a trap line was a lot of work. Some fellows preferred to train hounds to find the raccoons in the early morning darkness. This had advantages because you could move around in the darkness crossing onto anyone's land. Sure you were trespassing, but damn who is going to crawl into the swamp at two in the morning. If you placed traps you had to work them in daylight and leave them in busy game trails where they could be found. Once found they were usually stolen, or worse, the game warden could watch it until you crossed onto the posted property. Then you got arrested and your traps were confiscated. The leg iron traps were also expensive.

The art of using dogs to hunt raccoons had preceded this boom, but now it became a lucrative habit. After midnight you could let the dogs out on someone else's property and listen for them to tree a raccoon. Then you could hobble your drunken butt down into the woods and shoot the raccoon out of the tree. It was easy, exciting and money- making fun for folks with good dogs. Dogs with talent were entered into large competitions for huge prizes. A champion would get stud fees, prize winnings, and make good money for the furs. In the early 80s, the fur industry was destroyed by groups like PETA who waged war against the trade. This, coupled with the invention of synthetic fur-like material, ended the lucrative trade. You could still make money, and some still do to this day, but the pay now is probably less than minimum wage. While the industry collapsed the competitions still thrived. People love dogs, and now the hunters rarely even shot the 'coons,' preferring to run the critter another night while training their dogs. Okay, so now you know about 'coon hunters' and their expensive hounds. These guys hunt for raccoons with dogs throughout the swamps and because they are out after dark, from 8 pm to 4 am they roam the county as they like. Rarely does anyone know that this mysterious bunch has been crawling all over their expensive hunting land. Naturally, this bunch avoids the game wardens, and they keep their mouths shut about what they find while stumbling around in the woods.

Knowing about this code of silence, I was surprised when one of the raccoon hunters called to 'rat out a landowner.' This particular fellow was so pissed off that he called and had to have a meeting the next day. The guy had made a pretty good living running coon dogs and being a home boy, and he had a large extended family of aunts and uncle with plenty of land to get started in the business. I drove down to his ranch style house in rural Campground. He met me at the door, and it was the damndest thing you ever saw. He was nearly seven foot tall, probably in his early fifties, and silver haired. He looked like one of those Viking or Norsemen you see in books. He was wearing overalls and was barefooted. He greeted me with a big smile and firm handshake. His huge hand made me feel like a little boy. I couldn't help but think that this guy who had a reputation for being an outlaw might have some kind of trap for me. No way was I going to fight him, my hand drifted casually to my Berretta. He was sincerely upset about a problem that he had to show me. As he started to talk, two tiny Dobermans came charging across the room and started snapping at my shins. They were the damndest things you ever saw. They couldn't have weighed more than two or three pounds each and looked like something you would buy at 'Toys R US.' We were trying to talk, and these little monsters where tearing my pants legs apart. The big son of a bitch just ignored them until finally the little bastards decided that they were going to kill me, and they started leaping up and snapping at my groan.

"Goddamn!" I let out.

"Get off him!" The big guy hollered.

I swear I was just about to shoot the little son of bitches when the owner kicked at his little demons.

They froze and stared up at the big guy as if in trouble. And then without a word leap onto his overalls pants legs. They were just hanging on, shaking their heads and growling. They didn't take shit from anybody. He was standing there and just ignored the two dogs who just hung on with rage. They were ornaments hanging from his pants legs. As they hung there shaking their heads and growling, he continued with his story and we set up a meeting closer to the property that he wanted to show me.

I met him later that afternoon and we made a tortuous journey on his tiny three wheeler. I was on it behind him and honestly it looked a little gay. I was glad, at first that no one was in the field we crossed. No witness to make some smart ass remarks about my manhood, or to ask the giant of a driver who his new girlfriend was. No witness, not a soul. Shit, then I got worried that this was a trap again. He wouldn't tell me what the problem was, but it was damn unsettling because I knew that he knew where every 'body' was buried in this area near Sweetwater. We drove for several miles, and I began to wonder if he was taking me to the woods to kill me. I sat behind him trying to remember if I had arrested any of his kin. My anxiety rose as I realized that I had indeed arrested relatives…shit… most of them in fact!

We crossed a property line and damn if I didn't see paper plates scattered down the logging road. This is what he wanted me to see. We stopped and he said that he thought it was poison. I noticed that it was green and looked like antifreeze. You know the stuff that you put in your car radiator. In those days that stuff was incredibly poisonous to dogs and cats who liked the taste. There have been thousands of pets who stumbled on a careless shade tree mechanic's pan full of waste antifreeze. Many times these careless events would cause a shit storm of complaints to the game warden about some murdering bastard killing the local pets.

Well, this was an entirely different operation. Some genius was mixing sausage and antifreeze and then scooping the mixture onto white paper plates. I guess he used the plates so that he could see if it was being eaten. There were over fifty greasy plates and very few had any sausage left. I told the coon hunter what I thought it was. I told him that I didn't think anyone would be stupid enough to claim it, but that I would try to catch the bastard. I would be happy to catch the bastard except for one problem. I didn't have any idea where the hell I was. I honestly was lost because we had come across miles of pastures, fences and private properties. I was totally lost. He tried to explain the location, but it was pretty hopeless. He was frustrated, but I came up with a plan. He let me borrow his 3 wheeler and I rode onward until I hit the paved road. Once I hit the asphalt, I quickly recognized the location on Highway 43 south of Miller. I had been intending to patrol this dirt road but the gate had always been locked. I returned to my informant and I told him where it came out. With this information he knew the camp owners and where their hunting camp house was located. I made plans to check it out. It was really weird because he couldn't do anything about the poison because he wasn't even supposed to be on the private lands. He broke the code only because he was concerned for his prize coon dogs

Fortunately, this hunting club was non-resident, so there was never anyone on the place during the week. Later that day, I tiptoed around the camp. It was empty and the trash had been properly disposed of, so there wasn't anything much to see. Cleanest campsite I ever saw. But I noticed an old military jeep parked under a leaning shed. I checked it out. Low and behold in the back of the jeep there was a white five gallon bucket, and it had sausage stuck to the side and green antifreeze pooling in the bottom. *Jackass*, I thought to myself.

This was interesting because there was enough of the poison mixture in the bucket that if I could catch the guy in the woods where the poison mixture had been placed, then I thought that I could make the case on him. I made plans to work the guys the following weekend, which was the opening weekend of turkey season. I realized that I was going to need timing and luck because I didn't know a game warden that had ever made a case on a poisoned *Jimmy Dean* sausage complaint. This evidence helped, but it seemed like an arrest would be unlikely.

Friday night I drove down Highway 43 around 11 pm, just to check and see if any hunters had driven in from Mobile. If they weren't in town, then there was no reason for me to get up so damn early. The drive from my house was 35 minutes, followed by a muddy hike down a logging road. For some reason I felt that my chance would be better if I got there before them. If I came after and they were in the woods, then they might see or hear my vehicle. If they wanted to, they could just fade away into the woods. I was delighted because two fancy cars, a Cadillac and a Lincoln, were parked in front of the plantation style farmhouse they used as a hunting camp. Why was I so happy? There was no way they could drive those cars down the muddy road. They would have to take the jeep! The jeep with the bucket of *Jimmy Dean* sausage and antifreeze! Hopefully, they would be up so early that they would completely forget about the evidence in the back of the jeep.

For the record, I hate working turkey season…those guys get up and are in the woods before 4: 30 am. That meant that I had to get into the poison area earlier. I wanted to be in the middle of the poisoned plates when the jeep came through. About 3a.m., I left the house and made the lonely drive and walk to the strange land of paper plates, my only companion was a hot thermos of coffee. The air was crisp and cold, and the night sky was clear and sparkling with stars. The only sound was the thud of my muddy boots. I had hid my truck beyond the intersection of the 'poison road.' I put the truck in a place that I felt the idiot would never think of hunting. It was down a steep hill and in a thicket. I walked back to the road in the darkness. Although it was spring, it was forty nine degrees and was bone-chilling cold. My nose was running and I was shivering when I finally got into position near the poison-laced paper plates. Well, I sat there until 7 am, and I began second guessing my actions. Defeated and frozen and while cussing to myself, I started walking out. Dang…this was going to be an impossible task. I couldn't help thinking about my wife all cuddled up under the comforter. I got near an intersection and stopped dead in my tracks. *Hello and Bless My Heart*! I thought as I rounded a bend in the road. There it was the old Willis jeep parked in the middle-of-the-road. I stopped and listened, and I heard a turkey gobble about ¼ mile to the north. I eased over to the jeep and leaned into the back under the canvass cover. I was fully expecting the bucket with the residue to be gone, which would leave me with no way to make the unusual case. Not only was the bucket in the back seat floor board, but it had been refilled with more antifreeze and sausage. I still had a shot at this case! I slid under some brush within sight of the jeep, and about an hour later a lone hunter came up a trail in full *Mossy Oak* camouflage. He had a head net on and was carrying a Remington 870 Shotgun. I let him sit his gun in the jeep and while he is looking the other way, I quietly eased up behind him. He turned around and nearly jumped out of his skin.

"WHERE did you come from?" he squeaked in a voice like an 8 year- old girl. *I could tell you ...but then I would have to kill you. .*Okay I really didn't say that, but I was thinking it. Pretty satisfied with my big entrance, I introduced myself and walked to the back of the jeep and looked at the bucket... He shuffled along behind me. I pointed at that bucket.

"What is that?"

"That's antifreeze with sausage." He said arrogantly (turns out this old bastard is stinking rich…he could afford the arrogance).

"We have a coyote problem and I have been treating them." He continued while cocking his head and giving me a look like I am retarded.

"I put the paper plates out. Each one gets a scoop."

"You do know that putting poison out is illegal right?"

"Yes, but nobody cares."

"I care."

"Who are you?" He asked.

"What would happen if someone was walking their dog and the dog saw the sausage?"

"Serves em right if they think they can just walk their damn dog on my place."

He explained.

Whoa! I thought this guy is really making it easy for me to write the ticket. I mean he was an old guy and deserved some respect, but damn he was an arrogant asshole.

"I am going to have to cite you for this."

"Okay." he said giving me permission like he couldn't care less.

It was about then that I got the feeling that he was being a little too cooperative. It wasn't like a chill ran up my spine but it was like something else was there. You know the saying the '800 lb gorilla in the room,' just quietly sitting by himself. I thought that it might be another hunter, but it didn't feel like that, and there weren't any extra tracks or empty gun case. Something was wrong. I was missing something. *Maybe another hunter?* I have been in situations where there were other hunters with the guy, and the guy under arrest typically gets nervous. Maybe he is wondering if the other guy will show up and get caught. But I just didn't feel threatened in that way. *No.* I walked over to the jeep and noticed that he had thrown his jacket on the floorboard. I lifted it up and there was a half empty bag of cracked corn. He had been putting cracked corn out somewhere to bait turkeys. Now it was clear what had my 'spider sense' tingling. I walked down the road checking the pine straw and kicking over the oak leaves. Ten steps later, there it was! It was the yellow brick road of corn, which was illegal to hunt over or near. No wonder he was so nonchalant about the poison. He hadn't even thought about the poison, he was expecting to get arrested for hunting turkey over bait. That also explains him giving me the 'you aren't so smart' looks. He hadn't thought much of me because the road was covered in damn corn. It was paving the trail. Not only was this old fool a poison user, but he was such a terrible hunter that he had to bait up the turkeys. I looked up and grinned at the arrogant bastard. He just grunted. I wrote him a ticket for both offenses. Sure enough, he didn't seem to give a shit. Like I said the guy turned out to be wealthy, and now he had just gotten some cool game warden story to tell snobby friends over his scotch and whiskey. Unfazed, he began to tell me about some poaching that had been occurring during deer season. He took me to a field where they had a problem.

Now this is pretty typical behavior and most everyone will begin to tell me about their severe problems with poaching, and not being able to get any help from the game wardens. You know, 'why don't you go arrest a real violator.'

I will always just look them in the eye and reply, "I had no idea you had a problem. This is the first time that I have met you or had an urgent conversation with you regarding the need for a game warden. How in the world would I have known about it?"

Then they will take a step back from this bitch session.

"Do you think the reason that you didn't call me was because you had all this turkey bait and poison out here?"

This is typical banter and I would have dismissed him and his whole complaint, but I found a little blind made of cedar limbs and an empty pack of *KOOL* cigarettes. I asked him about the stuff, and he said it wasn't his and he didn't smoke.

When I showed him the stuff he was shocked. I really think that he had been bull shitting me and that he didn't really know anything about a poaching problem.

I imagine him thinking, *DAMN, where the hell did that come from? Oh my God, I do have a poaching problem.* Unfortunately for him, I believed that he had a poaching problem. Unfortunate for him because I would come back, and you will understand why I say this as you read on. As we went back to his camp, we passed a house where he said the guy who poached lived.

"He poaches when we are out of town," he insisted, red faced and with his fist shaking.

Well, I put this in the game warden computer and actually made a written note to check the place next gun deer season. I was busy as hell through the following gun season, but as usual by the spring I had some time to check on the complaint. I hadn't heard a peep out of the old rich guy, but I figured that the guy poaching would hunt Trumps' lease the week before the season.

As an aside, I have always wondered why most poachers wait till the gun season to start poaching on other folk's property. It just doesn't make good sense to wait for the owners to hunt the place and catch the wildlife relaxed. Hell, if you are going to start out hunting illegal then you might as well go all the way. But most of the poachers will wait until the opening day and are certain to run into landowners. I guess it just shows that most poachers don't start out with the intention of blatantly crossing the property line. I thought that this guy, because of his proximity, might want to have his way on the place before the other legitimate hunters got in the area to shoot the few turkeys or to make them gun shy.

Well, I worked the weekend before the season, and I searched the property. I didn't find the poacher, but the old guy had put out a ton of wheat. He was obviously going to bait the turkeys again. And he obviously forgot about asking me to catch a poacher on the place. I honestly think that he got himself lost in all of his lies, and the resulting confusion was going to get him another ticket. He should have just 'shut the hell up.' I love the comedian Ron White, and he has a statement that he was getting arrested for public drunkenness.

He says, "I had the right to remain silent, but not the ability."

It's the same way with the violators and especially the old arrogant ones. They have to get the last word in…big mistake.

Well, I got busy with some hot tips and more complaints than I could handle, and figuring that it was just the old pathetic guy, I chose to work a couple of other clubs. These new opponents represented contacts that could spread the legend of *Batman*. After all, the old guy had already met *Batman,* and wasn't a fan. It was a great weekend, and I rounded up a bunch of turkey hunters who where in blinds shooting turkeys over bait. It had been a spectacular and victorious patrol.

The second weekend of the season I went by Trump's camp, and they had been there Friday and Saturday. Sunday morning the bottom had dropped out and rain had hit the whole county. The old guy and his crew had left early, probably convinced the weather was too bad to chase turkeys. As I passed the camp, I confirmed that they weren't there. The gate was locked tight, and the trash can had been pulled down by the road. They were long gone. I looked at the house just down the road, and there was an extra pickup at the house where Trump had said the poacher stayed. I guess the suspect was off today. I called the paper mill, and the Chief of Security said the guy was home sick. After collecting my information, I drove by the camp house road again and noticed a track where someone had driven up to the gate and turned around. The mud on the tire tracks led right to the little *Datsun* pickup parked in the yard of the suspect's house. It was a clear track as if it had been spray painted on the ground with grayish-white spray paint. The only thing missing was an arrow head and a sign reading, 'this is the truck that the poacher is using.' Why had the suspect driven down to Trump's gate and turned around? Well, he knew that the nonresidents had gone home to Mobile, and I figured that he was just making sure that the old bunch was gone and that no one was hanging around at the camp. I trusted my hunch and eased up the wet clay road. I drove quietly, careful not to rev the engine or worse, get stuck. The woods were foggy, and the road was just muddy enough to leave an obvious track. I could see a small pickup truck track going deeper into the woods and could tell that it had just come out this afternoon. Now it had rained in late morning, and there is no legitimate reason for anyone going up this road unless you are dropping someone off. I mean this mud is treacherous. There was always a good chance of getting stuck or sliding off into the ditch. When it rained, these types of gray clay roads seemed to just melt like warm butter. I followed the track for several miles, and they turned around at a locked panel gate. You guessed it, the 'yellow brick' or 'yellow corn' road. This was the very road that old man Trump had been poisoning coyotes and hunting baited turkeys on. I stopped and looked around the intersection. There it was one set of boot tracks headed down the road to the field where I had found the cigarette pack. I mean just bloody obvious. The little rain shower had literally erased the weekend traffic of tracks, and it was just like wiping a chalk board. Even if you didn't notice trivial things like tracks, you would have been creeped out to see the big muddy boot tracks. You would get scared when you knew that you were following a lonely walker into the unknown forest. Lucky for me, I knew or thought I knew, who the guy was, and so for me it was just looking for my old nemesis. But after I got away from the truck tracks, even I couldn't help but have flashbacks to Bigfoot and the giant. I got into my vehicle and hid it in the same little thicket where I had placed it before when I first worked the poison complaint. I then slipped into my knee high *LaCrosse* rubber boots and started back to the road. It was an easy track to follow, beautiful imprints. I could tell that it was one guy and his tracks were close together, so he was calmly and cautiously stalking into the area. I reached the first intersection and he had gone down the road to the left but I could see that he had come out. I finally started back down the road to the right. I took four steps and saw his boot tracks headed back out.

Oh shit! Shit...shit ...shit! I thought. Milliseconds seemed to last for an eternity as the realization hit me. It was a slap across the brain. Remember, I had come down the road, now I was seeing his tracks coming back out.

Don't sit there calmly…I am tracking an armed unknown illegal hunter. He has to be right here!

I grabbed my gun and spun to my right. As my head turns, I see another track headed across the road to the trees. As I unsnap my pistol and complete my turn, I see him. He is laying on all fours like a lizard with his head staring at me. He was either doing a pushup or some kind of strange Yoga stance. Yes, a modified downward dog. That's it. *Yoga? Don't judge me*! He is staring at me bug eyed. He must have sprung to the side of the road and been watching me. Quietly balancing like one of those lizards in the desert that lifts it body up off the sand and alternates putting its feet on the blistering sand. Instead of sand, he is balancing himself above wet 'post oak' mud.

I holler, "Where is the gun? Where is the gun?"

He is terrified too and screams, "It's over there by the tree!"

Trust me, if you see a 6 foot tall game warden drawing his gun in a panic, I guarantee you won't recognize your own voice when you answer him. You will forget about your right to remain silent and your attorney privilege. Milliseconds pass. No more than a millionth of a second and I see that he is unarmed. My pistol is half out of the holster. In the seconds of the encounter he has watched me looking at his tracks. The whole time he must have had the scary realization that I was tracking him like game or prey. He must have been praying I would just miss it. He must have been horrified when he saw my recognition of his being right on top of me. It must have been heart- wrenching as I turned to discover him.

I pushed my pistol back into the holster and snapped the retaining strap. I kept my hand on the butt just in case. He relaxed his posture and dropped into the mud. He was exhausted and obviously relieved that I didn't shoot him.

"I need your license."

He sat up and handed it to me. I see his shotgun in the dirt at the foot of the tree. He had seen me and tossed it. The barrel was packed was with mud. He had plenty of time to watch because I was being a dumb ass looking down and acting like this kind of thing was 'routine.' He had more than ample time to kill me if he had been inclined. I had made another stupid mistake, but fate had smiled upon me. I cuffed my prisoner, who was mentally exhausted because for a split second he thought he might get away, and then when that failed for another split second he thought he was going to get shot. I unloaded his Remington shotgun, and noticed that he had buckshot in the chamber followed by turkey shot. He was covering his bases and was not overly concerned about the season. Once I am satisfied that there wasn't anyone else hunting. I walk him backed to my truck.

Now I have caught several pickup vehicles and arrested the occupants, but because of a few reasons I chose not to invest the effort. One reason was that it was still early afternoon, and a pickup vehicle wouldn't even consider coming to get him before dark. And that meant a three hour wait. No thanks. The other fact was that he appeared to be walking out. I figured that his wife had dropped him off, and that he was going to stalk out. He would quietly hunt down the dirt road until he got back home just as darkness fell. He would hunt all the way home.

I went down the road a piece just to see if anyone else was in the road. There was no sign of anyone else, and by this I mean there weren't any other shoe tracks. But there was something. The road had a fresh layer of wheat seed spread for a hundred yards! Sure enough, the old turkey hunter was up to his old tricks again. I took the guy to jail mainly because I was out of ticket books. Like I said, I had a big weekend. He didn't need to know that and so I let him think it was standard operating procedure. I asked him who had driven the truck and he got all cocky and told me.

"I want an attorney. You can't arrest me I was lost! You are violating my rights."

The jailer heard the guy's threatening voice and stepped into the booking room.

"You going to put him upstairs, Pat?"

"Naw Billy, this guy is a poacher. I don't think anal rape is a fitting punishment."

The prisoner's eyes widened as our conversation continued.

"I could put him in the cell three. Joe Jackson is 'the bull,' and he ain't queer."

I thought about the offer and then replied, "No thanks Billy, but I appreciate the offer."

"My attorney is going to tear you up!" The poacher offered.

"Sure pal. Oh yeah, I am going to cite you for hunting over that baited road."

"What! You can't do that! I didn't have permission to hunt that place. Old man Trump has the lease on the property. That's his bait."

"You should be more careful of where you decide to poach! But if you and your attorney want to plead guilty to the hunting without permission case, then I am inclined to drop the bait charge."

"When do I get my attorney?"

"When you call one," I stated, pointing at the phone

"You are free to leave."

He asked me for a ride home. I told him that he could use the phone and call someone. In fairness, it was a forty minute drive and it would have taken me and hour and a half to get back. It clearly wasn't my problem.

"You have to take me back to where you arrested me," he insisted.

"My problem is taking you jail. Getting home is your problem."

"It's Sunday. Who the hell am I going to call?" He said getting a little cocky, again.

"Call your attorney." I offered as I walked into the kitchen for a cup of coffee.

The dispatcher let him use the phone because he didn't have any change.

"If you're going to poach maybe you should carry some quarters for the pay phone, or maybe bail money!" The jailer laughed.

I hung around with the dispatcher and we chatted and pretended not to listen.

After scratching his head, the poacher finally dialed a number. Instead of calling an attorney he called his wife, big mistake.

"Honey…could you come pick me up…Linden….my truck is at home….ugh…the game warden drove me to Linden. I am at the county jail. I asked him but he told me to call my attorney for a ride home!"

Pause and compete silence

"Yes…around $350."

"But the warden charged me for hunting over bait too….About $1,100 total."

A torrent of profanity ended by final "you stupid son of a bitch...my daddy told me you were worthless!"

The jailer who was walking by was caught off guard by the language, and he even blushed. Hell, he had even been in the Navy. The lady's command of the language was that impressive! Everyone could hear her now, as he pulled the phone away from his head she proceeded to call him every name in the book…

"Geez. The mouth on that lady!" The dispatcher commented while grinning, displaying all of his bad dental work. The jailer finally started biting his forearm to keep from laughing out loud at the idiot. Remember there is no right to privacy in the jail.

"Oh yeah...I am coming to get you!" Her voice came booming out of the speaker. He turned a paler shade of white, and I thought he was going to puke.

He looked through the glass divider and spoke in a weak voice.

"Is it too late for you to put me in the jail for a day or two?"

My work was done and I felt pretty smug about the whole deal. I sat in the parking lot doing paperwork and watched my ex-prisoner. He sat on the curb in front of the jail looking all depressed. I really was there to be a witness of his ass whooping, and maybe get his wife's autograph for being the best 'cusser' in the world.

Of course I chickened out after a little thinking. I noticed that all the prisoners were pressing their faces at the bared windows, and the dispatcher and jailer decided to take a smoke break outside. Everyone wanted to see this insane bitch kill this guy. It's a good thing that she had a forty minute drive to "settle down." Right on cue, she came screeching into the parking lot and hit the parking curb with a bump that bounced her off the seat. I was thankful that I had remembered to put my vest on that afternoon. We all held our breath and waited. Nothing happened. She sat looking straight ahead as the poacher stood up and walked to the driver's side of the *Datsun* truck.

"You want me to drive, honey. Remember the last time you drove when you were upset."

She growled at him without even looking up at him. She continued to stare straight ahead.   He gave me a desperate look...*HELP ME!* I heard his mental plea. I just smiled and waved. He reluctantly moved to the passenger side of the truck and cautiously sat down and closed the door. He quickly grabbed the seat belt as she started to back the little truck up. Once pointed at the highway, she must have stood on the gas pedal because the tires started to spin and smoke. The vehicle shot out into the street and bounced out of sight. My last view of the guy was his right arm out the window grabbing at the top of the window frame in a desperate effort to keep from slamming his head into the ceiling of the truck. I never saw the guy again and never had another complaint about the fellow. He paid his fine on Monday morning.

You probably think that the story ends here, but remember I had discovered that my old friend the poison man had again baited his hunting area. You're thinking he has already suffered enough, and I should probably just forget about the old man. *Hahaha! Really... you should know me better by now!* Nope, the game is back on, so I called my friend Chester and he agreed to help me with the old guy next Saturday. I told him that I figured that there might be more baited roads, and I expected that there would be more hunters.

We entered the woods and went to the intersection with the panel gate. We walked down the road to the area where the cracked corn and the poisoned plates had been laid before but now was simply covered in wheat seed. When we got down the road, we immediately found the old Willis jeep. We heard some yelping, and it was terrible, so we figured it would be the old guy. Sure enough, we finally saw him about twenty steps off the road. He was sitting there with his back to an old oak tree. He was yelping away. I use the term yelping generously because what he was doing was making the most God awful sound. Even the crows and other birds had run away from the sound. It was just this horrible scratching noise followed by silence. He was a terrible turkey hunter, and it's no wonder he had put the bait out. Well, we just listened to the racket and watched him until he finally noticed us. He pulled off his mask and lit into me.

"You are messing up my hunt. Why haven't you caught that poacher...? You are a real nuisance...blah...blah ...blah!"

I opened my ticket book and read the name of the boy that I had caught hunting the very place he was today.

I said, "I caught your poacher."

He was obviously staggered by this and while his mouth was still open I added,

"While I was working your poaching complaint. I noticed your turkey bait. I am going to have to write you another ticket."

He stood there a second trying to process all the information. He looked at me seriously.

"How many times are you going to check this place?"

"Sir, I wouldn't have checked it for years...except that you specifically asked me to check it. Don't you remember complaining about me never checking your place?"

He put his little folding chair down and just sat down while I wrote his ticket. Now this should be the end of the story. *Nope!* There is more.

The following year I got a call from a federal game warden. It seems some timber people had come up on a buck deer and a doe carcass covered in dead scavengers...dead possums, raccoons, bobcats, and most importantly a dead golden eagle. It turns out the last day of the season someone had killed two deer and poured a powerful chemical called TEMEC all over the carcasses. It looks like black powder or pepper, but it will kill within minutes. Further, it would kill secondary feeding animals, third feeders, forth echelon, etc. Simply put, it would kill the things feeding on the previously poisoned critters. Gary, the federal agent, wanted to know if I knew anything about the club. He felt that it was pretty hopeless to try to figure the case out, but he was going to give it his all. From his description, it was my old buddy's club, and I filled him in on my poison plate subject. I promised him that I would nose around the camp and see if I could find any traces of the poison and perhaps the empty container. The next day, I went down to the camp. It wasn't the same as my buddy's, but the lands bordered each other. That's how things get started, seems like bad ideas spread like a cancer. Some rural genus decides to kill all the predators with poison because they are eating all the turkeys. He tells his neighbors, and they get all excited and try the same thing. When in fact it was just that the genius was a terrible turkey hunter!

This club was the cleanest camp site that I had ever seen. No way was I going to be able to sift through a burn pile or trash. All the evidence was gone.

Well, I noticed that this club was behind a locked gate, and that there was a jawbone collection box. The locked gate meant that the property had controlled access. And privacy meant it was probably done by hunters who would be motivated to protect their turkeys on their private club lands. These facts help narrow the list of suspects down to a select few individuals. The jawbone collection box has special meaning because these clubs prepare a harvest report and pull the jawbones off the deer. They are required to send the report and the jawbones to the biologist's office. This report includes the hunter's name and address, and the weight of the deer. This information helps the biologist make harvest recommendations and helps determine the need for doe or unaltered deer tags.

I drove to the wildlife office and met with the head biologist. He knew the club and found the report. The report listed a buck and a doe killed on the last day of the season. Now we had the when, where, and who had killed them. Now, being the last day of the season, and knowing that the deer had been laid across the road practically blocking traffic, it was pretty clear who was involved in the matter. We might not prove it in court, but we had a strong lead on the responsible parties. What seemed like an impossible case to make suddenly started to get possible. We faxed the report to Gary, the federal warden. All those guys had to do was keep their mouths shut. I mean all they had to do was just plead the 5th. Just shut the hell up. This is a good lesson for future would-be violators, 'when you have a hunting camp and twenty members. Someone is going to squeal on you.'

Gary called the club president, and true to form he didn't know anything about the incident. When Gary told him that he was going to subpoena all of the club members to federal court, he started singing like a bird. He rolled over on the guilty parties. The guilty confessed, and paid thousands of dollars for using the poison and killing the eagle. They were also placed on probation and barely missed jail time. Serious stuff! Turns out that the bunch was from Mobile, and they had all talked with my old friend. It turned out to be a disastrous idea. I realized after getting older myself that it is a real shame to get older and not get wiser. Their flaw was trusting the poison plate guy. Just because he was old as dirt didn't mean he was a genius.

I would later have dinner with the old guy, thanks to my friendly supervisor's encouragement. I think in the end, poison man had lot of respect for me regardless of the severity and the quantity of the tickets. I learned that although he was a terrible turkey hunter, he was a self made millionaire and probably someone that should be respected. He even invited me to the camp for supper…respect…I don't know… maybe he **just wanted to keep an eye on me.**

Chapter Four: Robot Turkey?

Ahhh. Turkey hunting. What can I say? In the world of hunting, turkey hunting is in a league of its own. Let me put it in terms you can appreciate. It's like comparing putt-putt golf, or miniature golf, to Tiger Woods playing the Masters. Let me explain, anyone can put a pile of corn out in a field and then at ten in the morning shoot the bird from 200 yards away with a scoped rifle. In Alabama, this would be illegal. Alabama has some of the strictest rules that make the sport of turkey hunting quite a challenge. To begin with, there is no bait. You must call the gobbler (male turkey) into close range. You have to use hand or mouth calls to fool the old bird into thinking that you are a lonesome hen looking for a 'quickie.' You must use a short range weapon like a shotgun or bow and arrow. All of these rules make turkey hunting a challenge. There are a lot of hunters but few turkey hunters.

The turkey has one great defense weapon… they have amazing vision and can see in front to the side and almost directly behind themselves. Their eyes are mounted on the side of their heads, giving them an almost 360 degree field of vision. While they can't identify a human sitting in front of an old oak tree, they can see the tiniest of movements. The birds can see you blink. There isn't a second chance, a blink or twitch sends them trotting away. Because of these rules the hunters must become masters of camouflage, calling, and stealth. As I said, the idea is to use calls to lure the bird into close range. There are even laws prohibiting the use of electronic calls. This requires the hunters to spend countless hours practicing calls that imitate the females call or yelp. They use wooden box calls and pieces of slate, which use friction to create the high pitch call.

The most common call is the mouth call, which is made from a u-shaped piece of metal with a latex condom stretched across the gap. The hunters put the call in their mouth and blow across the condom. I hadn't thought about it before, but damn that's odd. I wonder who the first hunter was to put the condom in his mouth. I understand now that there are flavored condoms. I guess that just adds another dimension to the sport. All in all, it is kind of fitting because the gobbler who is responding to the noise is strictly interested in sex. The 'calling' is an art, and each year there are hundreds of contests conducted to find the best callers and calls. These competitions pay generous cash prizes. The turkey hunters are unique types who are fiercely competitive. Fiercely competitive, but you would never know it by listening to them talk. Old turkey hunters have one common characteristic; they are fabulous liars. During the season all it takes is a slip of the tongue, and then everybody is in the woods, hunting your favorite spot or chasing the legendary bird you foolishly mentioned.

The absolute secret to being a great turkey hunter begins with acquiring the property that provides habitat for the birds. These great places are rare and hoarded by these charming resourceful hunters. Alabama is blessed with lands that turkeys can thrive on, but due to the timber practices some properties may be impossible to hunt. Most of the land is covered in young pines, and while a turkey can make a living on this ground, the thick undergrowth and briars become impenetrable.

The best and most sought after properties will have tall old growth timber where the turkeys can roost at night. Under the shade provided by the canopy, the land is clear and allows the turkey to move about with ease and maximizes his amazing vision to detect predators. These are the dream spots for turkey hunters.

A turkey hunter will risk his marriage and a loyal friend to succeed in obtaining these fine places to hunt. I have watched two old hunters, who together would hunt deer, rabbit, quail, and tailgate at the ball games. Nearly inseparable and easily called best friends, these two become bitter rivals in March and April during the spring turkey season. I remember one conversation at the wildlife office.

Both Steve and David have a gaunt appearance. They have bags under their eyes from lack of sleep, chiseled check bones, and hollow cheeks. They need a shave for their three day old 'five o'clock shadow.' It is now two weeks into the turkey season, and they obviously have been getting up at four in the morning, hunting every weekend, and even before work during the week. I know that David is driving an hour to his hidden hunting site, so he must be up and moving around three in the morning.

Steve steps into David's office.

"Hey. What's up?"

"Nothing, how about you?" David replies.

"You want to go hunting Saturday?"

"Naw, I think that I will help around the house."

"Have you had any luck?"

"Naw, I don't even have a decent place to hunt."

"Really?" Steve is not buying it.

"Yes. This is obviously going to be the worst season ever."

Steve looks at me, "Really?"

I just shrugged my shoulders even though David has just shown me three sets of spurs and beards.

"Well, you want to go with me tomorrow...I have been working an old bird."

"Naw. I have to work."

I start to feel sorry for Steve because he must be having a bad season. He says goodbye and that he will check back next week. I finish my business and stroll out of the office. Before I can pull off, Steve pulls up in his truck and rolls down the window.

"Pat, how many turkeys has David killed?"

I grin… "He's taken 3 birds."

"Why, that lying son of a bitch. I knew it…I knew it!"

I can't help but notice two sets of spurs and beards on Steve's dashboard.

"Well it looks like you have had some luck, STEVE."

100

"Oh, those are from last season."

He grins and stuffs the evidence into the center console. This is all part of the game for these masters of the hunt. The Monday after the season, they will meet at the 'Camphouse' restaurant and sit at the big round table by the front door. Over coffee, they will eventually slap the trophies on the table like a royal flush. Steve will sit across from David as if in a high stakes poker game. They glare at each other, trying to read each other's hand.

Steve plays first, "How many birds did you get David?"

David lays three sets of beards and spurs on the table and says, "I only got three, but one had an eleven inch beard and 1 ¾ spurs."

Steve breathes a sigh of relief and plays his three trophies, laying them on the table, "Me too, it was a tough year. Looks like we had about the same luck.

It's all over. Each has played his hand, but wait, Steve watches in horror as David sports a gigantic evil smile.

David reaches into his jacket pocket, "What's this...? Oh I forgot about these!" He says laying two more trophy sets on the table.

"You son of a   !" says Steve suddenly stopping...remembering where he is at.

"Hahaha," David laughs victoriously. "You probably would kill some more birds if you knew how to call...hahaha!"

The 'exhausted' will be relieved that the season, the contest, is over and now they get to tell their stories. And everybody has to listen! That means you too, if you casually ask about the season or simply ask them politely, "How are you doing?"

"Fine!" they eagerly reply.

You panic and start to move past as they grab you.

"I nearly died from exhaustion chasing a monster in the swamp!" He continues, while pushing the empty chair next to him backward and motioning you to sit down. You being polite ...again... you're trapped like a caged animal, and now everyone at the table is welcoming and lining up to tell you these fascinating stories. You sigh, and in the corner of your eye you see a blur of green polyester pants, a black pistol belt and a khaki shirt drop a ten dollar bill on the counter by the register. The door is closing before you realize it's the game warden escaping out the door, and he is using you as a distraction. As the story tellers get up to leave the restaurant, David asks Steve if he wants to go crappie fishing today after work.

"Sure," Steve replies because they are buddies again.

Luckily for everyone, Alabama only allows 5 birds per the month- and- a -half long season. If it was any longer, or allowed more birds, then I am sure that some of these hunters would die from fatigue.

Turkey Poaching

Turkey poaching presents particular problems. Let me set the scenario of a typical detail because I think it will help you understand my problems as a game warden. The turkey hunter will arrive at the area to hunt just before daylight. And in the twilight he will stand quietly and lift his face upward like a wolf about to howl at the moon. He will take his left hand and cup it over his mouth like a harmonica player. He will turn his body toward the tall growth timber that he can see across the property.

After taking a huge breath of morning air he will let loose with loud "WHOO…WHOO…WHO-WAW!" (*Work with me here this is difficult to imagine much less spell.*) He is trying to imitate a large hoot owl. After his call echoes across the land, he will turn his ear toward the roosting area of the turkeys.

The turkey and the owl are mortal enemies. The mature turkey is called a gobbler, and in the spring is especially boisterous and proud; the turkey will likely answer with a booming "gobble…gobble." As I said before, the professional turkey hunter takes great effort in perfecting his calls. And if you haven't ever attended a turkey calling contest, then you should. I promise you will get a kick out of it. Talk about prima donnas, you would think these guys were going to play a flute in a symphony. Of course this could be a side effect of the latex rubber in their mouth, talk about prissy. Dramatic! That being said, I have heard the noble birds gobble at a slamming truck door, a crow, and even a distant gunshot. *I'm just saying.*

Well, in the darkness the 'artist' formally known as Joe from the Jiffy Lube will listen for this gobble. He will try to get the turkey to give away its roost, which is where it spent the night in a tall tree. This process is called 'locating.' Once the bird is located, the hunter will try to close the distance, so that after daylight when the turkey flies down from the tree he will be right on top of him. He can then make the seductive yelping of a hen and hopefully end up fooling the bird into strutting into gun range.

Turkey poachers will drive around and park on the roadside, or ride a boat around the river, or park near the private lands and play this game. If they locate a bird using the owl call, then they will leave the safety of the public road or river and cross over onto the private lands and try to 'sit up' on the bird. The problem for enforcement is that if I get into the area before the poacher arrives, then there is a chance that I will spook the wary bird. If I am lucky enough to have a bird in the area, then I must then sneak around and try to find a stealthy and well-camouflaged hunter. I have to find the hunter and not GET SHOT by accident! If there isn't a bird answering, the poacher will get back into his vehicle or boat and move to another location.

As a rookie, I tried to get all these variables to work for me, and sometimes I would manage to run up on the hunter. We would both be shocked. Just a thought here and you will further appreciate it as you read on, NEVER SHOCK A MAN who is carrying a loaded weapon capable of blowing fist size holes in your body. Usually, I would be hidden in the beautiful woods where the turkeys lived and where my research showed that poaching was being conducted. I would be shivering in the spring morning's damp cold, and I would hear a loud hoot owl that I knew was my target. He would hoot then he would move and hoot again. He would walk the marked and painted property line listening for a turkey to make it worthwhile cross the fence. The turkeys, now spooked by my being in their range, would quietly disappear. The next day, the poacher would be in the same area working a bird. The poacher and the landowner would be closing in on the same bird. On a collision course chasing the same bird, they would run into each other. Usually the poacher would jump up and run like hell across the property line. Thirty minutes later, my phone would be ringing.

"Why can't you catch this guy? What's wrong with you?"

This and more. I would really get chewed out like I was tech support in India. Later, my crabby supervisor would call and chew me out.

It got worse because the local newspaper ran best bird contests and published pictures of proud hunters displaying their kill. Why is it worse? Well the jerk of a publisher decided to stir up shit. He would add captions that confessed to killing the big bird off someone else land or even in their backyard.

Imagine Steve smiling with a bird in a newspaper photo, and the caption reads, 'I killed it in David's back yard over his corn pile.' Sure enough, these two had a sense of humor, but I promise you quite often they were making these cracks toward paranoid landowners.

It's truly amazing that nobody on record went 'postal' on a taunting rival. Hmm! You know they've been thinking about it. There have been numerous hunters shot 'accidentally' while turkey hunting. I know for a fact that many of these landowners were seeing 'shrinks' and taking Prozac to deal with their anxiety. Of course, you can dismiss this as speculation, but every year we have turkey hunters getting shot at close range. I am serious; they are getting shot multiple times by accident EVERY year. Imagine an aggressive turkey hunter who is tired from the early mornings. Imagine him getting the drop on a poacher who has messed up his turkey hunt! Imagine the rage! I swear. I believe that I have stumbled onto something, perhaps an unwritten method for dealing with poachers. After all, hunting accidents are the most difficult to prove criminal intent. Maybe these hunters are going 'postal' all the time!

Well, back to my story. These telephonic ass chewing's get old, and I was determined to put an end to it. By my way of thinking, the decoy deer had worked well to reduce the night hunting. The truth is that we rarely got any night hunting calls anymore. I didn't need an extravagant decoy deer, but I did need an electronic voice. Most of the hunt was entirely audible communication with the visual part only coming into play seconds before the turkey is shot. I began looking in hunting magazines searching for turkey calls. I found some tapes with crows, distressed squirrels, and rabbits, which are used to lure in predators such as bobcats and coyotes. I did find one cassette that was instructional audio to teach a turkey hunter how to make the sounds. It turned out to be too much work to make a tape with multiple calls, and in the end they sounded like a turkey hunter. In those days we would go to the Movie Gallery and rent VHS tapes, and I was there with my kids when I noticed the professional hunter videos. I finally rented a turkey hunting video and it had great sounds of an old gobbler making all kinds of racket. I made a 'mix' tape, with one side being single calls spaced out by several minutes. On the other side I loaded the tape with multiple calls, which sounded like a flock of turkeys was coming toward you. For my player, I used a personal Walkman recorder. It wasn't really loud enough to carry any distance, so I went down to the Radio Shack. I had met a sound technician at the shop and figured he could help. After telling me about all the circuit boards and boosters, I finally stopped him and said that the player needed to be as loud as a real turkey, and not as loud as a 'PA' system. And it needed to cost less than 10 dollars, which was my lunch money for the day. He thought about it and then reached under the desk. In a dusty old box of junk there was a small outside speaker that had come off a BellSouth telephone truck. It was designed to play the incoming radio traffic outside the truck, while the worker was climbing a pole. We spliced a micro plug onto the end of the speaker wire, and then plugged it into the headset connection. Boom, it was just right. It sounded like the gobbler was right in the room with us. The store owner, who was a turkey hunter, leaned his head into the hallway and looked toward us.

"Relax I said, It's just a recording!" He smiled and went back into his office. It's not surprising behavior because after all it was spring

I had a device that I thought would work and had a plan. I needed to exploit the poacher's weakness. One of these was his movement. An experienced turkey hunter expects that a turkey will only come so far, and they are notorious for not crossing fences, creeks or even walking down hill. The turkey hunter expects that he will have to move closer to the bird. For example, if the turkey is across a creek or on a ridge, then the hunter will cross the creek and then try to get onto the same ridge as the turkey. No one knows if the turkeys are lazy, stupid or just arrogant. Regardless of why they act this way, it was a trait that I could exploit.

I was excited to use my junk device the next weekend. I could hardly sleep and finally I got up at 3am and drove to a spot where I had been burnt so many times before. I froze my ass off, but this time it was going to be different.

At 4:30 a.m. I heard him. "Whooo…Whooo …whowaa!"

I played one booming gobble at full volume. In the still, crisp morning air, the gobble echoed up the bottom. It was almost too loud. I didn't want to scare the guy, so I turned down the volume. I knew that he had heard my call because he hooted again, and he was in the same place. He wasn't sure where my turkey was roosting. All was quiet until daylight. I pictured him slowly crossing the property line and fence and then tiptoeing toward my location. He would probably set up 50 yards or so in front of me. Well, at daylight I was disappointed…He yelped but he was in the same place that he had 'owled' from. Shit. I had the volume so loud that he figured that he was close enough. From the sound I pictured his location to be two ridges over and probably right at the barbed wire fence that separated the two properties. If I moved on him he might be on the proper side. If he was across the property line, him being camouflaged he would see me first and quietly cross back over the line. I let him yelp, but didn't reply. He continued to yelp, and I had a hunch that he was getting frustrated. A few minutes later, I heard the owl call and it sounded like he was moving again. I turned the volume on my call to the lowest setting and gobbled. *Nothing. No reply.* I turned it up a little louder and gobbled again. He yelped back and I turned it down a little and gobbled at him. Again we had quiet, and this was a good thing because it indicated that he had heard me. Another hoot owl call indicated that he was definitely hunting me now! I nearly ran when I heard a loud 'YELP.'

Oh shit! The sneaky guy had moved within 30 steps. This was no small movement because it included crossing a barbed wire fence, wading a wide creek, and then crossing another ridge. I definitely could make the case now! *But how?* Now you must understand that turkey hunters wear incredible camouflage, he might very well be looking at me at this very moment. In the dim light, he might mistake the ungloved flesh on my hand as a turkey head. I slowly tucked my hand in my pocket and froze. I was in a panic. I didn't want to get shot with hundreds of tiny pellets from a shotgun. I had to make sure he didn't come any closer. I took my hand out of my pocket turned the recorder on loop playing and then set the volume to high. "GOBBLE...GOBBLE." The call echoed through the hardwood bottom. It sounded like a terra-dactyl! I heard the crush of leaves that I imagined was the sound of my hunter's ass crashing to the ground. He would be dead, still afraid to move a muscle afraid that the turkey was hidden behind a tree. He knew that this monster turkey would have super vision, and in a second it could catch a twitch of movement and in a blink of the eye it would haul ass. He yelped softly, and as if on cue the tape bellowed another booming gobble. I could imagine the guy's heart beating out of his chest. I bet his hands and feet, which had been frozen, would now be pink with new circulation. I know that I was warming up.

I was in a dangerous situation. I couldn't just start walking up to his front. He would have his powerful shotgun barrel pointed 'dead on' a forward approach. Not even I am that crazy, I might get shot. If not, I might not even be able to see him in the green spring undergrowth before he ran across the line. If I lost eye contact with the fleeing hunter I would have to follow the sound of his retreat, which would be a dangerous game of cat and mouse. I would be stumbling forward highly visible, and he would be sneaking slowly, practically invisible in his 'head to toe' Mossy Oak camouflage. It would be like the *Predator* movie with Arnold Schwarzenegger.

After pondering the attack, I finally decided a retreat was in order!

I slowly backed up. I really just crawled away from my electronic call. I went downhill off the top of the ridge until I felt that I would be out of his vision. Once out of his 'kill zone,' I made what is called a box patrol. I went west for 150 yards and then north until I hit the property line. I then moved back east for 150 yards and turned with my back to the well- marked property line. When I hit my spot, I found exactly where he had crossed the property line and left a back-pack. I picked it up and headed down the ridge to the creek. I walked in his very steps to cross the shallow, sandy creek bottom. As I slowly got back in line with the electronic turkey and the excited hunter, I would stop and listen. "Gobble" went my tape. Then a soft "yelp" from the hunter. I was behind the hunter now, and I knew that his back was to me. I figured he had his back to a tree and was facing the electronic turkey. I slowly tiptoed toward his back. The player sounded a loud "Gobble," then the hunter would yelp, and then I would move a few steps forward. You have no idea how hard it was to see the guy. He was in oak and brown-colored camouflage, sitting in brown leaves with his back against the grey-black bark of a young oak. He was nearly invisible, and I was within three or four steps when I finally saw him. I would have walked right by him if it weren't for his persistent 'yelps.' Standing within arm's reach and up close, I watched him answer the fake turkey. He would raise his gloved hand beside his mouth and cup his fingers like he was trying to push the noise straight at my turkey calling machine. He was really into it, and you would have thought he was performing for an audience.

"Hello."

He froze like a statue.

"Pat Reid, State Game Warden. I need to check your license."

His shoulder sagged. *Haha...priceless*! I thought.

He sat his gun down and took his gloves off.

"GOBBLE" went my tape player, a few dozen yards and just over the ridge.

I heard him catch his breath as he pulled his mask off, and he looked longingly toward the sound of the fake gobbler.

I took his license and asked him for his permit. He admitted that he didn't have one. My tape was doing multiple calls now. *Sexy as hell*! I thought. And mentally I was cracking up and trying not to bust out in laughter. The poor guy was totally buying it; he thought it was an old tom. He was thinking that possibly a super record breaking turkey was just a hollow over.

I made him get up, and we walked to the property line. I wanted to move him away from the tape player just in case he cracked and ran screaming toward it, determined to kill it with his bare hands. I filled out his paperwork at his truck, and he had no comment. He was defeated, busted, caught red-handed. I sent him on his way. I angled away from the electronic call because I didn't want him to suspect that it was all a fake. He never knew what had happened. This was the first time, but I would eventually get so good that I could make the hunters move around, climb a fence, cross a creek, come to me, and sit down just like a puppy.

If you are a serious turkey hunter, then I know you took a deep breath and swallowed hard. I know that you have sat on that property line debating whether you would cross and poach. You are probably thinking something along the lines of "you dirty bastard." Well relax; I am no longer a game warden so you are probably safe. I bet you are wondering what you would do when hearing a monster bird. And the answer is no, you wouldn't be able to tell it was a fake. It was a real turkey on tape, and it was one hundred percent real sounding. Would you cross the line?

It was a couple of seasons before I finally let anyone help me. After seeing my rig, Mike, the game warden in the adjacent county, got someone to buy him a nice system. But he eventually gave it to me to keep and use. It takes a mischievous person to go to the effort to work it. You really have to enjoy the prank to put in the extra effort required to make the detail work. It is not needed often but when you have this type of poacher, it works wonderfully. I really don't think that very many hunters have any idea that such a device is used. I have never told anyone whom I caught.

I turned the store bought device that Mike gave me into the department, but I don't think anyone uses it. The unit had a built in rechargeable battery, and I am sure that it has long been kaput. You know, maybe reading this might inspire some young warden to give it a try. So reader, when you are hunting and come to the property line, remember it could be a turkey, or it could be the sneaky warden hoping to 'PUNK' you, and arrest you! Or it could be a paranoid, turkey hunting, fanatical landowner who will shoot you until his weapon is empty. *Haha!* This is pretty funny because I have messed with your head. Oh my God, I might have given some crazy landowner the idea to just shoot your poaching butt. Geez. I am still a deterrent after all these years! But seriously, be careful out there!

Chapter 5: Alligators Are Cool.

A game warden in the southern United States is bound to run into nuisance alligators. Well, at first they are interesting, but I promise after a few years on the job you want them all covered in batter and deep fried. When you first get close to one these of amazing creatures, they evoke many different feelings. They are both frightening and amazing, with lots of teeth, and an appearance right out of Jurassic *Park*. The work of handling these critters and dealing with issues arising from their presence falls under the 'wardens' job description.

 Once thought to be in danger of over- harvesting, they were listed federally and labeled 'threatened.' This eliminated commercial hunting of alligators and the population thrived. After the designation, it now became a Federal crime to screw around with them. They say that 'hind sight' is 20/20, and now we can look back and see that it is clear that this is one of those times the 'feds' sorely screwed up. The legislation was enacted in the 70s.

People my age contracted an illness called *Saturday Night Fever* which caused seemingly normal 'rednecks' to wear silk shirts, bell bottom pants and fancy leather shoes and belts.   Prior to catching this illness, many of the same people had been questioned, "Do you look into a mirror before leaving the house?" The disease in a later stage manifested as *Urban Cowboy,* and other folks my age might remember the alligator shoes, handbags, belts, golf bags, cowboy boots and wallets. Curse you, John Travolta! It was the age of the 'loss of innocence.' Simple people who had never worn anything but white high top Converse tennis shoes now found themselves coveting alligator boots, belts, and wallets. There was an amazing cash market for alligator hides that would be shipped to Japan and converted into these coveted fashionable items. I have to give it up for those creative Japanese because I even met a fellow in the 'service' that said that he had some alligator underwear! *Ewww and a big gross*! It was truly the rage and like other hot items would truly prove to be a fad.

The reason I gripe about the 'fed' is not that they tried to protect the critter, but rather they hadn't adjusted policy. Even as the popularity faded for these products, most of the hides were being produced in alligator farms. Yep, those industrious 'Cajuns' started to raise the scary creatures like cattle. The 'fed' did nothing as the incredibly prolific alligators thrived in short order. With the designation as 'threatened' status, now every animal rights activist had a 'big stick' to interfere in the handling of alligators. By the time I began working in the early 90s, the alligators were in every piece of open water and literally began eating pets and even attacking people. I have had many a liberal biologist defend the 'noble' creature, saying that you can swim with the gators and they don't feed on humans. That naive attitude has gotten a lot of puppies eaten and people bitten. The problem occurs because as humans use the water way, invariably the gators begin to associate the humans with food. *YUM.* Whether it is simply stealing the stringer of fish lying in the shallow water, or from people tossing them treats of Kentucky Fried Chicken, the alligators begin to lose their fear of humans.

Nothing pisses me off more than when a jackass defends owning a "pit bull," or an educated blowhard defending alligators. If I have upset you, let me say one thing, pit bulls and alligators are not humans! They do not share the human emotions and in most events simply react to situations like a machine. While you don't have to hate or fear the creatures, you do have to respect them and the damage they can inflict. You can pretend that an alligator has feelings and recognizes you as noble creature, and that you have a spiritual connection, but you are just fooling yourself.

During my stint as a 'game warden,' the alligators went from a neat summertime distraction, to an absolute 'pain in the ass.' I remember my first alligator call in south Marengo County. At the time, most people had never even seen one in the area and everyone stopped to investigate. They wanted to find out what all the fuss was about. The call for assistance came from a remote location; it was a home down an endless dirt road. Behind a large ranch style house is an eight acre lake of lily pads and weeds. At the time, Wesley was still my training officer and was still trying to be all business about the process. The first problem was he hadn't received any training. Secondly, we didn't have any equipment to capture the strange beast. Truly, looking back, the equipment was as important as the training because a good trap or hook rig quickly handles the problem. Without the proper training, the task of relocating the beast would be monumental. Luckily, the area was so remote that we didn't get the audience that usually comes along with the spectacle of the 'alligator hunt.'

Lucky for us...Very lucky, Wesley called a few wardens from the Mobile area.

"Shoot that bitch!" was the advice that he got from the weary wardens.

Due to hundreds of calls, they were truly sick of the creatures and would simply call the federal officer and get permission to shoot them. Unless, and this is important remember. Unless there was an audience standing looking over their shoulder. Look, these wardens were not doing anything fishy. You have to appreciate that they were getting hundreds of calls annually. When you translate that into money and time you are talking about thousands of dollars wasted and the very real possibility of someone getting hurt. It just didn't make any sense to waste the resources to relocate the alligator when they were already overpopulated.

I remember one very large gator that had commandeered a small creek and pond on a major golf course. This gator was drawn to the little white golf balls and would eat them. Now this adds a whole new dimension to golf. Talk about a handicap.

Two golfers are standing facing the 12- foot alligator that has the Jack Nicolas golf ball between his front legs. The alligator opens his mouth and hisses.

"I don't mind loosing the golf ball," he says. "But I'll be damned if I am going to take a stroke! I am going in!"

Now the alligator has a golf ball and a chipping wedge. The poor game warden's phone begins to ring off the hook. I know what you are thinking! This is a no-brainer right. It's still Alabama, and somebody like me should hustle down there early in the morning and 'bust a cap in that ass.' I promise after a decade of fooling with the beasts there is nothing else I would rather do! Well I have to give Alabama credit we have our share of 'tree huggers,' and they showed up in force to make sure that this behemoth didn't get killed. Big deal, right? An Alabama game warden would just walk by and BLAM, he blows its brains out. *Game over.* Unfortunately the tree huggers brought TV cameras with them. While the same cocky attitude found in most of the 'game wardens,' none of these bad asses was stupid enough to get caught decapitating the old gator on live television. After quite a struggle and several weeks, they managed to lure him into a 'culvert trap' that was used to capture black bears. (Yes we have bears in Alabama.) This trap was nothing more that a large diameter metal pipe, the kind of corrugated pipe that runs under the road to allow drainage. It had a drop door on one end and a bait system in the closed back end. It was a simple device that really worked because of the stupidity of the creatures.

Well, let's get back to my first gator, which was a tiny guy about five foot long and he probably didn't weigh more than 40 pounds. I swear you would have thought that Wesley and I were trying to capture a dragon. We would tiptoe around the lake looking for the gator.

"Is that an alligator track?

"Let me see. No. I don't think so. What the hell is that?"

"Wouldn't they have a drag mark from where their tail drags behind them?"

"I think they pick their tail up when they run."

"How do you know that?"

"I was watching Mutual of Omaha...and saw a crocodile run off the bank...its tail was in the air."

"I didn't see that one...Did Jim catch it?'

"Yea...ha-ha...but it whooped his ass."

"What did Marlin do?"

"Same as always, he just kept talking to the camera about Jim struggling with it, and he kept reminding the viewers about how many Indians get eaten by crocs each year."

"Did you see him with that big boa constrictor?"

"Yeah, that was a good one...even Marlin got in the water...I thought Jim was a goner."

"What the difference between a croc and an alligator?"

"Hell I don't know? I think a croc is meaner."

"Is that him over there in the water? Naw that's a turtle, never mind."

At first we were so naive we didn't even believe the homeowner.

"Oh an alligator...sure...yea." (Wesley cuts his eyes at me).

The guy is adamant and getting a little pissed. We stalk around the swampy pond. And after an hour we gave up. I didn't ever see the dang thing. After we left, Wesley admitted that he hadn't seen it either.

"Well, maybe he left." Wesley offered.

The man insists "NO! There is an alligator in this pond!"

This guy's house was literally a 100 mile round trip to work, and his complaint was getting old. Wesley finally told the guy that he would set some baited hooks on some parachute cord. This was on a Friday, and we both were off for the summertime weekend. On Monday, we checked with the guy who had called us.

He informed us, "Yeah, you caught the gator, and I tried to reach you all weekend but nothing...I could not reach anyone. After struggling on the line, the gator finally chewed through the rope."

Dang.

Wesley and I investigated the line, and sure enough a small piece of rope was left tied to the tree. After seeing the chewed up parachute cord it was like magic, now we could see the alligator. I am not sure if it was that we had some kind of mental block or whether the hook had hurt the alligator. Of course, he probably was just wondering if we were going to put some more delicious chicken out. We were so tired of working this complaint; you have to remember it was July, and both the average temp and humidity were at 95. You can imagine us in our cotton shirts, heavy leather gun belts, and polyester pants. I mean we would be soaking wet with sweat. Wesley went to the radio and called Gary the federal agent, and got authorization to shoot the gator. Our landowner was going away for a couple of days, so we decided to harvest the creature that evening.

Wesley had just bought a Remington A-bolt rifle, and he was just itching to break it in...he fancied himself an expert marksman. He was a good shot. I know this because I would stand beside him on the firing range and he didn't miss. Ever! As I said before, he had a band and he was quite the performer. Evidently from his attitude change, killing or rather 'sniping' the gator was about to be a show too. After parking the green sedan under a large oak tree, Wesley carefully laid a green wool army blanket across the hood. (He was all business). I looked around to see if there were any cute girls watching. *Nope...no visible audience! This must be for me.*

Wesley was just in "sniper mode!" He strutted back to the open trunk of the sedan, and gently, with both hands lifted an old patchwork quilt out of the car. He moved to the front hood, and laid the 'baby' wrapped in a blanket on the hood. He flipped the quilt, exposing a long brown gun case. I mentally heard a *Ta-dah!* Gently, he reached with one hand and tried to unzip the case with a single pull. The zipper snagged, and he nearly pulled the gun case onto the ground. He grabbed the case with his left hand and struggled to get the zipper open. After he broke the pull ring, he ended up getting a pair of needle nose pliers from his tool box, and pulled until he tore the zipper to open position. The sniper show had kind of lost the magic for me, but old Wesley was still trying to pull it off. "Sniper mode" continues! He pulled the shiny 'long gun' out of the case, and it glittered in the sunlight, He had oiled the heck out of it. He held it up and admired it (Insert Holy Grail music).

"Emily."

"What's that…?"

"Emily. That's her name."

"You named your rifle…?"

"Yep… it's my 3rd ex-wife's name."

"Did you name it after her because you love her so much?"

"Naw…cause she was a mean bitch."

"Haha." I cracked up.

Well, thank God we were in the shade…old 'prima Donna' was taking his time. Finally, he managed to get the ammunition into Emily. He softly pushed each round into the magazine…I thought that he was saying a silent prayer.

Perhaps he was blessing each bullet. What a showman! Over the top!

He turned his baseball cap around backwards and then removed his aviator glasses. He wrapped the leather sling around his forearm just like the Marine snipers do and lay across the hood of the car with the barrel resting on the blanket. Right on cue the 'giant' 5-foot gator's head came out of the water. Finally, everything was coming together for us now.

"Shoot! Wesley. There it is." (This was the first time that I had even seen the thing).

"Yeow…shit!" Wesley jumped up "Dang!"

"What's wrong, Wesley? It is getting away!" I loudly whispered.

"The hood is smoking hot! I think I burnt myself!"

The gator cruised around the lake behind the limbs of a willow tree.

"Come on!" Wesley hollered as he ran to the edge of the swamp.

There, we were creeping along through the knee deep weeds and mud, expecting a cotton mouth to bite us and looking for the head of the dragon. It was creepy as hell, wondering if the gator was going to grab our boots and drag us under the murky water. I was right behind Wesley…step by step…just like *Abbot and Costello*. Wesley raised his hand.

"Whoa!" he dramatically whispered.

He raised the rifle. We were dripping with sweat, and the sun was sitting on our necks. Standing in the water, it was a humid 101 degrees in the blazing Alabama sunlight.

"I can't keep it still enough," he complained.

"Pat, you quietly come up front, here."

I obeyed and moved in front of him. Before I could turn and ask him what he wanted me to see, the barrel of Emily came by my face and rested on my shoulder. I looked at Wesley horrified.

"Put your fingers in your ears Pat." Wesley calmly reassured me.

I turned back to look at the gator, and it had surfaced. I jumped from under the barrel.

"Hell NO!" I said, "Ugh huh? No way!"

Splash and the gator went under. I was a rookie but not an idiot.

"No way are you firing that cannon balanced on my shoulder!"

"Pussy," he whispered as he walked by.

"What?"

"Nothing," he sourly replied.

He shrugged his shoulders innocently, and we struggled and squished back to the car. The whole thing was pretty silly, but it really ended sadly.

The gator surfaced, and Wesley stood in the muck wobbling around. He began blasting away. BOOM. A water spout appeared about two feet away from the gator's head. The gator just ignored it. I can't imagine anyone reading this would have ever had the opportunity to try to eradicate a nuisance alligator but it is a difficult thing. The rifle bullet just doesn't penetrate the water, and it tends to skip along the surface. The bullet impact makes quite an impressive splash, but does little to kill the animal. Mike McNeil, the warden from Sumter County, pulls up as Wesley finally connects with the alligator.

BOOM. SPLASH.

"Alligator is gone." Wesley announces, and slings Emily over his shoulder using the leather sling.

Wesley then fills me in with the details that I hadn't expected.

"Okay. Pat." he said while pointing at the lake. "Get into that little aluminum boat and go fish him out."

"What? You are kidding right."

"Nope. We have to measure him, weigh him, and sex him?"

"How do you sex an alligator, Wesley?"

"Well Pat...YOU have to stick your finger in its butthole and pull out its penis."

"No I don't Wesley."

"Yes Pat you must ...you are the rookie."

I looked at Mike, and he shrugged his shoulders.

While Wesley walked to the boat I whispered to Mike, "Please call Gary the Federal agent and ask him how to sex a gator...I think Wesley is full of shit!"

I didn't like the idea, but I was still in training so off we went.

I remember Mike asking, "Are you going to take your shotgun?"

Wesley gave him the 'Are you a jackass?' look. "Hell no! What in the world would we use a shotgun for?"

Embarrassed, Mike said, "I just thought that if you have to shoot at his head again...9 pellets would cover a larger area. Definitely be able to hit it solidly in the head."

I think that Mike got his feelings hurt because he left the area. He made my call and then walked to the edge of the lake and gave me an affirmative on the finger 'sexing thing' and then waved goodbye. That is how I knew he was mad...it was almost lunchtime. I know he didn't drive all the way over here and not plan to eat lunch. I truly thought that Wesley had been a little hard on him, but his patience was running thin. We were both covered in sweat, and the damn sun was burning our hair off.

Wesley helped me drag a small aluminum boat off the bank and paddle to the area where the alligator went down.

Wesley has brought Emily along…for what reason I have no idea. Geez, it had a nine power scope which was great for shooting 200 yards but damn impractical for shooting something three feet away. I was in charge of paddling the boat, but I wasn't sure that I wanted to find the dead alligator and perform any analysis on his privates. Wesley stood on the bow with Emily, very much like that picture of George Washington crossing the Delaware. Wesley loved that gun. Once in the right spot, he held Emily in one hand and he began working a paddle along the bottom of the pond. It quickly became clear that we were ill equipped for the recovery operation, but we gave it a try anyway. Like I said, time was urgent because it was lunchtime! Wesley was leaning over the side of the boat and with the paddle; he was probing into the shallow bottom. His other arm is up in the air and Emily is waving around like a counter balance. I tried to hold our position while ducking under the swinging muzzle of his rifle. I remember thinking *I hope he has that thing unloaded*. The little boat is leaning to the right, and the water is only about an inch from the gunwale. Suddenly, the gator comes up two feet from the side of the boat. Wesley nearly shits himself and leaps backward. I am already standing on other side of the boat, trying to get as much distance from the pissed off gator as physically possible! I don't remember moving to the side, but when that ugly lizard stuck his head up out of the water I think I teleported. With this movement, the boat rolls in the opposite direction and water sloshes in. For a moment it is like we are on a log roll. We both start moving to the right and to the left trying to stabilize the rocking boat. It was like some strange dance. Trying to save Emily, Wesley hugs the big rifle and dives in the middle of the deck of the little boat. It was either that or it goes sailing over the side.

The boat was still rocking, and Wesley screams, "Shoot it!"… *(His deep voice was now a lot higher pitched. Not girlie, but definitely having more of a tenor quality).*

I stand up and pull my .357 revolver pistol. Oh baby was I dreaming! I didn't need any encouragement.

BOOM…BOOM…BOOM…BOOM…BOOM…   BOOM.

I blasted the water like Clint Eastwood. Go ahead alligator, make my day!

Click…click….click. I ran out of ammo as water began showering down on us. I swear, none of my bullets were within a foot of the beast, but I was sexy as hell blasting away. I know I looked cool.

"Did you get it?"

"Nope."

"Damn."

"But I think I shot a hole in the bottom of the lake. Does it look like the water level is dropping?" I asked.

"No, I think it is lower because of the water that you sprayed into the boat." Wesley added never missing an opportunity for a smart ass remark. *And there is always room for comedy, even during life and death situations.*

The alligator, who was watching the show, gave us a confused look and then submerged again.

Wesley, having lost his hat and now dripping wet with pond water, gave me a different kind of look and we quietly paddled back to shore. We were both disgusted with the whole operation. We talked with the pond owner, who now knew for a fact that we were a bunch of jackasses. Of course, I am sure he suspected it from the first sight of us sneaking terrified around his pond, but now it was undeniable. He patronizingly guaranteed that he would call if the alligator resurfaced or floated up.

I get nauseous just thinking about the mess. What I didn't tell you was that the alligator had been hit. If you've seen pictures of an alligator's head, then you've seen that they have a long flat head with snout. The rifle had blown the snout off just in front of its eyes. It was horrifying. No way could it survive. It didn't have mouth or teeth. I can't tell you how sad it makes me, when thinking about the suffering that we inflicted on the little animal. Truthfully, that was one of the reasons I so urgently tried to blast it. After the damage that we had inflicted it had to be euthanized. We transformed a beautiful creature into a freakish abomination fit only for hell.

Behind the bravado, Wesley was a family man and a pet lover, and he was obviously tormented by the botched detail. I couldn't help but notice that he was 'down.' Yes, he was depressed…sad…vulnerable! .*Muhahaha, a silent mental laugh sneaks across my brain.*

"Wesley you might want to rename your rifle." I innocently said catching the vulnerable guy off guard.

"Yea maybe you got any sug__?" He stopped mid- sentence and grimaced as he could tell that I indeed had a smart ass comment.

"Wesley." I said pausing for effect. "Have you ever married a blind woman? Hahaha."

Wesley was going to his required Annual National Guard training for two weeks, summer camp for soldiers, so I was left in charge. Yep I was in charge! After he deployed, I called the pond owner and he said that the gator had come up and he had finished it off. I told him that I was sorry about the mess. He said that he appreciated the attempt.

I wanted to vomit. Thinking about the misadventure, I promised myself that I would do better on the next complaint. I really wanted to be a better conservation officer. I had learned one thing during the whole unfortunate mission. I knew for a fact that no one in our district had any real experience handling the alligator complaints. I was beginning to think that the only requirement for the job was a smart ass since of humor and 10 year-old maturity level. I was going to cut it close.

Our county was in the southern tip of the district, and the alligator problem was migrating north. I wouldn't have to wait because the very next week I got a call from another pond owner just a couple of miles from the fiasco.

The call came in on a Monday from a complainant that lived down the dirt road from the original call. The lady was quite concerned but was leaving today for two weeks. The area was fresh in my mind, so I drove down looking for the pond. After driving around for about 20 minutes, I finally stopped and asked directions at a plantation style, old wood frame house. I was greeted by a middle aged, graying blonde haired woman who was wearing those black schoolmarm glasses. I had interrupted her class for her son, Junior who was about nine and was being home-schooled. She explained that her son's name was Johnny. He was named after his father, Big Johnny.

I thought for a moment "…So this is little Johnny?"

"That's right but we call him Junior… it's easier to keep them straight!"

She was too nice to appreciate any comment I could make about "little Johnny," so I kept my mouth shut!

She made me sit down and have a piece of lemon cake and tea, while her son just stared up at me with his mouth wide open. Being that school was in session, she made me give a full report about my job and activities. It was like a private career day. The kid listened and then opened up with questions. Wow! Kids have a lot of questions. For a moment I felt like I was part of a Norman Rockwell painting titled 'trapped policeman with starry eyed young boy pointing at my badge and guns.' I let him play with my handcuffs. I was his new hero. Mom just watched and helped with the third degree.

"That a big gun!"

"Yes it a .357 revolver."

"Have you killed anyone?"

"Not today (his smile drooped visibly disappointed)…but it's early." I replied.

"Wow."

"I am not allowed to shoot anyone unless they are trying to kill me. Last week I was in a shootout, but nobody got hit."

I talked with his mom and turned and watched in horror as he locked the handcuffs around his wrists through the armrest of the chair. I didn't say anything as he snatched the cuffs trying to break them apart. My mind was racing, wondering if I
had a handcuff key.

Oh shit! I thought. I looked at my watch, "Oops. I need to radio into headquarters. I will be right back."

My mind was racing as I stepped out onto the porch. The little guy tried to follow but luckily he had handcuffed himself to the arm of the chair. He jumped up and then fell backward. He then tried to drag the chair along.

"Maybe Junior could see your radio?" the lady asked.

I pretended not to hear as I hurried to the vehicle.

I climbed into the cab of my truck and started the engine. I knew exactly where my handcuff key was located. It was in the bowl where I dropped my wallet and keys at the house. It was right by the refrigerator at home. I called the county jail asking if there was a deputy in the area. It was at lunchtime, and all available units where either eating or tied up in other calls. *Why couldn't this have happened near the Church's Chicken restaurant? I could have gotten 15 officers to respond!* I looked into the rear view mirror and saw sweat beads covering my forehead.

Oh shit. I don't have a key. I thought.

I heard a loud 'Owww!'

I looked up, and Junior had the chair caught in the front door, and he was tugging at it determined to get to my truck and play with my radio.

His mother was concerned now, but luckily she was trapped on the inside of the house.

I just smiled and pretended to be in an important conversation. I crinkled my forehead and nodded as I faked the radio traffic.

My mind was racing. *How the hell am I going to get those handcuffs off the little guy?* I kept flashing back to a conversation with my supervisor.

"I need an extra handcuff key," I said sincerely.

He laughed, "Putin' the cuffs on the violator is your problem. Getting the handcuffs off is his problem...hahahahaha."

Brilliant. I guess he just decided to put the key on backorder. Seems pretty obvious that I would need an extra key! I glanced up at my prisoner who had almost gotten the chair through the door. The little guy was in a frenzy now, and I thought *oh shit he is going to chew his hand off at the wrist. Talk about determination.*

In the corner of my eye I saw mother heading around the side of the house, and she wasn't smiling.

I was about to drop the mike and start apologizing...and asking if they had a hacksaw or something. I had resigned myself that I was fated to become a part of another 'little Johnny' joke. *Damn!* I leaned forward to hang up the mike and happened to glance in the ash tray. In among the old ashes, crude and old chewing gum there was a tiny stainless steel key, a remnant of the previous game warden's life. *Finally a reward for not cleaning my truck.*

"Thank you Jesus," I gasped.

"What's that?" the mother asks now standing in my truck doorway.

"Just appreciating this beautiful day."

"Amen." She replied.

Whew! I thought.

I grabbed the key and handed it to momma as I pretended to wait for a reply from headquarters. She took it, and I bowed my head and said a little prayer. *Please Jesus...let that key work.* I thought with my mind racing.

I was holding my breath and trying to think of a good story if the key didn't work.

"My son is trapped to a chair and you don't have a key."

"No ma'am. Your son is so strong that he must have damaged the handcuffs...wow... you should be very proud! My dog ate my other key...No. I mean I was working with a rookie last night and had to loan it to him. It was an emergency so I let him keep it. Damn those incompetent rookies. Do you have a hacksaw?"

My thought process was interrupted by a tugging on my sleeve.

It was Junior, and he held up the cuffs proudly.

"I escaped." He exclaimed.

"Yes you did! You would make a good magician."

I took the key from his mother and said, "You have an amazing young child here…you must be an amazing teacher"

She just beamed. *Smooth…real smooth. When in doubt…lay it on thick!*

I grabbed a paper towel off the seat and dabbed the sweat off my brow. I got up and let Junior climb onto the seat and play with the siren and blue lights.

"Are you okay?" Momma asked

"Yes ma'am. I am just dizzy. I think I got up too quickly."

As luck would have it, they knew the pond and the folks who had the alligator in the pond. She politely asked if little Johnny could ride with me. At first I told her that it probably wouldn't be a good idea, but I swear that I watched the light go out in the little guy's eyes and his checks dropped. She was catching my drift and starting to back me up.

"Yes, we have some more work to do"

What the hell I thought as I said out loud. "I could use some help though…

I might need someone to call for back up on the radio if the gator gets me."

I looked at the kid…Do you think you could push the radio button and say help."

The lights came back on, "Yes. I could do that."

At least I knew the little fellow could work the handcuffs in an emergency.

We loaded up and he showed me the way to the pond.

"Do I get a gun?"

"No you just work the radio and I will do the shooting."

He was clearly disappointed about this news.

I handed him back the handcuffs. "If I get 'em down you put these on em."

"Yes sir!"

There was my grin… he was all happy again.

I couldn't help but think that he would make a good wingman. A real improvement on some I would later train.

The pond sat right beside the road. There was a short driveway that ended at a barbed wire fence. We parked in front of the gap in the fence and walked down to the pond. This was a small pond. It was about a 100 foot rectangle with no vegetation around it. We sat down and got out the binoculars and scanned the pond for the alligator. Nothing at first, and then a small brown bump came out of the water. It looked like a turtle head. When I looked closer I saw the eyes rise up just behind the first bump of the nose. I was relieved that it was not the other alligator we had tried to euthanize. I am sure that it would have scared the wits out of anyone. It would look like some kind of freak 'zombie' alligator. Nope. This was just a typical four-foot long juvenile alligator. You might even call him a cute alligator. After I was satisfied that there was truly an alligator, and that I had answered all of Junior's questions, we returned to his house. For a finale, I let him turn the blue lights and siren on. He got a real kick out of that, but I thought I was going to have to get his mom to get my handcuffs back. She gave me warm, sincere thanks for my time. I tipped my cap and told her that if I caught the gator that I would stop by and let them have a look at it. I drove off wondering about the kid being home-schooled. I wondered if he was missing out. It seemed kind of a lonely existence. I wonder if he would grow up to be a game warden, or maybe an escape artist. *Oh my God...do you think little Johnny is a game warden?*

The Bear Trap

My new problem was that I didn't really know anything about catching an alligator. *Don't laugh. Ever seen a college catalog with trapping Alligators 101?* I didn't think so.

The lucky thing was that it was summer, and all the old wardens where at drill, vacation or just hiding out. It was hot as heck with no real complaints to work. I would later learn that you could use a reel and rod to catch some...hook em' with a gaff, lasso them, or spear them with a barb point, but at the time I only remembered that someone had used a bear trap to catch one. *A bear trap...I know...looking back it seems absurd...what was I thinking?* I liked the idea of a trap that I could bait and leave to catch the alligator. If I didn't have to touch the wild things then it was unlikely that they would get a hand or finger. I could load the trap and gator and make a clean getaway. No blood, no TV cameras and no written reports.

The basic configuration for a bear trap was a culvert trap. I know that you have walked by a road and seen the metal pipe that runs under the road to let rain water or creeks pass underneath. It is a big diameter pipe and looks like a bunch of hula hoops glued together but made out of galvanized steel. I wanted a trap that I could keep and have available to use over and over, but I was shocked to find out how much the pipe cost. They were $10 to $25 a linear foot, which was probably a good price for a road construction project, but well out of my price range. My budget was about fifteen bucks, plus the change I could get out of the seat of the truck. I stopped by the Demopolis Street Department. These old boys loved to 'talk shit' to the game wardens. I swear they greeted me like an old friend. Three of the guys gave me a grin and they had maybe a full set of teeth between the three of them, which didn't speak much for the municipal dental program. I make fun of them now, but honestly you could not have met a better bunch to help you with such an outlandish project. They would have weeks of entertainment talking about the alligator mission. I had only been on the job a few months but had already learned that the best way to get some assistance was to bluff. I spoke of the trap with specifics, and confidence that these items were mission critical to the capture of the dangerous alligator. I even threw in a story about how alligators eat puppies. In the Army, an ancient warrant officer told me "If you can't overwhelm them with brilliance...then baffle them with bullshit."

As I rattled off my ridiculous stories, I was satisfied that I had learned the lesson well. *Thank you sensei.*

I told them about my budget problem, and they said they had some culvert that I could borrow but would have to return. This also meant that I couldn't cut it. It was 10 inches in diameter, and 10 feet long. I decided to go ahead and borrow the pipe, at least I could develop a detachable trap door system that would give me the ability to put one together on 'borrowed' pipe as needed.

I was really curious to see if I could pull it off. The clock was ticking, and if the old wardens got back and got wind of the exercise, I was sure to catch hell for my effort in futility.

I got a lot of stares when I was driving down Highway 43 south of Demopolis. My four wheeled drive Chevy pickup had a tool box, and that meant that I only had about five feet of space in the bed with the tail-gate down. Anywhere from five to six feet of the huge 10 foot long culvert pipe was sticking out of the back end, depending on whether I was going uphill.

At the Diamond gas station, a drunken hobo named Henry asked me if I had a jet truck, accompanying the comment with another toothless laugh.

Hahaha…very funny! I thought.

"No. This is an alligator holding trap."

Laughter stopped.

The hobo leaned to one side and started sneaking up on the backend of the truck. He bent over and did some type of 'pimp step…pimp sneak.' Bent over at the waist, he would make a sort of skip step towards the truck. When I came back outside he was scratching his head.

"I don't see no alligator."

I looked into the pipe 'all careful like.' "Oh shit!"

I looked left and right pretending to be nervous like I had lost an alligator. I continued my charade as I ran and hoped into the driver seat. As I sped away, I saw Henry, now at the half-open door of the store. He was looking around, and he wasn't smiling anymore. As I started eating my honey bun and drinking my coke, I began to think that I might have some fun with alligators. I admit that it was a cruel trick to play on someone who clearly had mental issues, or at least couldn't tie his shoes. I drove the *Batmobile* home and just kept looking ahead. I was picking up some strange head movements from other drivers and pedestrians who must have thought that I either had a secret weapon, or that I had just ripped off a construction site.

When I got to my house, which sits on top of a steep hill, I decided to unload the huge pipe so that I could run some errands to the hardware store without all the advice and questions from the curious citizens. I hopped in the back of the truck, and with a ninja smoothness sliced my thin little yellow rope. You may remember that at least 6 foot of the pipe was sticking out of the truck bed and that I parked at the top of a large hill. These added factors now gave the pipe a 'will' of its own. It decided to leave! I, in my wisdom, had straddled the great pipe which now bucked me backwards onto the tool box. The greatest part of the pipe slammed down onto my new asphalt driveway. I guess this end of the pipe decided it was the head. The head proceeded to drag the small remainder of the pipe off the slick surface of the truck bed. It hit with a bounce and paused. I watched in slow motion as the newly freed end pivoted down toward the bottom of the hill. That side had a head start but the other side decided catch up and the whole thing started to roll. The huge 10-foot long pipe began slowly rolling down my driveway like a huge rolling pin. I caught my breath and checked the neighbor's houses for vehicles and kids. No traffic. No kids. No witnesses.

Living in the country has its perks and two of mine where Labrador retrievers. They would wander the neighborhood and countryside all day long, but if they saw a vehicle at the house they would start galloping home. They would arrive like they had been on guard duty all day. Well, they had seen my truck and had started up the driveway to my house. They were hauling ass up the driveway as the pipe monster was hurtling down. The dogs went stiff-legged and came to a screeching halt. My drive was about 140 feet long, and although it was just gravity, the 'runaway pipe' began chasing the startled dogs back the other way. Guard dogs my ass! They left the county. As the pipe got near the end of my driveway and approached the freedom of the main road, the left side bounced up causing the whole thing to turn left. The tail hit a pine tree and it spun out into the grass yard, and it stopped against a holly bush. After breathing a sigh of relief, I grabbed a piece of rope and ran down the hill to hog tie the pipe. I didn't want to even think about the paperwork that a 'pile up' of cars would have caused by the possessed piece of pipe. I went down to the pipe, and I swear that I felt like shooting it, but I couldn't remember which end was the head. I decided to work on it at the bottom of the hill, just in case it decided to run away again. After I was sure that it was dead, or no longer possessed, I began my alligator trap by closing off one end of the trap with a scrap piece of plywood. I left a small opening to allow me to look into the pipe and to service a bait bag which was suspended by a small pulley to the pipe. The small wire ran back to the other end, and connected to a small pin that would be pulled out from under a metal sheet door. If the door was working properly, it would drop straight down on U-channel rails to close the entry end of the pipe. I had the devil figuring out how to attach all of this   hardware to the pipe. Finally, I decided to drill holes in the pipe and set 2x4 framing boards on the outside of the pipe. Then, using decking screws from the inside, I would screw the boards to the pipe. It worked pretty well. All I needed was a flat board and some old u-channel from a shelving project. When I backed up and examined my work, I was pretty satisfied with my design, but I needed to test it.

My two cowardly watch dogs, both Labrador retrievers...a beautiful snow white named Mac and a coal black dog named Bear, decided to return to investigate the contraption. I called to the dogs, and Bear came over wagging his tail. Mac on the other hand wasn't coming anywhere near the possessed piece of pipe. He gave me a look, and then headed off towards the neighbors. I tried to get Bear in the pipe where he could see the bait trigger with his sock toy tied to it. He was trusting but wasn't going inside the contraption. I was dripping with sweat and honestly was done with the effort, so I went inside the house and got some boiled chicken out of the refrigerator. Bear sat patiently watched. He began to salivate when he caught scent of the chicken. Bear loves human food! I reached into the back end of the pipe and pulled the bait string with the sock toy out. I attached the chicken thigh bone to the bait string, and then tossed it down into the pipe. I glanced at Bear he was looking to the side like he hadn't noticed me. He was definitely playing it cool. I could tell he was thinking ... *Your gonna just leave that chicken out here. Hmm so that's where you leave the chicken...hmm...good idea...whatever...big deal.* He was definitely playing it calm displaying amazing self control. I went inside. I stopped at the door and caught him watching me through the window on the kitchen door, intently. He caught me looking and lay down like he was going to take nap. I could hear his little brain, *Yea you go take a break...and I will guard the house from this chicken...aw... I mean this pipe monster. Gosh my work is never done!* I went inside, and after a pitcher of cold sweet tea and an afternoon nap I got a call from McNeil. I told him about the trap and asked if he could help me. He said he was on his way to help me load it and set it. He was feeling better about alligators. I guess he wanted to show up Wesley because of his smart ass remark at the first gator call. He also wanted to know how to build an alligator trap because now I was the division expert. He was very complimentary, but I am sure that he was on his way to get an interesting story' for the next meeting. He asked me if it would work.

"Hold on." I replied.

In my sock feet, I walked over to the kitchen door and saw that the trap door was down. I could just make out a long black Labrador nose sticking out of the back access hole. I could tell it was mouthing the words. *Help...this thing is eating me!*

"Hell yes!" I confidently replied. But I was thinking, *well it works on dogs.* Mike arrived about the same time as the boys got home from kindergarten. You can imagine twin boys all wound up from day care. They were climbing all over the trap and, of course, had to pretend that they were alligators and pretend to get trapped in the pipe. After they each had turns dragging Bear into the trap, Mike and I went inside to get a glass of tea. When we came out, Alex had trapped Neville in the pipe. Bear evidently had taken Mac's advice and left the county. Neville thought it was great fun until Alex started poking at him with a stick through the access hole. Luckily we had some chocolate chip cookies, so I was able to steal their new toy and go off to do some work without too much of a fuss.

Mike rode with me in my truck with the 'super' trap sticking out of the truck bed. "That's a big trap." Mike commented.

"Yes. It's made like a bear trap."

Mike raised his eyebrows. "You know how to make a bear trap?"

"Sure...doesn't everyone."

"I can't wait to see your alligator!"

When we arrived, we quickly dropped the pipe out of the truck bed and onto the bank by the small pond. Mike helped me get it near the pond but said that I had to get into the pond with it. He was not going to get his uniform wet. He helped push from the hillside end of the trap. At first, the pipe tried to float, but it slowly began to sink in the cloudy water. As it filled with water it began to get heavy. Very heavy! Now when I built the trap, I had envisioned sitting it in the shallow end of the pond. The problem with that was that this square pond didn't really have a shallow end...it was like a bowl. I quickly realized that if I got the whole thing in the water so that the alligator would swim into the back and grab the chicken, then the front end would be at least 10 feet toward the center of the pond and in three feet of water. As the steel pipe began to fill, I quickly realized my folly, and that it would have to be laid or positioned parallel to the bank...right alongside the bank. I grabbed the now nearly sunken trap door end, and had to lunge with all my might to twist the end toward the right and closer to the bank. Of course, my boots where already above ankle deep in the soft mud. I stepped right out of my left boot and my right foot got hung up just enough to trip me up. I thought *TIMBER* as I started to fall with a lover's hold around the end of the devil's pipe. That's right, face first into muddy water. No time to bitch or listen to the laughter coming from the 'land lover.' I did manage to push the pipe beside the bank. But I didn't have any time to catch my breath because the pipe, now approaching a couple hundred pounds in weight, did sink parallel to the bank. Hooray! The square frame at the front acted like a lever...one side in 4 inches of water, and the other sinking side going down to 2 feet. The whole dang thing began to roll over. I was already a wreck, so with muddy hands sliding off the steel I began trying to stop it. The pipe definitely weighed around 800 pounds now, and again seemed to have a will of its own. I watched helplessly as I began to slide down the side of the steel. My sock foot buried in the mud, I went to my knees and the pipe threatened to roll right over me...squishing me into the cow shit smelling mud of the pond. *Why does this pipe hate me?*   "Mike. Mike stop laughing and help me!"His laughter went to concern as he detected horror in my voice.

While I know he would have loved the story of my silly death, I am sure he didn't want to do the 'paperwork' and explain how he had gotten me killed with a piece of pipe from the street department.

"Yeah, Pat was killed by a bear trap that we were using to catch an alligator."

I bet he would have had to rewrite it a couple of times to make any sense of the accident. *That Mike he was always getting me into messes! What a character!*

Just as I was going under, the pipe stopped. I struggled and half swam to get out of its way. After catching my breath, I eased back down to the water's edge and baited the trigger rope and then raised the trap door. I crawled up the bank and laid on my back with one muddy boot on and a muddy brown sock on the other foot. Right beside the trap I noticed something curious. The alligator had been in the water right beside me and had watched the whole show.

Mike looked at the gator.

"Pat that's a lot of trap for a three foot long alligator."

"Shut up!" I gasped.

"Well he looked bigger yesterday…must be two or three in this pond." I growled.

Now I got the smart ass look, and Mike again decided that he needed to get back to Sumter County before someone connected him with one of my schemes. The son of a@@# probably just wanted to get somewhere to call the other wardens and laugh it up without me hearing.

The next day I got up and made the long drive down to Surginer to check the trap. I was shocked because the trap was tripped. Great! But damn it, I honestly could not tell if the gator was in the trap. I changed into my swim suit and eased down into the water. I peaked and honestly couldn't tell if I had caught the gator. Years later, I would not be able to see an 11-foot long gator in a smaller trap because with only a few inches of muddy water he was able to hide. Alligators have the skill of 'acting small.' Well, this was a tiny alligator in a huge pipe filled with water and I had no clue. This pipe was nearly impossible to move. I had some real engineering problems to work on. I was determined to find out if I had the alligator, so I lifted the trap door end of the trap and just held it up until enough water had drained that I could lift that end onto the bank. I had put the door pretty close to pipe so I was having to peak in the cracks above and on the sides. It was hopeless. I needed some help. Nobody was home at the farm, and I didn't want to call any wardens. I thought of Mike, but figured that I shouldn't risk overwhelming him with my skill…hell he had enough material for a comedy show already! I had already made a fool of myself with the dang trap. Luckily, I come from a big family, so I called my brother who just happened to be off work.

"Hey, Charlie. Do you want to help me move an alligator?" I was all confident sounding, even though I didn't have a clue to whether the gator was even in the trap.

"A what?" came the confused question?

"An alligator…I have trapped one and need someone to back me up in case something goes wrong."

"Hell yeah!" Charlie replied. *I didn't even have to offer him a beer.*

I drove to Demopolis and picked him up. He was standing on his front porch eating a moon pie and washing it down with a Budweiser. I noticed that he had a cooler beside him. He already had his beer. He had bags under his eyes and was wearing cowboy boots and *Levi's* jeans. He had a blue golf shirt on and still had his orange ear plugs draped around his neck. He looked tired and had just gotten off the graveyard shift at work.

"Hold on…I am just finishing my lunch."

"Charlie," I said while looking at the cooler, "you can't take a cooler of beer."

He looked at me incredulous, "You mean to tell me that you are going to catch an alligator sober."

"Charlie, this is a police vehicle. I can't be carrying a cooler of beer in the cab."

"Who the hell is going to care? You think the alligator is going to give a shit?"

"No. But I don't want to get into any trouble if my supervisor makes a surprise visit."

"Well why don't you call that son of a bitch to help you."

"I can't. He is an asshole, and he is on annual summer drill. Hell... all the wardens are at summer drill."

Charlie cocked his head and grinned.

"Okay...but you have to put the cooler in the back and your drink in a McDonald's cup."

"All righty then! Let's go whoop us an alligator's ass!"

Understandably, he had a million questions and I acted like I had invented alligator trapping.

"How did you catch this thing?"

"I built a trap and caught him the first night."

"What kind of trap?"

"A bear trap."

"You know how to build a bear trap?"

"Sure, doesn't everyone."

He totally bought it. It was an easy sell because he had only eaten a moon pie for lunch and drank three beers. Also, he had just worked off a double shift. He was feeling no pain. When we got back to the trap, Charlie eased up to the pipe.

"Man that's a big trap…How big is the alligator? "

"Well, Charlie, this one is only a little fellow, but this is the only piece of pipe I could get on short notice so I had to make do."

"Shit you could put *Godzilla* in that trap."

Silently I was praying that I had caught the alligator. *How much crow does a guy have to eat anyway?*

Well, by this time, I had come up with a plan. The pipe was still resting with 5 or 6 feet of its bulk in the pond. I quickly wrapped a rope around the pipe and hooked it to the towing ball on the truck.

"Charlie, I need you to pull the truck forward slowly. Now please remember that the pipe is full of water and probably weighs 1000 pounds. I need you to slowly pull so that the water drains out as we go, or the force will blow the back door out. When it is mostly out of the water I will lift the back end up so the frame doesn't catch the bank and get torn off."

I figured time was critical because one more beer and I wasn't sure if Charlie would be able to distinguish the drive gear from the reverse gear. He complied, and we slowly worked the huge pipe out of the pond. It worked like magic. I couldn't believe we pulled it off. Once totally out of the pond, we let the pipe finish draining. Charlie had his eye pressed against the crack trying to see the alligator, while I was sitting on the tailgate of my truck. I was calmly holding my breath and pulling off my LaCrosse knee high boots.

"Cool…Cool." Charlie whispered.

"What?" I asked hoping on one booted foot to the trap.

All the sudden there was a sound of a hiss and a sound of a toilet flushing. It turns out that even a small alligator can make this horrific noise.

"That's a nice one, but maybe you should have used a minnow trap. Haha"

I got up and peaked in, and to my delight there was about a six-foot long alligator in the trap. *Bless my soul*!

Although this was a miracle I played it cool.

"Yes, Charlie alligators can be very vocal. They will hiss and grunt. In fact, they have matting calls which are grunting sounds and can be heard from up to a mile away. What you are hearing is a warning hiss and growl." Blah…Blah…Blah, man I was laying it on thick.

We managed to load the pipe by lifting one end at a time into the bed of the truck. This activity and the bumping associated with the movement, really pissed off the gator. What we didn't know was that the alligator had slid down to the back end of the trap. As we lifted that end off the ground, his little toothy snout shot out of the crack between the frame and the galvanized pipe. It was like a steel toothed bear trap snapping out right at crotch level. *Why am I making an analogy here?* Just like a toothy alligator sapping at your groin!

We both screamed and dropped the pipe. The pipe crashed to the ground shattering part of the trap door. Again, I had teleported 20 steps away. *I was getting good at this.* Charlie grabbed a tree limb and pushed on the little guys head until it moved back into the trap.

By now Charlie wasn't scared of anything, and if he hadn't acted quickly the critter might have gotten out because when we dropped the heavy pipe; the impact tore most of the trap door loose. Fortune smiled on us, and the alligator didn't understand that he could make a break for it.

Although he was a small alligator, he was quite the prima donna. He was tiny, but he had quite a roar. Scary as hell! There were only five or six gas stations on the way home, but I made a point to stop into each one and buy a drink. If no one acknowledged me, I would go back inside and stand in line and ask if they had a water hose that I could use to 'water down' the alligator. I would use the bathroom and loiter around until quite a crowd would circle the *Batmobile*, which now had a thunderous alligator in the back. I played it cool and would answer folks' questions, talking about the nesting and movement of gators. Their threatened status…etc. I got quite good at the production. As the people got bolder and would press in very close to the pipe, I would accidently bump the pipe and the tiny dragon would flush his toilet and hiss. The people would jump back. I was pretty smug and having a grand ole' time until a guy asked me.

"What are you going to do with him?"

"Huh?"

"You aren't going to put him out around here?"

I hadn't thought about where I would release the alligator.

Thinking fast I lied, "Oh no! Sir. This one is going to a…a…a reserve."

He bought it, but honestly I had never even thought the trap would work. It never really occurred to me that I would be in possession of a real, live alligator. My plan really didn't have a destination for the alligator. I couldn't just drop it anywhere if someone got bit…I would catch hell.

After I finished the traveling show, Charlie asked if he could be there when I released the gator. I told him sure, but I would have to do it the next day. The gator would have to spend the night in the trap. Charlie needed to find some film, and I had to find the gator a new home.

I called the supervisor, and he said he didn't know what to do with the alligator either. He said that some people would put the captured alligators in their ponds, but his experience was that in a couple of years they would want it removed again. You know when it lost its cuteness and started eating the family pets. I finally decided to take it to a bridge on Highway 80, which had a lot of traffic but no homes nearby. I could pull off the four lane highway and let it scurry down the rocky slope. No one would know where I released it, and there were probably hundreds of alligators in that area anyway. Charlie met me at my house, and we drove to the remote site. I had made a catch stick with a 15 foot long metal pole and a piece of rope. Charlie raised the door and I worked the pole, which had a loop of rope sticking out of the end. It went pretty well, and the loop slid around the tiny alligator on the very first attempt. Charlie removed the door and got the camera. I pulled the little guy out pretending to be struggling. I flexed my biceps and grimaced like he was putting up a fight. The pictures came out funny and ridiculous looking. It looked like I had an iguana lizard on the end of a long pole, like maybe it was fish bait or something from the pet shop. I released the loop from around alligator's neck and he just lay down. He didn't move a muscle.

I gently poked him. "Go on. You're free."
After a few moments, he rose up and started waddling down the hill to the river. I walked along just behind him as he slid into the water.

This had been the job from hell, but I felt pretty good about the whole alligator rescue. I felt all noble and shit. (Rookie thinking). Now, and especially with the photos for evidence, the veterans were about to defer all alligator calls to me. Big mistake. The old wardens had been waiting for a sucker like me for years!

As luck would have it, the Department had just approved a provision for private alligator trappers to remove these nuisance alligators. The requirements to become a certified trapper were that the applicant had to have some experience, and he had to provide his own trap. Enter Leroy Overstreet. Leroy was a lanky old fellow who was 72 years old at the time I met him. Despite his age, he hopped around like a teenager. He was convinced that his good health came from drinking coke-a-cola every day.

Leroy was one of those amazingly interesting ancient people who still moved like they were kids. He had no patience for the idea of retirement. This was in the early nineteen 80's, so you can understand that his life was like the history of America. His childhood was horse and buggy and he had lived through those hard times until the age of routine space flight. Leroy wasn't an average guy, and when you talked with him you got the feeling that he had lived many lives. He grew up in Florida. His days as a child were lived in the swamp lands that now house the famous Walt Disney World.

He would walk to a one room school along cow trail roads. He would take his .22 rifle and try to kill some game for lunch, something like a rabbit or quail. Instead of a book bag, he had his knife, fire starter, and salt. Imagine taking your rifle to school today! Cattle ranching and farming were the livelihood of his family. Unlike most of the "wanabe" alligator trappers, he actually had a lifetime of experience. He had made a good living trapping alligators until the government stopped the hunting. Later, he would go to school and learn drafting and machining. With his 'can do attitude,' he had made a fortune or two in manufacturing special parts for a wood flooring factory in the rural county where he lived.

When I first met Leroy, I was suspicious. After all, he had made a living on the trade a 'hundred years' before. I was naive and too uninformed to realize that the alligators were no longer in danger and that they were not only a nuisance but had become a deadly problem. The fact that they remained listed as threatened on the federal list was bizarre.

Mega-Gator

As the alligator population continued to grow, the complaints moved further north. These persistent reptiles would walk miles up dry creek beds to scattered farm ponds which dot the Marengo county landscape. It was in late June when a farmer near Dixons Mills called to tell me that he had an alligator that kept running off his clients. He had a catfish farm and would allow people to fish and pay by the pound for their catch. I met Mr. Turner and his son at the intersection of Highway 43 and Highway 10. Mr. Turner was selling watermelons from his truck. You know I am sure that most people would simply dismiss the old man and the fruit stand as just another poor farmer. Ah... *look at that old guy he must be starving to death trying to make a living,* you are sure to think. A big fellow approximately 6' 2" and white-headed, he was personable and insisted that I meet his family. We went to his house and said hello to the wife and his daughters-in-laws. We had a friendly conversation as we crossed his farm...large farm...like I said you might dismiss the old guy, but he was retired military, a retired state employee, and had a huge farm scattered throughout the little community. He didn't need to sell watermelons for money, but he was just one of those folks who were 'old school' and just had to be busy.

We rode to his pond and watched the surface of the water for about an hour. Finally, the old gator rose up. He was smart one, and he had tried to lie low, but finally needed to come up for air. He was a big fellow, but I figured that my 10-foot trap would hold him. I think, looking back, that Mr. Turner had a little of that 'karma' stuff working against him. For years, he had told the locals that he thought might be sneaking in and fishing his pond after dark that he had a pet alligator that was active at night. Well, his story became reality, and now his paying customers where to afraid to fish in the pond. The episode was threatening to put him out of business.

The next day I returned to the pond with my giant culvert pipe trap. I wrestled it into the water and sat the bait, which consisted of fresh chicken legs from Food World. I figured that I would need to train him, so I hung some legs a few inches above the water on bamboo sticks, so the alligator would easily learn that the chicken was easy to catch and delicious. I then hung some bait at the front of the culvert pipe, and then baited the bag attached to the trigger at the back end of the pipe. For the next couple of days I would return to the trap and it would be sprung and all my chicken would be gone. I couldn't figure out how the bastard was getting out.

One day while baiting the trap, a cow came down by the water's edge and knocked over a trash can. A single coke can fell into the water, and the can drifted like a leaf across the surface of the water. In the center of the pond it drifted with little circles of ripples cascading in every direction from its sides. The old gator surfaced a few feet away and moved purposefully to the coke can. He opened his great jaws and picked the can up like a Labrador retrieving a ball. He crunched it and twisted his head and then dropped it out of his mouth. He then sank back into the muddy water. I had an epiphany watching him; *he was a machine reacting to a stimulus.* You could name him and pretend he had feelings, but if you hopped into the water and drifted across the surface, you could bet he would bite you and see if you were something edible. It wouldn't matter to him how nice a person you were.

It was at that moment that I put a call into Leroy and told him I had a problem that I needed help with. He said he would be delighted to help out. I met him in Sweetwater the next day and asked him to follow me to Dixon Mills. This was the first time that I had seen his trap. OMG! It was a 16-foot long steel box on huge rectangular frame that was floated with foam-filled pontoons. It looked like a Civil War Battle Ship. We returned to the Turner farm, and I introduced the two old gentlemen. They took to each other right away. I could tell that Mr. Turner was glad to see the silver-haired old alligator hunter. As we convoyed to the pond, we got some of the most amazing looks from the locals who were staring and pointing. I mean this was a huge trap. "What tha…you guys trapping Bigfoot…?" By the time we got to the pond we had quite an entourage of people watching. *A crowd! Are you kidding? Where the hell did all these people come from?* Curious locals had followed the battleship parade float like it was the Pied Piper. And, of course, Mr. Turner had called all his family, including the grandkids, the cousins, you know the works. Leroy insisted on doing everything himself and backed the huge trap into the pond. It looked like a small shack or boat house with a chicken coop suspended in the middle. Leroy jumped onto the boat and then began lowering the steel cage section into the water using a hand winch.   After Leroy was satisfied that it was positioned correctly, he retrieved a metal can from his truck. Unfortunately, I was downwind when he opened the top. Ugh! I gagged and circled around trying to get upwind. I nearly trampled one of Mr. Turner's grandsons. I, we, the crowd watched in horror as he reached into the can. From the smell, I thought that he would pull a dead baby or something hideous from the can. Instead it was a maggot infested mullet.

"Yeah, I bought these mullets in Mobile. I have to hang 'em out for a couple of days until they get just right." Leroy proudly told us.

He had stitched a heavy cord through the corpses with a sewing needle so that they would be difficult to just bite and pull away.

He placed a couple of them on sticks around the edge of the pond and then baited the trap.

"Leroy...you think anything will eat that dead stuff."

"Oh yea...alligators love rotten mullet"

"This one loves chicken," I offered.

Leroy gave me one of those... 'Are you kidding me or are you just retarded looks. One of those looks that only a hundred year-old person can pull off.

Ouch...my poor feelings. I felt about two-feet tall and quietly withered into the crowd.

"Must be turtles eating your chicken. Ain't no self respecting gator going to be fooled by chicken...hump...why I never heard such..." Leroy replied with contempt.

The crowd, now enthralled by the amazing 'gator hunter,' gave me a look and unanimously rolled their eyes. My five minutes of fame was totally over!

"Well Leroy, if you need to euthanize the gator you have state authority...I think Mr. Turner is ready for the gator to be gone ...it is really costing him."

I retreated to my pipe trap and hooked a rope onto its head and drug it out of the pond. It mostly came to pieces, which was fine, because I was out of the gator removal business. I loaded the big pipe by myself while being completely ignored by the crowd. After stopping at my house to remove the screws and the frame of the trap door, I returned it to the city street department. I was over it!

A couple of days later, Mr. Turner called and he was over it too. He wanted the gator gone! I called Leroy, and he said that the gator just wouldn't touch his prepared bait.

"Please forget about the trap and get down there and harvest/kill/remove it. Evidently, the alligator had cultivated a finer palette. After all, he was use to Pepperidge farm 'Grade A" Chicken legs.'" That night, Leroy went down in a small aluminum boat with a harpoon. You know like *Moby Dick*. Lucky for Leroy, the gator avoided the attention. He did, however, go for bait hung on a huge hook that Leroy left for him.

It turns out that the most effective way to catch an alligator is to bury a large hook in a piece of meat. Hang it just high enough above the water so that the turtles can't get it. The 'gator ' will easily rise up and swallow the bait. He will swim off and swallow the dead mullet whole. You give him a good lead of rope, which drags behind him. Enough slack so that he can get the fish down. After 30 feet or so, the rope tightens and the hidden hook impales the gator through the stomach wall. He will struggle, and the huge hook will tear his insides to pieces. After a while, the alligator will bleed out through his mouth. The next day you just pull him up and drag him to the bank.   Leroy called me the next day because he was looking for a winch. The alligator was too big to be pulled out of the water. I was over it, but I couldn't imagine a gator that was too large to be drug up and out of the pond. I was shocked and drove down to the pond. By the time I got there, Leroy had winched Godzilla up off the ground by a wrecker truck. I stood beside the dead beast in the accompanying photo. He was 17 feet long, and weighed almost 700 pounds. I had grossly underestimated his size.

Curious, I looked at his back, and he had a fresh scar just in front of his hind quarters where the thin metal door of my pipe trap had been hitting him. The problem was that he had 7 foot of tail still sticking out of my trap. Huge! This beast was an unimaginable creature by me or the local folks. Even old Leroy was impressed by the beast. I showed the scar on the back of the alligator to Leroy.

"See Leroy, the son of a bitch liked chicken here is where my trap was catching him."

"Hmm." Leroy grunted.

Looking back on it…I wonder if Leroy recognized how big and valuable that old gator was and wanted to definitely harvest it. I mean we were looking at a hell of a lot of boots, belts, and wallets. Maybe he knew that the gator would not hit that horrible bait, and then he would get to kill it. I kind of suspected that from the crafty old rascal, but I would later see it worked on others he caught, so I am not sure. Naw, Leroy wouldn't do that, but sometimes when I think about it I smile. And while it might sound strange, I like to think he pulled one on me.

Regardless, this alligator had to go! It was not cute and would have been a hazard to man and beast alike. It would have been scary on a 40-acre lake, but on this ½ acre pond is was surreal and dangerous.

(It was not a pretty ending for the mega-gator but for a creature that can swallow a pit bull in one bite, it was allowable.)

We had the alligator, but now we had to load it out. We finally decided to use the boat trailer for his aluminum 'harpoon/whaling boat,' to haul the giant lizard to his rural home which was 90 miles away.

The next day, I met Leroy at his trap, which was still sitting beside Mr. Turner's pond. We had another alligator near Sweetwater, which was around 20 miles away. Leroy had a hell of a time pulling out the metal behemoth of a trap, and during the process he must have torn the leaf-spring loose. Unnoticed at first, but a few miles down the rural county roads, the left side of the trailer began to smoke. The axle was torn loose on the left side, and the tire was hitting the trailer frame. After an emergency stop in the most dangerous curve on the narrow road, I got out of my truck to help Leroy, who had hopped out of his cab and slid under the trap. The weather was clear and hot at 104 degrees. It was one o'clock in the afternoon with at least 60 percent humidity. It was steamy hot, and I was covered with sweat after only a few steps. This was Alabama summer! It was like being in a sauna, but with some giant kid with a magnifying glass holding it over the back of your neck trying to burn you up like an ant.

As an aside I want to tell you that while growing up, I was always told that the heat in Alabama was worse because of the humidity. *It's a wet heat....or in winter a wet cold.* It was just one of those things that you hear growing up. You repeat this information, but you begin to believe that it is just whining and bitching about the heat. Well that's what I began to feel about the old saying until Desert Storm. Yep. I got called up and shipped to the desert of Saudi Arabia. Hot and dry...I remember walking between some buildings and getting hit with some water

I looked up. "Who spit on me? Where are you? Show yourself you son of a bitch." I hollered to the alley. I was ready to deal some Alabama justice...but I was alone.

I looked around but no one was in the area. Later on watching the news I saw a report of rain fall in Riyadh. That is where I was! Well, I bring this up because we routinely played volleyball in the sun with the temperature around 114 degrees. I mean we played in comfort by drinking loads of water. When we went back inside we would have great salt circles around our underarms, circling our collar and on the bridge of our caps. We were comfortable because as the sweat evaporated and it cooled us down. In Alabama, with high humidity, the sweat just soaks you to the bone. No evaporation so you get incredibly hot. *SO it is TRUE!!!*

Now back to Leroy and being broken down on the road way. The '70 plus' guy in coveralls hopped out of the cab of his truck and slid under the trailer without a complaint, and he totally ignored the blazing heat. He wouldn't let us get down there because we would ruin our pretty uniforms. Here we are... three grown and fit game wardens sweating, and leaning on the boat trailer as an ancient lanky old guy jogs circles around us sliding under the trailer, beating on the axle stationed, and then jogging back and forth from his tool box on the back of his truck to the damaged trailer. In no time, he had the trailer axle ready to be moved back into position...We all heaved the trap up and he kicked it into position. We were wheezing as he whorled his wrench around onto the retaining bolts.

I was seeing blue spots and could hear the rapid clicking of his ratchet wrench…*click…click…click*…like a machine gun. I decided to abandon the old guy and hobble to my blazer and air conditioning

"To hell with this." I mumble to Mike.

"Okay let's go!" Leroy advises as he shoots out from under the trailer and jogs to the cab of his truck. Leroy puts it in to gear and I am left in his dust as he takes off like a bat out of hell.

Mike and I look at each other.

"Damn that old bastard is a robot!"

We hobble back to the blazer.

Mike stumbles. "Just go on without me Pat"

I give him a look and shamelessly utter "Okay."

He definitely reads that I am going on without him and picks up his pace. We climb into the vehicle, and I fire up the engine and the air conditioner. The cool air came streaming out of the dash.

"Ahhh!" We said in unison.

I look at Mike covered in sweat. "Mike I think we are going to make it."

I take off after Leroy and probably wouldn't have caught him except that he was towing 1000 pounds of steel alligator trap.

Mike wanted to pass Leroy. "Get a lead …and lead that old bastard into a station for some drinks."

"Roger that!" I agreed.

I punched it in a wide spot of the road. As we passed Leroy, I was grinning. Leroy was looking ahead, calmly and matter of factly. He was sipping a coke! *Amazing!* I thought.

We lead Leroy into the station, and I told him that we needed some liquid. At the checkout I noticed that Mike had a coke just like me. We were believers after watching the old guy.

After a big swig, I looked at Mike "Hey you feel any better?"

"Not yet," he replied. "I think we better get another one."

Leroy would have made a poster child for coke, but I don't think they ever heard about the amazing old dude who ran on high octane 'coke-a-cola.'

I began looking forward to seeing ole Leroy. He was one of those amazing characters that are unforgettable and precious. He couldn't have a boring conversation. A couple years later, I went to Sumter County looking for him. It was summer and I wanted to check in with him. His wife was still at their home, but Leroy was in Equator. He had bought a ranch down there and was going to farm gators and grow crops. What an adventurer! His wife was ill, but gave me a long letter which read like a diary that Leroy was keeping of his adventures down in the rural areas. He told of how he was learning Spanish from a little Ecuadorian lady and had some trouble when the school hired another tutor. He had really liked the first lady so insisted on her continuing his instruction. This upset the local boss lady and she flat out told him no. It was her way or nothing. Leroy then hired the lady, and ordered some Spanish books for his favorite instructor to set up her own school. This really upset the balance of power…and threatened a little Spanish feud. Leroy eventually managed to have his way without bloodshed. I can't help but think about Leroy's new toy, a titanium .38 caliber pistol. It was small and light but always in his pocket. Lucky for the locals the feud ended in peace. A 70 something year old country boy doesn't really care about your feelings if you pull something on him. Hell, that's the kind of adventure that makes him feel alive.

He also wrote about the construction methods down there. He was simply amazed at the concrete roofs on all the buildings. He also wrote about the little parades they had in the small village where he was staying. It seemed that everyone was in the parade so very few people where left to actually watch it.

"Funny," he said. "It didn't bother the marchers." I know this is odd to write so much about a fellow in the alligator chapter, and I don't mean to distract you from the subject. But one of the most special things about being a 'game warden' is the amazing inspirational people you meet in the woods.

Now retired, I watch my peers at their wits end, and they are afraid to try something new. I even catch myself thinking I *am too old to learn a new skill.* When I think about a 75- year old Leroy heading to Ecuador to alligator farm, I realize that it's all about your attitude. Leroy's lesson to everyone is to live! In the end, I think Leroy wanted some freedom if you think about all the rules and regulations that you have to read just to go hunting or fishing in America .Well it's a real tragedy. Of course, many depend on these rules and publish more every day without stopping to think about the repercussions on simple citizens.

You have to be bold enough, brave enough to let go of the training wheels that our government has put on everything we do today. If Leroy gets scared he just puts his hand in his pocket and grips his pistol...*man that's old school.*

I like to remember Leroy like this. The big gator is a metaphor for life and ancient Leroy represents man. The man is sliding a rope around 'life's' neck!

CHAPTER SIX: The Coward in Me

I remember at one of the first meetings of the division a young officer was being berated about not making an arrest. They were giving him hell.

During a break in the meeting, a 6 foot 4 inch tall white-haired game warden put his hand on the rookie's shoulder, and looking the kid in the eyes said,

"Don't pay no attention to those assholes. Take it from me; it is always better to make a good run than a bad stand! "

I put a lot of thought into those words and looking back they might have been some of the most powerful. It gave you permission to back off and re-approach under better circumstances. In those days, before decent radios and bullet proof jackets, it was taken as a weakness to call in for backup. There was this attitude that you should never back down and should 'cowboy up' at all times. In fact, the Alabama law said the police never had to back down.

For example if someone was holding a hostage, the 'old school' deputy would just walk past the barricade, kick in the door and go grab the drunken husband. Nobody would have thought to call him a fool. In those days, as I was learning the trade, I remember there was a television series called *Hill Street Blues,* based on the policemen working the ghettos and gangs of New York City. Thanks to housing projects and the despair they projected, the attitude about life and death became an entirely different thing. While we weren't in a metropolitan area, we did have housing projects. You would be driving in a really remote area like Epps, Gainesville, or Jefferson and run into a housing project. I am not kidding. For generations, these areas had populations of less than 50 or even 20 families. But now, thanks to the Federal Housing Administration, we had housing projects in the middle of nowhere. It was utterly absurd! Suddenly the population would be several 100 people stranded and isolated from the world. Placed in areas where there was absolutely no hope of legitimate employment. There was not a chance in hell that anyone would build a factory in the remote woods of Alabama. So now you have to imagine these hundreds of people living for a welfare check, sitting on the porches staring blankly at the road. Now imagine the 5 or 6 landowners or people who live in the area. You have the only house, possessions, and money in the area. Your idyllic life is now interrupted by these trapped indigents walking by offering to cut your lawn. Now understand that there is no infrastructure to support them and that means no police to enforce the laws. These areas became villages of the damned and spawned the same irreverent violence as seen on *Hill Street Blues*, the only difference being there were no cops walking the beat. Drugs, unwanted children, spousal abuse, incest, and murder became a weekly event. These are the same areas I had grown up in, and if someone had been murdered during my childhood the whole town would shut down. The whole world would stop until the killer was caught, and this happened only once or twice a year. With the invention of housing projects this changed completely, murder and violence became as common as the ball game on Friday night. The paper still only came out once a week but…you checked the high school scores and then check to see how many were murdered in these projects, or stabbed at the neighboring 'club.'

So you see the old game warden was ahead of his time when he gave the young rookie the permission to "run like hell."

The Giant

Well it was the end of April and we had begun to check some of our local fishing holes, some of them are just a places where the road cuts across the many creeks. There is a place just north of Linden where Highway 43 cuts across the Chickasaw Bogue Creek. People would turnoff and drive along the road side and park under the bridge. From there they would head off on foot and fish along the banks of the big creek. It was a beautiful spot, and I liked to pull down and check it out. Even if I didn't see vehicles, I could tell a lot about what was going on by the tracks and trash. It was a perfect spring morning when I decided to pull down and check out the site, and I wasn't looking for trouble. I parked, and strolled down around under the bridge…broken beer bottles…an old fire site…but on the other side of the bridge I noticed a set of tracks heading east along the bank. I searched, but didn't see any tracks coming back. These were 'one way' tracks. Someone had been dropped off and was still in the woods. I continued on along the bank of the muddy creek and had to stoop under some vines. When I stood up, I found another fellow coming out from under the vines from the other direction. He was bent over too and had gotten 'way' too close. He startled the crap out of me. That stuff can happen when you are tracking someone; you really need someone with you looking for the target. You are just really vulnerable when you have your head down looking at tracks. Well, the guy being bent over now began to stand upright once he cleared the vines. And dang, he just kept standing up. This guy was large! He was a freakishly huge black guy, at least 6 foot 7 inches or more. He was wearing ragged clothing like some hermit might have on. His hair was 'natural' in an unkempt way and pushed to one side like he had slept on a flat rock. He had a thick head and heavy brow line, and I remember it looked like it was cut from rock. I was relieved not to see a weapon or fishing pole but…damn it… he was caring a dead rabbit. It was a large 'cane cutter' rabbit, but it looked like a little mouse hanging from his huge hands. Unfortunately for me, it was not rabbit season. He was in violation of the law.

I greeted him with a friendly, "Where is your gun?"

He replied in the deep booming voice fit for a deity. "I ain't got no gun. I heard some dogs running. I saw it and chased it down. I beat it to death with a stick."

"Oh."

I looked at this giant and suddenly felt like an itty bitty mouse, and I saw myself scurrying from the pursuit of this giant.

"Where is your stick?"

"I busted it when I hit it."

I had my hand resting on my 40-caliber automatic. I remember thinking that it felt like a toy gun, and I could just imagine me shooting this guy and him swatting me and the gun down. Well, I quickly tried to justify how to get out of this situation. I didn't think the hobo had a license, and he had taken game out of season. I want you to realize how much it takes to walk away from two cases. I mean it's pretty slow in the late spring, and game wardens try to make the cases when they came. Still. This was no ordinary human.

"Oh you don't have a gun. Well that's good because it isn't gun season. Enjoy your 'stick' killed rabbit." I slowly eased away. "Have a nice day."

Talk about feeling of inadequacy. Size does matter! I got in my vehicle and got the hell out of there before he committed some crime that I would have to act on.

Well in fairness, I did tell Michael and Chester, and they thought it was hilarious the lazy genius was chicken shit. Okay. But I do know for a fact that Michael never checked another fisherman in the land of the giant hobo. God bless us cowards.

Chapter Seven: Death From Above

I know for a fact that every 'redneck' boy-child in Alabama fancies that one day he will be a pilot. I think this will always be the case until someone comes up with a flying recliner. I was no exception, and I had even been accepted to the Army flight training a month before my required enlistment was up in the U.S. Army. Sure I would have loved to learn to fly, but I was quite done with being a soldier. Airplanes and game wardens are really made for each other. You can use it to locate hidden hunting fields, feeders, and even stuff like corn thrown on the ground. The federal guys would always fly just before duck season looking for bait. Gary, one of the federal agents said you could see the corn on the bottom of ponds. I doubted this for years, until I saw some of his photographs. From a couple of hundred feet, he had a picture of a pretty little pond with blue water, but what you could really notice was a big brown muddy spot positioned right in front of a duck hunting blind. You could not see corn, but it was dang obvious the ducks are feeding right in front of the blind. He even had other shots of the rear ends of the ducks as they bobbed for corn. The Federal officers loved it because they could really cover large areas quickly. One day of flying gave them plenty of ponds to work.

The biggest problem was trying to figure out how to get to the ponds once you found them. When you look around, all you see are forests. Below you are the forests with thousands of logging trails. You have to find a landmark, like a major road, and then navigate back to the ponds. At this time, GPS devices were thousands of dollars and only worked with clear line of sight to the sky. Now everybody uses airplanes with one of those talking navigators like *Tom-Tom*. It was different in those days.

Our department had one airplane and one pilot. The pilot usually ferried the commissioner around to events, but from time-to-time he would stop in the counties and help locate violators. The local game warden would be flown over the county looking for feeders, duck hunters, green fields, 'telephoners'...etc.

I remember the first time I flew the county. I met Wesley, my training officer, at the Linden airport. 'Airport' is a generous term for this facility. It was a mowed green field with a strip of asphalt a couple of hundred yards long. There is one metal building with two small airplanes. Wesley and I got there early and walked around the runway...road. It had patches the entire length. It looked like it had been hit by a meteor shower and some of the toothless guys with the street department had filled in the holes. The runway condition didn't fill you with a lot of confidence. Wesley and I shared some coffee on the hood of his sedan, and I munched on a Slim Jim. I told him that I was hungry, and he just smiled and said that we probably didn't want to eat before we got in the plane. For the first time, I got the feeling that Wesley really didn't enjoy these annual airplane journeys. Well, he was an old timer I thought *...he is probably just bored*. We were standing there searching the clear blue sky. Then we heard a buzz and a little plane came into view just above the tree tops. At first, I thought that it was a toy plane...one of those remote control planes. Nope, it was a little single engine plane big enough for four people. It went right down to the front of the road, turned hard, and sat right down on the runway. It would have been pretty impressive, except for the fact that every time the plane hit a pothole patch it would bounce up off the runway. *Shit.* I was definitely disenchanted with the whole exercise. And as gung-ho as I was; I was thinking *you have got to be kidding.* The pilot pulled over in front of the vehicles and shut the plane off. The guy was about six feet tall and with fresh shave and with a crew-cut haircut. He was sporting a pair of those mirrored sunglasses. You could tell that he was a pilot right away. I had been in the army and had a pretty good stereotype in my mind. I pictured the loud, woman chasing and beer loving brutes that I had associated with in the military. But this guy was different; he was 'king of the nerds.' At the time I made a little mental note...*This is why we don't fly at night!* As I am older now, I will take the nerd anytime.

I remember how we used to dare and challenge the Army helicopters pilots. I mean, the Army chopper pilots could be provoked.

"Hey can we fly with the doors open?"

"No...we have got special instructions."

"I didn't figure you could handle it with the doors open. These things are hard enough to fly aren't they?"

"What?"

"Oh nothing....pussy..."

All the sudden the co-pilot would come back and check your straps. He would sport an evil grin and slide the door open with a slam. We would have them flying on their side with the doors wide open as we clutched the seats and stared at the ground. You would spend the next twenty minutes at 300 feet in the air with the helicopter on its side, while your arms and legs would be hanging out the door. Everyone would scream with terror and joy.

These pilots were crazy cool.

We had big fun with this until one of our comrades vomited and pissed himself...and worse dropped his M-16 out the door. We watched in horror as the pretty rifle sailed toward the stand of pine trees below.

I looked at the guy and figured that he should jump with it...because the Drill Sergeants were going to kill him!!! He just looked back at me and started to cry. When the chopper hit the landing zone, the rest of us extended our perimeter as far away as we could get. Nobody wanted to be near the guy as he told the drill sergeant that he was no longer a killing machine because he had lost his weapon. *What were those irresponsible pilots thinking?*

Airplanes Make You Puke

Well this State pilot was a different breed.   We greeted him and found out that his name was Bob. He was running behind, but he had to pee so we waited for him to walk to the edge of the runway and face in the direction of the woods. After making his adjustments, he ushered us into the plane. This thing was tiny; the front passenger seat leaned forward and to get into the back area I crawled over the seat. I ended up on to a tiny bench seat in the back. It was exactly like getting into a two door *Rambler*. The pilot and Wesley sat in the front seats. I felt like we had been stuffed into a telephone booth. The pilot was hunched over the steering wheel, and Wesley was pressed against the dashboard. I began to get a bad feeling right away as we bounced down the runaway. The little engine screamed, and after what seemed like an eternity it lifted off the ground. Our cautious pilot wanted to gain altitude so that if anything happened he would have time to find a place to land. We traveled gaining altitude for about 10 minutes. I was having a bad time…it was hot in the little backseat…the engine was noisily beating like a little machine gun, and I couldn't hear anything. I didn't have a window, so I tried to lean forward over Wesley's shoulder.

He screamed, "Try to find some baited dove fields."

I looked out the window and couldn't even see the ground. We both were struggling to see, and the thoughtful pilot saw our difficulty. He just nodded and turned the plane on its side. My stomach flipped, and I had a flashback to the fateful helicopter ride. I could smell the vomit, pee, and tears of fear that my army buddy had provided on that fateful helicopter ride. I was going to puke!

There we were, Wesley and I with our faces pressed against the glass windows together peering downward at the earth. Just like two kids with their faces pressed against the window of the Christmas display at the dollar store. I could see the ground and I could just make out some fields. I could feel all the blood draining out of my face. My stomach began to feel really tense. I sat back in my little bench seat, and I felt like I was trapped in a box. Noisy, smelly, bouncy …I began to sweat. Wesley saw my discomfort and with a wicked smile, he looked at the pilot.

"Can you go lower?"

Motherfucker! I thought.

"Sure?" The pilot cheerfully replied.

Now the plane began circling and spiraling downward. I could feel everything in my stomach. I could taste bile mixed with coffee and Slim Jim. I had to get out of the plane, but I didn't want to be ridiculed about it. Oh, the abuse that would be dealt at the next district meeting. I tried some breathing exercises and tried staring at the horizon…which was now spiraling around. It seemed like an eternity.

Finally I hollered over the engine. "I need to get out." The pilot turned and looked at me. "I am going to puke." I hollered.

He handed me a little bag.

"Fuck that! Get me on the ground!" I said and tossed the bag back at him.

I honestly felt a lot better after using the profanity.

His eyes went wide and he said, "I will have you down in 5 minutes, hang on."

He put the plane's nose down. The plane straightened up and began to lose altitude. I felt better almost immediately, but when the pilot looked back to check on me I had seen him flinch. I knew that my nerdy pilot was scared of puke. I puffed my checks out like I was fixing to blow cookies and Slim Jim all over his clean little aircraft. The next thing I heard was the screech as the tires hit our bumpy runway. I felt a lot better now as gravity pushed me down on the seat. I was going to make it. He pulled up to the vehicles, and Wesley hoped out and pulled the seat over. I struggled, and half fell out of the little phone booth. I was feeling relieved but walked to the edge of the runway and gave them a few gags…just for effect. I waved at them and walked to my truck. Wesley gave me a serious look, which transformed into an evil grin like he 'had something' on me. Then he loaded back into the plane like he had dropped the weakest link off at the airport. They took off and I watched them turn and head east like an eagle or remote control toy plane.

I thought about my childhood dreams of being a pilot. I was thirty–something, with two tiny boys and a wife who thought I was special. I was over it. *Yep. Totally done with the pilot thing.* I left head down…from shame not puke and drove to Crispy Chick for some fried chicken and a large sweet tea. Fried chicken always settled my stomach. I sat around and enjoyed my drink…imagining the torment that I would endure at our next district meeting.

"What's wrong Pat?" Mike would ask feigning concern.

"Why nothing Michael...."

"Pat…You look all pale and shit…maybe you should sit down. Are you going to get sick and vomit? Maybe we should Medi-vac you out to the hospital. Gene get a helicopter in here…oops…on second thought …this is Pat…Pat might soil himself. Too bad…looks like you are gonna have to just sit there until you feel better." Blah…blah…blah, a relentless assault followed by a unanimous "hahaha"

I will reply, "Laugh it up, mother fuckers!"

As I am daydreaming about my impending punishment, I hear the little bell on the glass door of the restaurant ring. Wesley steps in the door and he was pale as a cotton sheet.

"Wesley what are you doing here so quickly."

"Ugh, we ended the patrol quickly...I want to drive to Thomaston and check out some feeders I saw from the air."

I would find out days later…that even seasoned pilots and air passengers will get sick if they see someone else start throwing up…and get whiff of all that grossness. Something of a sympathetic reaction is likely to occur. Yep, old iron guts had folded up like a lawn chair once they where air born. The pilot made an emergency landing and booted my hero out onto the tarmac. At the time, I just thought Wesley was being kind and noble. *Yeah right.* The pilot had quickly informed our sadistic Supervisor of our weak constitutions…and the old bastard couldn't wait to see us. He even scheduled the district meeting two days early! I know he had stayed up nights giggling thinking of smart ass things to say.

"Okay gentlemen, let's take our seats and get this paperwork done. Pat. Wesley if you guys want to you can sit on the floor…those chairs are very high. Don't want to have you guys cleaning up your breakfast off the nice carpet. Hahaha." *Sick bastard!*

The Maiden Night Flight

The Department had very tight limits on the use of airplanes, and at the time I thought this was just a 'stick in the mud' lazy attitude. Looking back, they were actually ahead of their time, but they made a poor argument to help subordinates understand their reluctance to use tiny planes. Remember this was twenty years ago and the administration had the George Wallace leadership which said not to question, just do it. After a few years, I began to understand the reasons why they were steadfast against it. Their main objection was the safety issue and liability. A night flight in a small plane over rural forest was extremely dangerous, and honestly the odds were that eventually someone would be killed. Today, most people will recognize the repercussions of a catastrophic flight. The lawsuits and damages would be staggering for the Department, and the loss of life would be unjustified. Remember the penalty for night hunting was $250. (Truthfully, if they had legalized night hunting it would not have affected the deer population in our county.) Honestly, at night in our county you have to dodge the deer. One night I was sailing down a county road and slammed on brakes to avoid a deer lying in the middle of the road. After stopping, the deer got up and walked into the woods...the bastard was sleeping in the middle of the road!

The Department was completely satisfied with our ground efforts, which kept the night hunters at bay. These days, I watch *COPS* and these high speed chases where a guy takes off from a traffic stop for expired tag, something minor but the manic tears ass through vehicles and intersections. Everyone at home is watching as he crashes into vehicles, causes accidents, and then T-bones a van with a mother and a child returning from the grocery. The guy has done nearly a million dollars worth of damage and injured or killed an innocent mother and child. The asshole always, and remarkably, will jump out of the destroyed vehicle and take off, only to be tackled by pursuing police. We cheer "take that asshole to jail." We change the channel and forget about it. What if it had been your wife or child in the van? Is it still worth it? They never follow up on the asshole, but my experience bets that his case is continued for years...he doesn't have any money   to pay for the damages...so you and I pay for it. He spends 6 months or less in county jail. It just isn't worth it...PERIOD. Okay so this was a side bar, but my point is that the supervisor had a progressive understanding of these issues that we now take for granted. If they had been better at articulating the message, the whole department would have benefited.

Well, even though I was naïve to these things, I was determined to get an aircraft up at night and started looking for a pilot who was bold enough to fly a mission. This was incredibly easy for a couple of reasons. Every redneck wants to be a pilot; it's a pretty common dream. Many will take lessons and get a pilot's license. What then? The new pilot gets a couple of flights, or maybe a trip to a ball game, and then has nothing to do. I drove out to the local airport and talked with the manager, and he put me into contact with a local pharmacist who had a pilot's license and his own plane. I liked the guy immediately. He was a successful pharmacist and an adventurer. The great thing about this guy was that he was smart and a natural leader. He really thought out the process of navigating and communication with the police, which was great because as you know I had kinda flunked the whole flying thing.

Once he had one of our radios, he could handle the air support which left us the time to concentrate on getting to any located 'spot lighters.' The department finally came out with a release form that said that under no circumstances were employees of the state allowed in the aircraft, and that the pilot had no claim to any benefits, money, etc if and when they died. Stan signed it immediately. After all the hassle we had, we pretty much decided to keep the whole thing quiet…even from our bosses. We did have the foresight to get some extra chase vehicles, and to make sure they could communicate.

Even though I had pushed to set the whole thing up, I did have some doubts about the whole process. Alabama was playing on Saturday so nobody wanted to work that night, all my buddies would be tailgating, eating and drinking. So we picked the first Friday night after the opening of gun season. I met my buddy Pat Oliver, the Marine policeman, in Demopolis and after filling our thermoses with coffee we headed south to a little town called Myrtlewood. This was a tiny village consisting of one gas station, but it had some circumstances that made it perfect for spotlight hunters. It sat on the Tombigbee River, and there was a one mile stretch of road that ended at the railroad and vehicle drawbridge. The shoulder of the road was wide, and on one side a power line provided a field-like area where deer could feed at night. You could always count on seeing anywhere from three or four deer to fifty deer. When you got to the river bridge you had a stop light. It would be red or green because traffic was only one-way on the bridge. A red light meant traffic was coming toward you, either a train or car, or maybe there was a tugboat passing under the bridge. If a tugboat was going under the bridge, then the whole center of the bridge would raise up.

Now if you where night hunting, you would pull off the side of the road at this intersection and let all the traffic pass onto the bridge. Once they crossed the light would turn green and instead of proceeding across the bridge, you would turn your vehicle around and start back up the long stretch while you whip out your spotlight and search the ditches for deer. You could see a mile ahead, and at night you would easily see if anyone entered the bottom before they got close enough to make the case. The truth was that it was a sucker's place. While you could see if a game warden was coming over the hill by the headlights, you were really trapped on a one way road. The old wardens would hide in the woods and let them hunt all the way back. After they had let the guys work the spotlight, shoot, and load their deer, the wardens would simply pull out and block the road. A great place to night hunt, but if the warden was working then you were going to get caught.

The locals were paranoid about the flats. And the landowners that lived there would set up stakeouts to watch the 'flats.' They worked it with a mad fervor and paranoia, which resulted in some mental problems. Okay I ain't no doctor, but some of these folks where crazy! No kidding, some were actually committed for insanity. There was debate among the spectators as to whether the hunting paranoia caused the mental problems or whether it was hereditary. Still, some said it was related to rot-gut whiskey that the families had drunk during prohibition. Regardless of why these folks were as crazy as a 'run over dog,' they made for constant security surveillance on the Flats. So this truly was a place for dumb asses to hunt, still every other weekend or so, somebody would get caught in the area. This was the area I chose to make my stand on the night of the first airplane patrol.

I didn't sit directly on the flat but instead backed off Highway 69 in a long bottom just south of Myrtlewood. I backed into a logging road with my front end facing the highway. As we where shorthanded we had gathered up some help. Wesley had picked up Jesse Langley and moved north, and a couple of deputies were scattered in there squad cars. Mike McNeal was in south Sumter County. I had gotten my new acquaintance, Pat Oliver the Marine policeman to work with me.

As soon as Stan lifted off at the Demopolis airport, he got contacts, a bunch. The problem was that our area was very rural and split by two rivers. In fact, in North Marengo, Green and Sumter counties the property line is made by two large rivers. There was no way that we could work all three counties because we would have had to go 50 miles just to find a bridge to get across the rivers. It would have taken hours.

Stan was on the radio and talking with Mike in Sumter County, and he was trying to get Mike to the 'spot-lighting' vehicle. I was familiar with the area where Stan had seen the large spotlights from night hunters. It was across the river from the airport, and at night it is 20 square miles of forest with no land marks. It was going to be an impossible and frustrating effort to find the vehicles. Stan had to find a landmark, and then see Mike in the game warden vehicle, and then try to find some way to connect the two paths.

Meanwhile, Pat and I sat the fake deer across the road in a small field because it looked like we were out of the ball game. We made some idle chat and pleasant conversation...this was before 'dog man' or 'Bigfoot,' so Pat was in good spirits.

"I have a pond on my farm. You should bring your wife out and go fishing." Pat suggested.

"Wow that sounds great, but I didn't think you liked company?"

"Well it is these new pistols."

"What do you mean?"

"Well I only feel comfortable in crowds if I have a bullet for everyone in the group. You see for the last 10 years we have been shooting the six shot revolver...so you can see I couldn't really entertain. But now I got this nine millimeter Glock and it hold 16 bullets at one time...so now I feel more comfortable around larger crowds.

"Wow. Congratulations, huh. Pat...sounds like you have made a break through!"

"Yea…I am pretty happy about it."

I stared at him incredulous…trying to work the math…looking to see if he was pulling my leg as old timers are known to do.

"So I thought," he continued, "I should make some more friends."

"I feel so special to be your first friend." I said jokingly.

I sat there frozen like a deer in the headlights and stared blankly across the road pondering his words.

He finally broke the ice, "How about some coffee?"

"Great idea," I said and finally started to breathe again.

I pulled my thermos out, and he reached into his Igloo cooler which was packed with food. He could barely close the top it was so full of items.

Stopping to pour coffee, I said, "Pat we are only gonna be out here about two or three hours. You brought a lot of food."

He looked at the contents. Yea I know. I think I have enough. I even have some Carmel cake."

"What?" I stuttered. "Did you say caramel cake?"

"Yeah, why."

I jumped from the vehicle leaving him dumbfounded and ran across the road. I grabbed the little stuffed deer and threw it into the back of the truck. I started to climb into the cab of the truck.
"Just getting ready. The last time I had caramel cake all hell broke loose."

He handed me a slimy, sticky piece and I took a big bite. My coffee was steaming in the brisk cool fall air as I took a swallow. *SSSHHSHSH*! The radio sounded in a stream of static.

"CONTACT!" screamed Stan on the radio.

I grabbed for my radio mike, and it squished out of my hand like a slippery critter. I grabbed it again.

"MEUNMB WHERE STAN?" As I tried to swallow my caramel cake. It was soooo good but time to run.

"Mrytlewood flats!"

I took a look at the sticky delicious cake. *Dang the sacrifices I have made*! I tossed it out the window. I fired up the engine and threw gravel into the pine trees behind the truck as I turned onto the highway. We were only one mile away and at Mach 1. *Color us there*!

Pat was determined to finish his coffee and cake and bounced along balancing the items. I watched him out of the corner of my eye. Cool as a cucumber you would have thought he was watching the laundry spin in the washing machine. Oh yeah, we were doing a 108 miles per hour, he just munched his cake.

It was pretty amazing to see him lean out to try to take a bite of cake. I would take a curve and his whole body would lean away from his left hand with the cake. He would just look to his right hand and take a swig of coffee. Another curve and a bounce sent him leaning to his left. Snap. A mouthful of that delicious caramel cake. He didn't seem to notice that the vehicle was leaning on two wheels. *Calm.*

Whatever maybe he was just a very focused eater? I hoped he

finished his food before we got into a gun fight or something.

"Ugh…Pat. …*Bullet whizzing by*…could you return fire?"

He would be calmly licking his fingers. "Sure. No problem. He opens his cooler, "You want a sandwich Pat?"

"Oh, okay. Could you hold off on supper until the shootout is over?" I would ask.

"Oh okay. Just a little hungry."

"Dang it Pat! We have only been working a couple of hours! "

"Yeah I know. Are you hungry too?"

"Aaargh!"

Fortunately, when I got to the flats I didn't see the night hunting vehicle.

"What do you see Stan?"

Radio static "There is a car on the Mrytlewood bridge…they are using a spotlight."

A spotlight is wonderful. It is illegal to work it or cast it on real property. It's a small case but more importantly a good reason for the game warden to make the stop and search the vehicle. We thundered onward into the darkness toward our unknowing night hunter.

"They are crossing the railroad draw bridge."

When we topped the hill to the flats, we couldn't see the car. But that didn't matter because a couple hundred feet above us. Stan, our guardian angel was still watching them and could see us, too.

We crossed the two miles of flat road but had to stop because the light was red at the bridge. We sat there disappointed.

"Are they still shining Stan?"

"No they have turned the light off and are passing through the American Paper Mill.

(A road passes beside and through the plant area; one side of the road is adorned with huge metal buildings with tall steaming stacks of pine trees, and the other side is a railroad yard. Inside there are several thousand employees busy at their jobs. It looks like a small city when lit up at night.)

Dang we are going to lose the suspects!

"Stan can you see the bridge? Is there any traffic on it? Cars or a train?"

After a few seconds he replied, "No. It's clear."

I started to run the red light.

As I punched across the old bridge, I had a sudden fearful realization. "Stan is the draw bridge in the up position?"

I held my breath and then Stan replied, "No it's down."

Pat leaned over toward me, "If it's up the road will be blocked. You will be able to tell. Go."

How the hell would someone know that? Had he done this before?

I stepped on the gas and headed across the bridge. You are not going to believe this bridge. It is made of wood. That's right it is made of railroad ties which are the big 8x8 inch beams used under railroads. You had to drive carefully because there was a railway track down the middle. As I have said before, it shared a single lane. This was a one way lane shared by vehicular traffic, two way rail traffic, and the bridge would rise to allow barges to pass underneath. If you saw a picture of it you would have thought it was a Civil War vintage bridge.

Looking back, crossing it under these conditions was pretty stupid. Fortunately, I could do stupid!

We fearlessly banged along and I was relieved when we made it across and hit the paved road. I punched the vehicle and sped through the plant.

The suspects were almost at the four-way stop in a little town about two miles west of the mill. It was gonna be hard to keep track of them with all the light from the many homes.

"Shit." I said to Pat.

"Oh well," he replied and he reached for his cooler, again.

I slapped his hand away, "Pat! Not now!"

He shrugged and grinned at me. I was panting and sweating, and he was sitting over there thinking about his sandwich.

Stan broke the silence. "THEY ARE TURNING AROUND and headed back to you."

Pat and I looked at each other. "YES!" We harmonized.

He said, "Let's go."

"I think we should just wait here by the mill there is plenty of light here so that we can make a stop." I could tell Pat didn't care for my plan but I was driving.

"Let them hunt back toward us." I continued. Pat gave me a dirty look.

"Look," I said. "It is a two mile strip with grassy places and deer. Let's see if they hunt."

Again with the stink eye, but he conceded to my wish with a grunt.

We backed into the parking space for the Human Resources Manager and cut our lights off. Here we were waiting on a night hunter while 3,000 people were making toilet paper a few hundred yards away.

This road west of the mill is another two mile stretch of great night hunting property and straight as an arrow. When I was a small child, my dad would ride out and we would look at all the deer. This was a great place to see deer, but probably not the best place to hunt. The road was usually pretty quiet except during shift change when hundreds of tired workers would race away from and to the mill.

"What are they doing Stan?"

"They are stopped." (Pat interrupted with growl) "Now they are moving."

Now I could see the headlights of the vehicle coming straight toward us. It was a little two door white *Dodge Colt*.

They entered the large parking lot and passed right in front of us. *I was a genius!* I eased in behind them and turned on my headlights and my tiny blue light. I saw the two occupants, wide–eyed; spinning their heads around to try to see what was going on. Suddenly the little car punched it with the wheels slinging gravel in all directions, and we were off to the races!

I was chasing the little car with my blue light and siren on full blast. We were passing around unknown buildings and the baffled security guards. Abruptly, they made a turnaround at the car wash and then sped down a dirt road that followed the river.

"Keep an eye on em, Stan. We might lose them."

"I got them," Stan replied in a sinister voice.

We hit the gravel road right behind the car. It was swerving left and right fishtailing, sending dirt, dust and gravel across my vehicle hood.

In truth, this was my first high speed chase I didn't have a clue. Not knowing what to do, I just figured that I would follow them.

I glanced at Pat, and he was trying to finish his coffee. *What was his deal?*

As we approached a curve in the road, I watched in horror as a black guy climbed out the passenger window and sat on the door frame, clutching the roof with his left hand and aiming a single barrel shotgun with his right hand. In slow motion, he pointed it right at me and the darkness was broken with a flash. BOOM. I tried to duck but my seatbelt held me fast in place. I ended up doing some sort of ninja turtle move. I tried to pull my head into my chest and behind my bullet proof jacket.

I sucked in my breath, grunted and hit the brake.

BOOM. The gun went off.

"Shit." Pat hollered.

I was shocked as I did a mental check of my body. I had just held my breath waiting for the buckshot pellets to hit me. Nothing.

I looked at Pat.

"Are you hit?"

"No damn it…I spilled my coffee. That son of a bitch! Go. Go."

"But Pat, they are shooting at us."

He looked at me, "Go! Go! They can't hit us!"

I hit the accelerator and a voice straight from hell came out of my mouth.

In a super deep voice I told him, "Kill him. Kill him!

Pat didn't even make an attempt to draw his weapon, which frustrated me. Now when I say frustrated, I mean for a whole 10 milliseconds. One thing about chases and gunfights the rules of time don't apply. Time slows down and events can't seem to catch up with your mind.

Right on cue, the guy that had fired the weapon slid into the seat as the car spun and nearly sideswiped a pine tree. I remember wishing it had knocked him out of the car. I was mad that he wasn't killed! Evidently after you get over the surprise and relief that the bullets didn't kill you, you tend to get very angry, angry enough to kill someone. I guess this is some kind of super-speed 12 step program, huh!

Pat reached down and picked my cheap little blue light off the floor where it had fallen.

"Go…Go. Let's get them."

I wished I had more time to get mentally prepared for the stop. But after another hundred feet and the little car spun out and stalled. It spun around facing us, but with the front bumper pointed to the ditch. I hit the bright lights, slammed on the brakes and slid up to the little car at a rapid pace. My big Bronco stopped about ten feet in front of their bumper. I could see the two men in the cab... eyes now wide...it looked like I was going to crash into the dash. For a split second, I seriously thought about plowing into the small car after all they were shooting at us. Deadly force is, after all, deadly force. If they had spun out with the passenger door facing us, I would have had to because the guy had now reloaded and stuck the muzzle back out the window. I slid to a stop a few feet in front of their car my headlights casting a blinding light into their dusty wind shield.

I jumped out drawing my .357 Smith and Wesson revolver and aimed it at the window. Pat sailed out his door and ran to the driver's door. I was watching the passenger, and he was staring at me. He had the shotgun out the window, and while looking right at me, he slid it forward in an attempt to bring it to bear on me. *Click.* The barrel hit the door frame before he could get it pointed at me. He tried again, but luckily he could not get it pointed at me. He had a shot at the ditch but would have to lean out to get it pointed at me. I watched in slow motion as he banged the barrel against the front windshield frame again and again, but he could not get it around. I, on the other hand, didn't have that problem as I walked forward with the front sight on his heart.

I hollered, "Don't do it. Don't do it."

Finally he stopped moving the barrel and starred at the giant pistol in my hand. I walked forward and was a few feet from his windshield. I was leaning over the hood. There was no way that I could miss if I squeezed the trigger. I don't know why I didn't just blow his head off. I knew that I was authorized to shoot, especially as he banged the muzzle against the door frame. But I knew that he wouldn't be able to get the muzzle of the gun around the frame, so I waited for him to settle down. Talk about playing it close. He finally got still, and I reached around and grabbed the barrel of the single shot twelve-gauge shotgun. I pulled it from his hand as he continued to stare at my gun. While my little saga was going on I could only faintly register what Pat was up to.

Pat had gone after the driver who was struggling to start the car. Every time he turned the key, the headlights would dim. Pat hollered at him to open the door, and he continued to try and start the car. I have the slight recollection of Pat reaching in and grabbing the man by the throat and pulling him up and out of the window.

The guy screamed, "My seat belt...my seat belt."

He managed to hit the buckle, and the last I saw were snow-white *Reebok* tennis shoes going over the steering wheel and then out the driver side window into the darkness. It was like some monster had snatched him right out of the car. *Pretty awesome because this guy was over six foot tall.* He was hollering like a little school girl.

Pat had him cuffed and put him in the ditch as I held the other guy at gun point. Without a word he came around and grabbed the other guy and pulled him out by the shoulder and neck; lucky for him he didn't have a seat belt on. Pretty impressive, Pat had these guys cuffed and ready for jail. The whole chase and arrest probably lasted less than two minutes. It seemed to last an eternity.

We had radio calls from all directions, and deputies from two counties were speeding to help. Somehow, word had gotten out about the incident.

Pat and I fixed a cup of coffee from my thermos and tried to get our heads together.

After finishing the coffee, I picked up the shotgun and opened the breech. It was loaded. *The son of a bitch had reloaded.* The son of a bitch really wanted to kill me. It just slaps you in the brain to think that he would have done this. I wonder what would have happened if the vehicle had spun further around. The guy would have had a perfect shot at me as I got out of the vehicle. *Lucky for me.*

Pat searched the vehicle and when he opened the hatch back and reached into it, the night stillness was interrupted with a loud, "OWWW!"

A bloody doe kicked the crap out of Pat's hand. She was kicking and hell bent on making a getaway. Evidently, she was what the two hunters had been doing when they stopped on the long straight away. They had shot her and were picking her up when Stan saw them stopped on the highway Well, now she was determined to climb out of the trunk and make her escape without any regard for the heroes of wildlife.

"What are you going to do?" I asked.

"Euthanize her! She is state evidence!"

I was standing over the two prisoners watching as Pat pulled out a pocketknife and dove into the trunk after the deer. After a minute or two and a final "blahhhh" the critter finally quit struggling.

Pat climbed out and stuck his blade into the dirt to clean off the blood. And then after folding it with one hand he put it into his pocket. I made a little note not to shoot at Pat or kick him in the hand! *Scary dude.* There is no way to describe the scene but I will try.

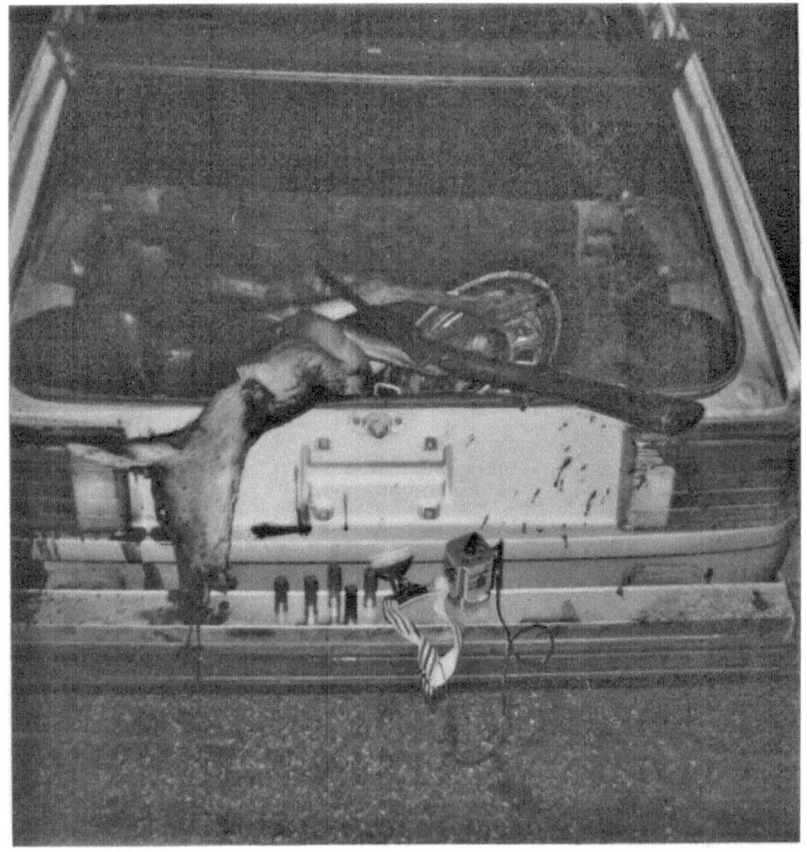

Stan was concerned and was now circling the scene in his tiny aircraft. He was helpless and wanting to help. He was circling and putting his plane in steep dives overhead. The sound from his engine was not unlike a buzzing bee circling around your head. I mean he was low, and I don't know how he managed to circle and dive so tightly without stalling. In the total darkness all you could see were his many lights, and from a distance it must have looked like an alien invasion the way he was maneuvering. I am pretty sure he would have hung out the window of his plane and shot the son of bitches if he could have seen everything. He was relieved when I got into the truck and radioed him about the catch. You would have thought he had killed a 10-point buck. He really was happy and relieved. I guess sometime during the chase I had radioed that we were in pursuit, but I honestly don't remember the transmission. I told him that we would be several hours processing the scene, and that he should move to Thomaston and work with Wesley and Jesse who were waiting. He flew off and I swear he was waving the wings of his plane as he left. *What a pilot*! *My brother!*

It was a long night and 3 a.m. before we got home, but as I entered the jail I notice Billy the dispatcher smiling. Billy, the jailer was grinning with his tobacco stained teeth.

"Hey Pat. Hehehe. Did those sons of bitches try to kill you? Hahaha."

Yes. Sometime during the two minute chase, I had grabbed the mike and hollered that we had been 'shot at' but in not so poetic words.   DANG. That explains how all the other deputies got word of the incident and the shooting. I went into the kitchen washed the caramel cake off my hands and then got a cup of coffee. I stopped in front of the window where the trustees, the dispatcher and Billy, the jailer were grinning.

"Yes, Billy, as a matter of fact," I said "Yes…those sons of bitches tried to kill us."

I made a mental note to work on my language. Especially during emergency radio transmissions.

That night I could not get to sleep. There was just too much adrenalin pumping in my blood. It was exciting, but I could not get the picture of the guy hanging out of the car pointing that shotgun at me.

I have told this to a lot of people and they always say "He missed you."

"Yeah, I guess he did, but I swear that I was looking down the barrel of the shotgun."

Nine marble-size lead shots should have crashed through the windshield and everything in the cab. To me, it was like they had just disappeared. Like time stopped and my vehicle had skipped the flying curtain of lead. A secret and scared part deep inside me feels as if I will wake up in the crashed Bronco in the ditch, with smoke coming from the hood of my truck which is smashed into a tree. And me bleeding to death in the cab of the truck. Maybe that is what happened and all this now is the dream of a dying cop. *Weird.*

Other times, I wake up at night from a dream where the guy is sitting on the window frame; he slides into the car as the pine tree skims the side of the car where he was sitting. I keep willing him to be crushed and to be knocked out of the car. In my dream, he always makes it and I am left disappointed and always wishing that he had died. Year after year the image gets clearer, now I can see his eyes and face and of course he is mockingly grinning. I have real sorrow that he lived. Sorry. But that's the way I feel. It is an indescribable feeling when you know that someone pointed a gun at you and squeezed the trigger. He wanted you dead rather than get a ticket. Pretty traumatic but in the end I had this feeling that I had been spared and that I had something special to do in my life. *Stupid huh*?

In the end, I have remorse for not shooting the guy with the same knowledge that I did the right thing. I was the cop that the public deserved. A cop who didn't want to hurt him, or more importantly kill anyone. Maybe I wasn't cut out to be *Batman*?

Chapter Eight: How You Got Caught

All right this section is a little boring and if you are a pleasure reader skip to "Telephones and Fish" (or so says my editor…but she is a girl). This is for the wardens and the outlaws. Without fail, when I was making an arrest, the poor violator would start trying to pump me for information. They were simply amazed that in a ninety-eight square mile area that a single game warden had found their pile of corn, or located them poaching. From their perspective, they were invisible to deer and humans. Still, even with the latest camouflage and being vigilant for signs of the warden, they got caught.

Truthfully it was easy. It was easy. Really easy. So finally, I guess I will reveal my amazing clues and then sum them up with my particular patrol style at the beginning of deer season.

Beyond any doubt the number one clue for the game warden is 'The Dirty Truck in Plain View.' That's right, the number one clue for me begins with that truck of yours pulled off on the side of the road. I will drive by your vehicle at normal speed and after going down the road a couple of hundred yards, I will turn around and drive very slowly back to that truck. As I near it, I will gently roll to a stop, and with the vehicle still in drive I will turn off the engine. After the vehicle stops, I put it in park and gently open my door. I quietly close it, making sure there is no door bang. I walk to your vehicle. I look into the windshield. Are there maps and marking tapes that foresters use? No. I see that there is an empty bow case. It is taking up the passenger seat and it appears that it is just one guy bow hunting. Now I go look into the bed of the truck. Here's the real magic. Yep, I see an empty yellow corn sack or even a few grains of corn caught in the bed liner. If you are a bait hunter and you have hauled corn, you will know that even if the bag seems perfect, the corn just seems to escape. I have made so many cold cases by just checking this out.

Okay now I am interested in you and suspect you are hunting a feeder or pile of corn. In some cases when an ATV has been used there is a trail of scattered corn all the way to your stand. Sure, it is only a couple grains every couple hundred feet, but they are yellow and easy to see. Right now I am ready to come get you. And my goodness, you have worn a trail out while running back and forth. I know you are alone. Odds are you are going to be sitting on a big pipe feeder or even just a pile of corn. I know you are using a bow and arrow. If its gun season I will notice if you left your hunter orange vest or cap on the dashboard of the truck. I can tell by the corn that it's fresh. Just a little dew or rain and it would have gotten soft, moldy, or even sprouted.

I have arrested hunters who have taken the corn with them piled it up and then climbed a stand right on top of it. Usually a bait pile takes a couple of days for the critters to find and start feeding on it. *COME ON!* If I know the property is only a small block of forest, I might leave my vehicle right on the side of the road. My main consideration is the time…if its 5:15 and its dark at 5:30...then I am coming f to check you right now. If it's just after 3 pm with plenty of light and a lot of hunter traffic is on the road, then I will try to move my vehicle down the road and hide it on a logging trail. No use to advertise. Your buddies might see the vehicle and decide to blow the horn and make racket to warn you. Heck, today they could just call you on your cell phone.

"Run you son of bitch. The game warden is at your truck!"

If it's a large tract of land with possibility of multiple hunters, I might wait and come back on Monday and patrol the whole property to locate all the feed sites. If I find a bunch of feeders on green fields, then I will wait until gun season in order to catch as many violators as possible. After I have decided to find you, and have hidden my vehicle, the tracking begins by me entering the trail or logging road. If it's a trail, I look for crushed leaves and cut marks from a machete or axe. It really helps when you ride the ATV down the trail to put up your ladder stand. Trails, although having less traffic, usually do follow along the painted blue or white property lines. YOU always hang your stand on the back corner, sometimes on a painted tree and always turn to face the adjacent property. You will try to hang the stand in an area with a view. As the woods open up, I slow down and begin searching the trees for your 200 pound silhouette.

When I get to the back corner, I see you in your climbing stand. There you are in full camouflage gazing down on a stump covered with yellow corn. There are several other piles and even a couple of trails heading off onto the neighbor's property. On another stump there is a syrup block. Hanging from the branches of a cedar is a cotton ball with deer urine dripping off.

I am standing right under you now.

"Hey. I whisper. "Hey."

You look around and then down. I can't see your face, but when you shoulders sag I realize that you definitely recognize who I am.

"Hey, I need to check your hunting license." Still whispering. Maybe I am just checking licenses, maybe I haven't noticed the bait or maybe I don't care. You wish!

"Just drop it down," I whisper.

You hang your bow onto a hook that you installed into the bark of the tree.

"Sir, I need you to just stay there for a second."

I pull my radio from its holster, and you don't see me twist the squelch knob. It whistles with static.

"Yeah, Wesley. I have found this guy. His name is Joe Blow. Will you please log it for me?"

I am watching you and your shoulders sag as I read your name into the radio. You are defeated. (I might have been pretending but you can't tell). I pull out my ticket book and copy your information onto the citation. After I have finished your ticket, (making sure to leave some space in the charges section just in case) I politely ask you to come down from the stand so that I might have a word with you. You attempt to leave your bow and quiver, but I ask you to lower them down to me. Once on the ground I introduce myself.

"Hello, I am Conservation Officer Pat Reid and I am assigned to Marengo County. I am investigating a report of baiting in the area." Your eyes twitch. Did someone rat you out?

After the introduction, I inspect your bow and arrow to make sure they meet the specifications for the game species you are hunting. I look for the rubber sleeves where poison pod is placed, and check the size of the arrow head. I then ask to inspect your back pack, looking for a pistol and documenting the items in the bag, deer grunt, deer urine, rattling antlers. Unlike other wardens, I carry a small video camera. I ask you to stand over by the stump and in one quick movement I video the climbing stand location and turn to you with the bow and arrow. I then capture a good shot of your face, a quick look at the bag contents, and then finish on the pile of corn. After putting away the camera, I read you the citation and explain the court dates and alternate methods for settling the ticket.

You will start trying to pump me for information, and somehow you get the idea that someone has told on you. Revenge is in your eye! *Muhahahha!* I write my phone number on the back of the ticket. *Oh yeah. You are gonna call me.*

Well let's look at my case. I have a photo of your truck and tag with corn in the back. I have a shot of you in your stand with a bow and arrow in close proximity of the bait. I have a photo of the deer grunt, urine, and the rattling antlers. I have these items to present to the judge. It clearly appears that you are deer hunting and using illegal baiting methods. Now this was a simple bait ticket. Nine times out of ten you will have broken a few more rules. For example, during gun season you will have left your hunter orange in the truck. Other times you will have crossed over the property line a few feet to place your stand. You will possess a high powered pistol while bow hunting. The list goes on and on.

You are wondering how you got caught. Now let's pretend you are watching from above. Let's speed it up. There is the game warden vehicle hauling ass on some rural county road at 50 or 60 miles per hour, and from our sped up view it looks like the game warden vehicle is a blur. The game warden zooms past your truck parked on the side of the road. Several hundred yards later, the vehicle slows and without missing a beat the vehicle makes a U turn using the shoulder of the road. Now we can see that it is the green State of Alabama vehicle used by the game warden. Our view is speed up so it appears that the state vehicle is moving back to the place where you parked at a good pace, but in reality it is creeping back slowly and quietly. It gently comes to a stop on the opposite side of the road.

A lone figure exits the driver's side, and he walks to your vehicle and takes a quick look at the passenger compartment, and then the bed of the truck. After one loop, the figure moves like beeline to an obvious path along the property line. The figure walks the path which is clear and heavily used and following the painted property line. The path leads straight to you.

Did you screw up? You stopped a speeding vehicle (warp speed vehicle) dead in its tracks and lead the warden to your secret killing field. *Easy.* A complete stranger to the property, he walked right to you! Yeah, your mistake was leaving the truck in plain view. If you had pulled out of sight, I would never have known you were there. If you had parked at another location, say up the road by your gate, then I would have foot patrolled all of the obvious fields. I probably would have found you because I would eventually get to the property line and walked it if time permitted. I thank you for parking in plain view.

During the drive through, I am going to take stock of how many vehicles are parked in the area. I have a property ownership map that shows the owner of the property and the adjacent property owners. If it looks like this is a big property, and there are possibly other hunters on the same piece of property, then I am going to process you differently. I am going to take your identification and not let you sign your ticket. I will tell you that I am going to check the other hunters and will meet you at the truck at dark. I advise you that if you hinder my operation that I will not accept bond and will take you to jail, especially if you attempt to warn anyone. By now I can see that you hope everybody gets a ticket. *It's okay...really*. I will relieve you of any phone or radios (Yes. I have checked people who would be trying to radio there buddy that the game warden was there). One time I was holding the guy's link phone when the first guy that I caught radioed "Look out for the warden!"

I replied, "Too late. Did you forget about what I told you about hindering my enforcement effort?" *Once bitten.*

I will sometimes jog back to the vehicle or if on a small property then to the next obvious vehicle. If it is a large property, I will run to my vehicle. No sneaking now. I am finding hunters. As I locate each, I take stock of their situation and photograph them with bait or other evidence. I tell them to meet me at the vehicle.

IT IS GETTING DARK now and I must find the others. Nobody likes moving around late in the evening, you could get shot. Listen the jogging thing was my little deal. No **self respecting game warden is going to hustle like this**. For me though, I will be having a ball! I am motivated because word would spread, and everyone, along with the evidence, would quickly disappear.

My real drive or hustle came after an incident in Greene County. There wasn't a game warden in Greene County, so I was asked to answer complaints. I worked the complaints a couple of times with success, but couldn't help but notice a vehicle always parked on the side of the road by a logging trail. It was obvious that someone was hunting the same spot every day. Come on folks the deer get spooky with this kind of pressure so I fully expected that some baiting was going on.

Now you have to appreciate that I had to use a map to work this complaint. Hell, I kept getting lost. You can't get any colder on a trail than that. Half the time I wasn't even sure if I was still in Greene County. But there was that vehicle. So, the following Monday I made the trip to where the vehicle parked. *Yep I got turned around again .Lost*. Persistence pays off, and I eventually located the spot. I like the weekdays for doing a reconnaissance, especially during business hours because everyone is at work. I was less likely to be seen. Sure, if they had seen me they would have temporarily stopped committing the violation *but that ain't any fun*. I parked at the spot and followed the nice logging road into pine forest. It was a beautiful walk with soft the brown pine straw carpeting the road. The pines were tall enough so that the view was clear underneath the limbs. Sure enough, when I got to the end of the road, and about 30 yards from the property line, there was a nice green field and shooting house. And 15 yards away I could see the camouflage green PVC pipe with a huge pile of corn at the base. The ground was torn to pieces. With an evil laugh, I jogged back to my vehicle and tore out of the area.

In Alabama, the area stays baited for 10 days after the feed has been eaten or removed by a spooked hunter. I made a videotape of this bait site with the date to document the condition of the area. Afterward, I stopped in at the Greene County Courthouse; I was looking to find out who owned the property beside this county road. If you didn't know, the courthouse has a safe room with maps of the entire county and the individual landowner's names are written on the maps. I didn't have any luck. I just could not figure out who the property belonged to. I couldn't even find the county road. This is not typical, but the person who was working was too busy to help me. Ideally, I would have seen the property drawn on the county map. I would then have identified the landowner by name. Then I could pull up the landowner's tax card, and it would give me the information to locate any additional properties. Yep, most landowners lease the property out to the same people, and if I can find additional property then you can bet that it will be baited too, or it might lead to the parcel where the outlaws have their camp site. Like I said, no luck in Greene County, but I was determined to check this one baited site the following weekend.

Just as a special note I will tell you that most counties publish a book with maps of all the county land parcels with the landowners name written on their particular property. It is easy to use, and it shows county roads, churches, power lines, gas lines, railroads…etc. In the back it has an alphabetical index of the landowners, with the page numbers in the book where I can see their particular property, or properties. It is a very helpful tool.

Once I got a tip from a chronic complainer that a group of Texas hunters had leased a large block of property in Mrytlewood and had been seen with a trailer load of corn driving into the property. I drove down the main dirt road and had to stop and pull over because the road was blocked. I walked to the center of the road and dragged a 50 lb bag of corn out of the way. Pretty good tip…littering with a sack of corn. Of course, I arrested six hunters on the property that evening. No big deal, except that I got the indication that these guys had more property leased. I pulled out my property ownership book, published by the Lion's Club. I found the particular property in Mrytlewood, and I saw that the owner was a guy named Boxer. I checked the index and there he was Boxer with two entries by his name. There was another holding on page 62. I went to that page and saw his name on a 600 acres parcel just west of Uniontown. The next week I drove 50 miles northeast to the other property and sure enough it was baited too.   The very next weekend I caught one of the same hunters that I had caught in Mrytlewood. He was setting in a camouflage golf cart, staring down a 300 yard strip of plowed dirt that ran though a thicket. The dry gray soil had been disked and planted, but they had also poured 500 lbs of corn down the whole lane. This guy was amazed and utterly stunned. He even tried to hire me to work for his company. He wanted to know if I was married because he had a daughter he wanted me to meet. I am just writing this because you have to know it is not magic!

Back to my bait in Greene County. It was a crisp November evening when I finally got up to the spot. *Yep I got turned around again. Damn.* Now as a rule I will not check a bait site, or even be in an area of the targeted property until at least 3:30 pm even if I am rushed for time. If I don't have other complaints, then I will wait until much later to enter the site. I don't want to spook any of the hunters in the area. I don't even want my vehicle to be seen on any of the roads. If you haven't seen the game warden in your area all year, and then you see him three times on the same day then you can bet somebody is getting a ticket in the area. It is a sure thing.

On this occasion, I waited until 4p.m. before starting the long foot march into the property. The gate was unlocked, but I had noticed a ground blind about halfway where someone might be sitting; I wasn't sure I could see them or catch them if they heard my vehicle coming down the road. I hid my vehicle around the curve in the road behind an old shack. It was a beautiful evening when I started my walk. The road was covered in pine straw so my feet made little to no noise. I walked slowly checking to my left and right under the pines for anyone sitting and watching for game. After clearing the little hidden ground blind, I picked up the pace to the primary hunting field. When I got to the green field, I was behind the shooting shack and I could see that the door was closed. I didn't have any more calls, so I figured I would sit down and watch the hunter hunt. If he took a deer, it would be even more evidence that he was hunting deer species. I sat for about an hour and it was approaching 5 pm. I had about 30 minutes of daylight left when I noticed smoke coming from the shooting house. The idiot was smoking a cigarette. I could smell it. There was no way a deer; even a tame deer was going to enter the kill zone twenty feet in front of him. I got up and paced to the shooting house.

Tap, tap, knocking, I ask, "State game warden, Could you step out of the shooting house, sir?"

There was a grunt and then the plywood door slowly squeaked open. A wild haired guy with a black and gray beard stuck his head out. I swear it looked like *Wolfman Jack.* I asked for his hunting license. He didn't have one. He was guest of a friend whose grandfather owned the property. No license. *Yessssss!* Bait. Y*essss!*

When I told him that he was getting a ticket for bait, he looked me dead in the eye and said, "There ain't no corn in that feeder."

And I swear to God his eyes crossed just like a fly had landed on the tip of his nose.

The hair on the back of my neck stood straight up and I stepped by him and picked up his rifle and then cleared the chamber.

"Well sir, maybe you could walk down here and let's have a look."

Truthfully, it was only twenty steps across flat ground and you could clearly see it from the shooting stand. My God he did have a scope on his rifle.

Again he looked me in the eye and said, "I can't walk I am disabled." He finished his statement and then his eyes crossed again.

I gave him a double take, and with his rifle over my shoulder I walked over to the feed and picked up a big handful of corn. I carried it back to him and showed it to my disabled prisoner.

"Oh. I didn't see it"

"Well it looks like the same corn in the back of your truck."

"That ain't my truck; it's my hunting guide's truck. He isn't here; he is with my brother at another field."

The wheels started turning in my head, but I played it cool with total disinterest.

"Well when he gets back you can tell him to clean up this mess of corn and then he can hunt here 10 days later."

Like I wasn't about to go talk to the guide...ha!

While filling out the ticket I got to the occupation section for the prisoner and wrote in disabled. I had a second thought, *Geez. What if this guy is dying of cancer? I might need to give him a break.*

"Sir, what is the nature of your disability?" I asked, honestly expecting it to be something that would keep him from walking.

"I have ADD." He replied proudly as if it was a major award.

"ADD." I repeated. "You have Attention Deficit Disorder."

"Yep."

I gritted my teeth. "Well I am sorry to hear that. I hope you feel better." I said, not at all using a sarcastic tone.

You mean to tell me that you can get a check for ADD. My word what is the world coming too.

I quickly wrote him his tickets and explained the process to him. He complained that he was disabled with ADD problems, and he needed to bait because he couldn't concentrate for long periods. It looked to me as if he ought to have back problems because he had a pot belly which had to weigh 100 pounds. I said goodbye before he could gather up his things and quickly paced down the pine straw road. As soon as I was out of site, I took off at a full run. I wasn't sure that he had ADD but I was sure that he was a NUT. I needed to hurry. Remember, this guy was a guest and surely there must be another vehicle parked nearby that I had missed.

I got back to my vehicle in the blink of an eye and patrolled the paved road two times. I couldn't find a vehicle or even another road or trail. The clock was ticking and I was desperate to find the hunting guide and his brother. It was about 5:20 p.m. and almost dark; I saw an old man working in his yard, so I calmly pulled into his driveway and said hello.

"Sir, I am Pat Reid, Conservation Officer and I am new to the area. Have you lived here long?"

"Oh, yes, I have lived here all my life."

"I am not familiar with the property and I see a vehicle parked up there. I don't want to mess anyone up hunting. *(Mental hehehe)* So do you know who that is?" (I tried to suppress my impatience because I was running out of daylight.)

He thought for a moment and cocked his head.

"Oh that is my property. What did the vehicle look like?"

"It's a blue Datsun pickup."

"Oh. That's my son truck."

"Great. So he has permission to hunt there. Do you own any more property?" I feigned innocence and hid my excitement.

"Why yes, down the road east of here behind a grey singlewide trailer."

"Oh that's interesting, but I didn't see any road into the property."

"The road is behind the trailer that's my son's trailer."

I was about to bust, and I needed to get to the property ASAP. My hand brushed my radio and the squelch sizzled. I looked at it.

"I think my supervisor is trying to reach me. I need to hit the road. Have a nice day."

I climbed into my truck and sped away.

Just around the curve I noticed the gray trailer. Damn the torpedoes or any buried septic tanks, I pulled into the private drive and around to the backyard. About 30 yards across a small field was another small truck loaded with all kinds of camping and hunting supplies and bless my heart a Louisiana tag. The truck was parked blocking a narrow pine straw road that cut through 10 year old pines which were about 15 foot tall. Bingo! I jogged down the road until I came to an intersection where a little voice said go left, but I decided to go straight using the rule that the hunter will hunt all the way to the back of the property. After about 150 yards I saw a figure standing in the road with a rifle. No hunter orange, no hunting license, and smoking. Smoking, geez. What an idiot. I got his driver's license and asked where the other hunters were, and he pointed to the end of the road where a trail cut to the left through the pines. I jogged ahead leaving the guy behind. I followed a trail to the property line where an old shooting house was falling down. It overlooked a clear bottom under some magnificent oaks on the neighboring land. I looked down and saw fresh cigarette butts, the same unfiltered Camel cigarettes that the guy sitting in the road was enjoying. The lying bastard had sent me to his stand. He must have been walking out. He had sent me on a wild goose chase. I took off running back the way I came. I was pissed. I ran full out. When I entered the logging road, I turned hard, running back to the intersection that I had passed up.   My lying friend was sitting down smoking a cigarette. He was grinning in triumph because he had delayed me until darkness had fallen. He tried to talk to me obviously an attempt to keep me busy. I stopped and told him that I would meet him at the truck. He tossed his cigarette down and I stepped forward to put it out. *Asshole*! I crushed the cigarette with my boot and something caught my eye. Something yellow, Sure enough. I started kicking the straw and found corn scattered underneath it. I looked up grinning at my lying hunter wasn't smiling anymore.

"I see you got some corn here. I want to talk to you at the truck."

He started to say something but I pivoted and ran as fast as I could to the intersection that I had passed, where my little voice had said, *Turn here*! It is around 5:45 pm and almost pitch black. I ran breakneck another hundred yards.

I entered a green field that is still visible only because the mint green grass is almost luminous in the evening twilight. I see a shooting house to my left and two figures are exiting. I walk over to the two and check their hunting licenses. It is a fellow from Tuscaloosa with his 17 year-old son hunting. I turn on my flashlight in the darkness.

"I need to check your field."

I walked to the end of the 100 yard field casting my light left and right. Damn it! I didn't see anything and started to walk to the two hunters who had moved toward the exit road.

NO! I said to myself, *every place on this property is baited. These guys paid to hunt this lying hunter's father's property. There has to be bait in this field.*

I heard a sigh of relief as I approached the hunters. *Bullshit.* I made an about face and walked back to the shooting house. I stood in front of it. The field was L-shaped and turned sharply to the right downhill. There was a small area of the field directly in front of the shooting house and some open area under the pines, not even 30 feet from the shooting house. I walked to the pines, and looked down. Now I could see it. Scattered like snow there was yellow corn under the trees, a large pile in a 10 foot circle.

I politely asked the two hunters to come over to my bait site. They stood in the middle of the corn, weapons in one hand, and shells in the other. I took my video camera out and turned on its light. I videotaped the trail of corn and them standing in the pile of corn. Lights, camera action, they are stars. Defeated stars. *SMILE!*

We walked back to the vehicle where the cocky-lying hunting guide was waiting. I wrote the bait tickets, hunter orange and hunting license tickets. As I am leaving, I told my the lying hunter,

"Oh yeah, your buddy from Louisiana is waiting at your truck at your other field. You will need to remove the feeder and clean up the corn and wait 10 days before hunting in the area."

In the light from my flashlight I could see the blood red flushing across the guy's face, and now he was pissed. I had gotten everybody. He had begun with a funny heroic story of how he sent me on a wild goose chase, but in the end everyone got arrested. I guess I got the last laugh. Well, that is what got me running and hustling after hunters. I was exhausted, but in the last 30 minutes of daylight I had accomplished the impossible and had written almost $2,000 in tickets. But for me, I had won the little game of hide and sneak and lie!

Chapter Nine: Telephones and Fish
`

A game warden in Alabama will typically get a boat to patrol fishing and duck hunting. I was issued a green sixteen foot aluminum *Duracraft* boat with a 75 *Mercury* motor. It was 20 years old but still ran like a champ. My first years were a learning experience, and I loved the river. Spring and summer are amazing on the Tombigbee and Black Warrior Rivers. Everything is green and alive, and the wildlife appears tame because the critters don't react so fearful of people in a boat. Que Sera Sera. Life is wonderful, etc…

I got to see some amazing things. Just beautiful!

By my third year it was a pain. Hot blistering sun and grouchy fishermen. The new was gone. It was pretty boring, and I worked extra hard to try to find some adventure. The most interesting cases to be made would be to catch someone fishing with electrical devices or explosives. Both illegal methods are especially effective means for harvesting a boatload of fish in record time.

The electrical devices are referred to as 'Telephones.' This electrical device sends pulses of electricity between two wires that are dropped behind a boat and usually weighed down by chains. The devices get the name because early devices were made from antique telephones. If you have seen an old black and white movie where the person cranks a handle to talk to the operator, then that is what I am talking about. The little hand crank is a small generator. Later, the devices were made with fence chargers and electrodes hidden in empty Skoal cans.

You can use most electrical devices as long as there is a resistor/capacitor that causes the electricity to pulse. Without the resistor, all of the electricity simply shorts out like a lightning strike.

Don't tase me bro! Yep, the 'redneck' fishermen were 'tasing fish' 50 years before the now popular self-defense device. During my early years I searched rigorously, looking for wires, fence chargers, and chains worn shiny from being dragged behind a boat.

Every day I would make sure to check for these indicators but with no success. My buddy, Mike had some luck and caught a few folks telephoning with the Skoal can device.

In Sumter County there is a university, and in the summer the combination of fishing and bored intellectuals really fueled the electrical fishing. At one time he had quite a collection. I actually assisted with a couple of 'stake outs' to no avail.

Scuba Adventure

One August day I got a call from a warden in Choctaw County, and he was sure that he could find a telephone that he thought a suspect dropped into the river below Lock 2 Park. He called me because I had access to some scuba gear from the Rescue Squad.

I was excited to try and stupid enough to think that it was a good idea, so I picked up the gear from the Sumter County Rescue Squad and met him at a muddy boat ramp. He hopped into the boat and we drove to a little recessed area along the bare bank of the Tombigbee River. We dropped an anchor, and I willingly suited up. This sounds like a wonderful adventure until you actually do it. I put my gear on and started breathing through the regulator. After climbing into the muddy water, I held onto the edge of the gunwale as I let the air out of my buoyancy vest and started to sink. I remember vividly as my mask sank into the muddy brown water. After only a few inches, all I could see was a faint glow from the surface. After 3 feet it was total blackness. I mean dark. No light. It was like the walls of darkness closed in on all sides. I had released the air from my vest so I could sink rapidly. It was only about ten feet deep, but the darkness was total. I wrapped my arm around the anchor rope and grasped for the flashlight at my side. I pulled it off my belt and switched it on. Nothing, still total blackness. Had I gone blind? I was breathing rapidly and started to get lightheaded. I concentrated and told myself that no alligator was going to gobble me up, no snapping turtle was going to snap a hand off, and that I probably wasn't in a nest of water moccasins. My 'self' talk was not helping. I was terrified. I raised the flashlight up and pressed it against the lens of my mask and could just make out a faint glow. It wasn't just dark here…I was swimming in muddy water with the visibility of chocolate pudding! I returned the flashlight to my belt and sat there on the bottom with an overwhelming sense of claustrophobia. It was terrifying, and I was panting almost hyperventilating. I concentrated until I got my breathing under control. I fought the urge to rush up to the surface and clammer into the boat. After a few minutes I relaxed and quit thinking of monsters or gators swimming up and swallowing me. Still clutching the rope I began reaching out to my side, probing into the utter squishy blackness for a metal telephone device that was supposed to be at this spot "exactly."

"I know exactly where it is," Larry had insisted.

I don't know how I managed to do it but I made a little circle around the anchor, and after a cycle I would lift it off the bottom and swim it a few feet and plant it. I would clear the area and repeat. I couldn't see my pressure gauge, but I knew that at ten feet of depth my air tank would last for a long time, probably an hour or so. Also, at this shallow of a depth, under 30 feet, you don't have to worry about the bends because there is just one atmosphere of pressure. Okay, I threw this information in only to show that I am not a complete fool and have been schooled in the sport. I tried to be brave, but I had no clue how long I had been down. After an eternity, I decided that this was hopeless and that I was tired. I slowly added air to my vest and rose to the surface. When I got to the surface, I was met with a blizzard of criticism and advice.

"What are you doing? Why didn't you find it? You must be blind." Larry was berating me for my incompetence between puffs on his cigarette.

I took it all with a little hidden smile and a knowledge that he was about to slip into the hell that I had just returned from.

"Sorry Larry." after all it was Mr. Cocky's turn.

I bit my tongue as he suited up. The cigarette was hanging out the corner of his mouth.

"Yeah, I will be right back. With the telephone. You obviously don't know shit about diving."

I took my scolding and relished his cocky attitude. He was relentlessly laying it on thick. *Merciless.*

He was really digging a hole for himself so there was no way he was going to be able to back out! He pulled his mask down and flipped his cigarette into the water. He sat on the edge of the boat and did one of those fancy back flip entries into the water. He forgot to hold the front of the mask with his hand, so the mask and strap slipped off his shiny bald head and wrapped a choke hold around his throat.

"Got damn it, this mask is to loose from being on your big water head!"

I just smiled. *Keep it up mother fucker!*   After all I knew my head wasn't abnormally large.

He reached to adjust his mask while letting go of the boat and of course he had taken his regulator out of his mouth to cuss me out. Now he bobbed up and down in the river one hand reaching for his mask and the other trying to find the regulator to shove into his mouth. He would swallow water trying to breathe as he continued to bob up and down. There wasn't any traffic on the river so I just patiently watched as he bobbed along and drifted down river. He would sputter, choking for air and cuss every time he bobbed up. At last, he finally got the regulator in his mouth which stopped the torrent of profanity coming from his muddy, water filled mouth. Did I mention that Larry had been in the Navy? Ever heard the expression that someone cussed like a sailor? Well I had a new appreciation of this branch of the armed forces. I grunted trying to withhold my laughter. I knew my face was probably red from the strain of holding back the laughter. I probably could have been more helpful, but I chose to wait until the expert told me.

Passive aggressive, ha, you bet. After all, an expert had just told me that I didn't know shit about diving in the river!

Well, the wise guy finally got his mask on and the regulator in his mouth and began swimming back to the boat. This really got funny because he was just managing to hold his position because the current kept pushing him back. I kicked my feet up on the dash of the boat and monitored his progress. I wasn't worried about him because he had managed to inflate his vest to maximum, and his head and chest where almost totally out of the water. He would swim for a few minutes and then stop and look up to locate the boat. After seeing it, he would put his head down and swim some more. I was dying trying to conceal my laughter. Poor Larry had a two pack a day habit. This was murder. I wasn't sure which would give out first, his pride or his stamina. He would look up and see the boat getting further away. Shake his head and then swim some more.

Just before he went around the bend he hollered… "Help…help me!"

I lifted anchor and drove the boat beside him. He was exhausted but still too full of pride to get back into the boat. Instead he wanted to hold onto the side and I was to drag him to the site of the dropped telephone. He was holding on right beside the boat cockpit. I accidentally gave it too much gas, and he was drug face first under the water. He rose up to cuss so I gave it more gas until his head went back under. After a second I would slow down and he would come back up.

"Oops, sorry."

"You son of a …"

Again I would gas it. And he would go under.

I slowed and he floated back up. *I am so stupid!*

"Oops, sorry." I admitted, "Okay the second time wasn't an accident."

He was too scared to make another crack.

Once back at the site I dropped anchor, and he grabbed the anchor rope and then Larry dramatically submerged. He went out of sight for about five seconds and shot back up to the surface. He sat there a moment clutching the anchor rope.

He pulled his regulator out of his mouth... "Having some buoyancy problems with my vest."

He looked at me and I folded my arms on the gunwale and leaned over the side intently watching him with a big smile. One of those 'I gotcha' smiles. He was just as terrified as I had been, but the proud mother fucker wasn't going to cry UNCLE!

He squinted both of his eyes at me and then gritted his teeth.

"Let me use the flashlight."

"Sure Larrrrry. Here you go." I said using my most naïve and polite voice.

He sat clutching the anchor line with his pale little water-pruned hands, obviously out of breath and struggling to get the nerve to sink into the water or 'pudding.'

Down he went and he came right back up. It looked like he was on a bungee cord. Now he pulled the flashlight out of the water, and he worked the switch a couple of time to make sure it was working.

He tested the light and then released the air from his vest. I could see the fear in his eyes as the muddy water covered up his mask.

I let him sink a couple of feet and then busted out with laughter. I had the river valley ringing as I heehawed about the master diver. After a couple of minutes, I noticed that Larry was just below the surface of the water. He was swimming around in little circles. That's how muddy the water was. He thought that he was cruising around just above the muddy bottom. He was wearing a full body wet suit, so he could not feel the air on his back. I stifled my laughter and leaned over the boat. When he paddled by, I grabbed the top of his tank which was sticking out of the water. It took him a moment before he realized that he was hung up, and then he started to flail around and grunt into his regulator. He was screaming in his mask as he struggled to get free from the monster.

"AHHHHHHH! AHHHHHH!"

I released my hold and ran back to the console on the boat as Larry surfaced. When he realized he was at the surface he clawed frantically at the side of the boat. Once his hand found a hold, he just hugged the side for a few moments while pressing his check into the side of the boat. He grabbed the mask with his free hand and yanked it off his head and choking said,

"GoGodljhfmmfff."

I stood up and walked to where he was clinging to the bow of the boat.

He spit out his regulator. GODDAMN it is DARK in this damn river."

He slipped out of his buoyancy vest and I pulled it and the tank into the boat.

I didn't wait for him to ask before I leaned over and pulled him over the keel of the boat. I bet he didn't weigh 128 pounds. He lay in a crooked little ball on the deck. I have to give him credit for his next words.

"I need a cigarette!"

Joe Cool to the end. My sides where aching from concealing my laughter, but I didn't let him know.

"Well Dive master. Let me get you another tank. You probably want to get back in the water."

He held up his hand in mock surrender, "Let me catch my breath." He said as he blew out a four foot wide smoke cloud from his unfiltered Camel cigarette.

It was amazing to watch him curled up like a cripple. Puffing those cigarettes.

Now if we had any sense then this would have been the end of the story. But no sir! And after 30 minutes of us recanting our individual dives into the blackness of hell, we decided that we had a plan and then both made another dive. Pig headed, I guess we both were cut from the same cloth. I must admit that I had a small thought that maybe he was onto my little laughing attack, and that he was luring me back into the murky depths for revenge. Fortunately, everything went well and we both survived the adventure with stories to tell, and it made us all the closer for the trouble. We didn't find the telephone and we never used scuba gear in the Tombigbee River again.

Money for Nothing

After just describing my scuba dive in the murky river I hope that you have an appreciation of how horrible the conditions were in this environment. Blacker than night and navigating by feeling along the bottom with your hands is beyond dangerous and terrifying. After saying this, I have to tell you that some of our citizens make a living at doing just this kind of diving. They are not looking for telephones but rather harvesting muscles or freshwater clams.

Before I get started telling you about these idiots, I would like to describe them to you. I bet you know one of these guys. They are white males 18 to 45 years old. They are lanky and skinny and have a wild tangle of hair on their head. When not engaged in the work, you will see them with a cigarette dangling between their missing teeth and holding a cheap beer in one hand. They will have lines around there eyes and damaged skin from many days of passing out in full sun. Whether it's the commercial fisherman pulling gill nets, the muscle harvester crawling blindly along the muddy bottom of the river, the coyote trapper catching live rabid creatures, or the rural crystal 'meth' technician/dealer cooking a 'batch,' these guys, all of them look the same. These guys would have you know them as 'outlaws.' too lazy and free-minded to ever work for anyone past the first payday. These 'free men' invariably chose these career paths which end up actually being hard work and that are practically suicidal. One special perk is that these careers do allow 'on the job' drinking. That's right; you can perform them completely drunk or high. No one's going to check you for being drunk or make you pee in a cup. OSHA doesn't even know you exist!

In the early 90s, mussel harvesting became a new industry for these 'would be' entrepreneurs. You can thank our industrious Japanese friends again because they had learned how to make cultured pearls. It turned out that by implanting small round seeds into the oceanic clams that they could make pearls. The Japanese could make these seeds from several different materials, but it turned out that the best material was made from the shells of our fresh water mussels.

If you could find a mussel bed and harvest them, then you might make $1,000 a day for a few hours of scuba diving. You needed a boat and an air supply, as well as the determination to get in the water and feel around the muddy bottom of the river for the shells.

My first experience with these guys came when I was checking fishing licenses in the lower pool of Lake Demopolis. I noticed that a horde of trucks and empty trailers had parked at the landing. I wrongfully assumed that it was a fishing rodeo. I walked down the hill, which was a slope made of granite rocks, to check a few bank fishermen. When I got down to bank level, I could see the lower pool area under the dam. I was shocked to see fifty or more small boats clogging the whole lower pool. I mean you could cross the river by stepping from boat to boat. I was stunned. I couldn't imagine what the heck they were doing but drove like a manic back home to get my boat. I launched and proceeded to patrol up to the boat jam. I approached, and one of the 'entrepreneurs' frantically waved me off.

"We have a diver in the water!" he hollered.

I shut my engine off and watched the mess of boats. Each of the boats had at least one of the typical entrepreneurs. I could tell by their wiry frames, beards, and wild unkempt hair that these folks were going to get checked today. I could see that most of the boats were out of compliance without safety equipment including life jackets, fire extinguishers, and emergency kill switches. Knowing the profile, I knew that I would find marijuana, and many would have outstanding arrest warrants. Heck, fifty divers in the water and not one dive flag. Further glassing the boats, I could see that many of the vessel registrations were years out of date. I just sat there patiently waiting, and happily confused. *Like a mosquito at a nudist colony*!

As the divers came up, I began doing safety checks and writing tickets. I saw the burlap bags of muscles but didn't have a clue about the law so pretty much stuck to the basics.

Some of the things that struck me were the equipment they had put together.

Their typical operation started with a gas powered air compressor which was hooked to a cylinder. These cylinders are where it really got interesting; instead of technical inspected air cylinder they had stolen those large silver and black cylinders that you see the soft drink man hooking up to the fountain drink machine. I guess any vending machine distributor is probably slapping his forehead after reading this, "So that's what happened to those tanks!" Mystery solved. Now from the cylinder they ran a hose to the diver, and it seemed anything would do. I saw garden hoses, vacuum hoses, flexible plastic pipes. You name it they would use it. Now this hose would lead to the diver in the water who would sometimes have a standard diving mouth piece, while others ended with the jagged end of the hose. They would use duck tape to attach this to a loop of rope tied around the neck of the diver. In this configuration, the diver would simply put the cut off end of the hose in his mouth when he needed a breath. When he wasn't sipping the air, the line would just freely bleed the air out the open end.

Now I am sure that this sounds reasonable, almost doable if you haven't used scuba before, but let me refer you to the previous scene when two well equipped game wardens nearly killed themselves in the muddy water of the same dirty river.

Now staying down is a real problem for a diver and we use a thing called a weight belt. Most divers will need ten percent dead weight of lead to hold them down, especially when wearing a wet suit or in strong current. When I dive, I typically carry 22 lbs of lead shot in my weight belt. A very important component is the quick release, and a standard weight belt will have at least one quick release and newer ones have two or more. The mussel divers were no exception to the weight belt needs and had improvised a suit. The typical suit began with old tennis shoes, blue jeans, a t-shirt and garden gloves. For a weight belt they would tie barbell weights with cord to their bodies. One guy had made a harness of those little red bricks with the two holes used in brick veneers on homes. I guess he had some masonry experience. As far as I know there is no record of the total number of folks who were injured in the muscle diving 'heyday.' I am sure that many an emergency room treated these uninsured rascals for carbon monoxide poisoning, ruptured ear drums, ear infections, cuts and numerous other injuries associated with diving. Probably there are dozens of these folks who are on the missing person's lists, but are simply dead and now are standing on the bottom of the river held down by some stolen dumbbells.

These lovely fellows were quite inventive and ingenious at improvising substitutes for legitimate equipment. They looked like criminals, and by gosh they certainly lived up to it. They quickly developed a scam which pissed off a lot of the local knuckle heads.

One of the problems was that once you got the 'mussels' then you had to find a buyer. That was the true secret to making any money. I mean, for two years everybody got into the business and then most were stuck with a pile of stinking dead muscles. I learned about one of the scams after a guy called to inform on some guys from Nashville.

"Hey, is this the warden?"

"Yes sir."

"I would like to report on some mussel divers who are holding a bunch of crack."

"Well thanks for the tip. Why are you telling me this?"

"I just want to help out."

I continued to talk to the guy and assured him that I would indeed check on the men.

As I began to hang up the informant asked if I could relay a message.

"Sure… no problem."

"Tell Joe that I put pesticide in his air cylinder, and if he don't clean it out then he might get sick."

"What? Why on earth would you do something so evil?"

"Well, Joe sold me $1,500 worth of equipment to get me started in the business, and then he won't tell me how to sell the mussels. I got a ton of them rotting in my back yard."

You know, I have heard of those 'home business' opportunities where you can make thousands of dollars at home. They tout how much you can make at home, sell you some equipment, and then wish you luck. Then you are ready to go but don't have any contacts. You are out of money. When you call them back, they say that if you need a contact list they can provide you with a list for an additional fee. So you fork over another couple hundred, only to receive a random list of names and numbers to cold call which is basically a list of people straight out of the phone book or business data base. You are pissed, but when you read all the fine print you find out that they met the broad terms of the contract and they are simply guilty of a little exaggeration about the market. Well, these non-resident muscle divers would end their season after the quota was met for their buyer, and then they would look for suckers to unload all the homemade equipment that they had fabricated using stolen materials. They nailed all the wild haired boys in the area, selling them their old equipment for good money, and then hauling ass before the new entrepreneurs figured out that they needed a place to sell all these dead muscles. For the record, if a shirtless wild haired man drives up in a banged-up 1972 Chevy van pulling a rusty metal boat, and touting the millions to be made by diving for muscles, I recommend that you wish him a good day and look forward to your day at the plant.

Chapter Ten: Training

<u>Weapons</u>

I have to give the Department of Conservation credit for training. Everyone made light of the training to begin with, but I know firsthand that it is helpful. The weapons training was excellent, and even a certified tender foot became very proficient with their side arms and shotguns.

When I began my service with the department, we carried 357 caliber six shot revolvers. These weapons had kick…or stomp. I am 6 feet tall and 228 pounds with thick arms. Those vintage pistols would spray fire, smoke and a huge piece of lead. Now this revolver has six rounds in a cylinder that rotates into firing position ever time you squeeze the trigger. My pistol was twenty years old, and had been pieced together from spare parts from other old pistols so the timing was off. This meant that the bullet would not be lined up perfectly in the barrel. When I fired the weapon, lead would shave off the bullet and spray out the side between the cylinder and the barrel. It would spray residue from the combustion left and right of where I was standing. It was constantly pelting the guys standing next to me on either side with hot lead fragments. It's kind of unimaginable but became obvious one night when we shot the guns at night. Paul Osborne was getting sprayed with the shavings. A deeply religious guy…man you should have heard him cuss. It's a wonder the damn thing didn't blow up in my hand. Most folks have fired shotguns and had bruised shoulders. Well this pistol would kick up and I swear my wrist felt like I had punched a brick wall. If you have ever seen a pirate movie and those cannons sticking out the side of the ship firing. BOOM. The cannon slides back into the ship. It sticks back out. BOOM. A huge cloud of smoke and fire. Now imagine you are holding that cannon in your hand. That's what it was like. My wrist hurts just thinking about it. I remember the first time I tried to shoot the pistol; the Department Chief had to reshoot me. I failed the first round! I passed it after I got the sight picture right, but it was really embarrassing. I made a promise to myself that it wouldn't happen again. I mean that was totally unacceptable. I was raised around guns from the time I was twelve years old. My problem was that my father hated handguns. He had four boys and we all had double barrel shotguns. He would not allow a pistol in the house.

When I got back from the initial firing tests, there was about a four month period while I waited to go to the police academy. I worked with my partner Wesley and patrolled under his supervision. I carried my shotgun with me everywhere we went. It was getting ridiculous. I couldn't carry it everywhere. Hell it was very intimidating and took two hands but I didn't have any confidence in the handgun in my holster. I simply had to do something!

I began buying cheap target rounds for the big revolver called wad cutters. I would go to the range and target practice. At first I had to stand about six feet from the paper plate target just to hit it. *Damn!* I sucked with the thing. Desperate, I finally went to the library and got a book on handgun marksmanship. I read the whole thing and finally got my grip and sight picture right. When I returned to the range I tore the paper plate to pieces. Hell it was even fun. I kept this up and even got to where I could nail the target at 80 yards. I had even learned how to lie on my back and steady the pistol and make shots at 100 yards, which was no easy task because the bullet dropped over a foot. I continued my practice until Mike called and invited me squirrel hunting.

On our hunt, he was using a shotgun but I told him that I wanted to try to take a squirrel with my pistol. He gave me one of those… 'Are you queer or something?' looks and I just smiled and said.

"I need the practice."

We split up and went hunting, but the wind was blowing so the squirrels weren't moving. After about an hour, I heard one barking and stalked to the bank of a large creek. Across the creek about forty yards away sat a fat old squirrel. I took out the revolver, carefully aimed and nailed it though the heart. It fell to the ground with a thump and not another movement. I crossed the creek on a fallen tree and picked up my game. When I got to the truck, Mike was waiting. He just stared at the dead squirrel.

"You shot a squirrel with a .357 magnum revolver?"

"Yeah," I said in a matter of fact tone. "I was using that cheap wad cutter ammo. And it was a long way away so I aimed at his heart. If I had had more confidence in the ammunition then I would have shot it in the head."

Mike was stunned.

I didn't think anything about it until the next district meeting when I overheard him talking about me hunting with my service revolver.

"No." he replied. "The son of a bitch shot the squirrel through the heart! He doesn't need a shotgun!"

Well, that was the end of my revolver training. I put my shotgun in the gun rack. I now had the confidence that if the fire and the smoke didn't choke or scare you to death; the bullet would definitely get you off my back!

The Department was under considerable pressure and lawsuits to hire women. One of the problems was this Clint Eastwood sized pistol we carried. It was nearly breaking the big men's wrists. The other departments had moved to a nine millimeter semi–automatic which held 17 rounds. The weapon fired a lot of bullets with no noticeable recoil. Our department was stubbornly against the smaller weapon but with all the different pressures was about to transition to it except for a tragic FBI shooting in Miami.

Several federal agents had been tracking some chronic violent bank robbers. After figuring out the suspect patterns, they managed to locate the two felons on the way to rob a bank. In an effort to stop them, the agents rammed the criminals' vehicle, and a terrible shootout occurred with most of the officers getting over powered by the semiautomatic rifles which tore through the agents' vests. Several officers were killed and wounded before the bank robbers finally succumbed to their wounds. When they autopsied the bank robbers, they discovered each had been wounded many times by the nine millimeter ammunition. Several of the bullets simply stopped short of the heart and vital organs. One of the criminals had over 15 hits from the agents' pistols. The brave agents had nailed the assholes over and over.

This event sent law enforcement agencies all over the country into massive rethinking of the very extensive and expensive mistake of the nine millimeter pistol.

This tragic incident caused an immediate rethinking of the weapon because it was clearly too small a caliber to take down determined criminals. The immediate response was to create a new round that had the expansion of a lead hollow point but had a steel post in the center that would cause the ammunition to penetrate through wind shields and car doors.

Lucky for us, Berretta developed a .40 caliber semiautomatic, it only held 10 rounds but would leave a 24 inch cavity in a jell target. Coupled with the new-type ammunition with the steel post, this gun satisfied everyone's requirement. I remember the first day at the range with the semiautomatic. It was a sweet weapon with very little recoil and smooth firing. Everyone's score went up at the range. People who scored 70 percent went up to 80 percent, and the good shooters went to perfect. One of the nice features was the trigger pull. The old revolver had an advertised pull of 6 pounds, but it felt like a lot more. The new weapons needed about three pounds of pressure to squeeze the trigger, which meant that you didn't pull the sight off target when firing the weapons. It got so easy for me that I decided that I would increase my speed. At the range you move forward to the target, and the final shooting position is only six feet from the target. You are supposed to react and not aim. This was to simulate you being attacked while talking with the subject. When the whistle would blow, I would raise my pistol and squeeze those rounds off as quickly as possible…drop my magazine…swap hands and empty my magazine at point blank range. OOOhhh…it was so good. I would holster my empty weapon and snap it in. Everyone else would be firing their first magazine.

The first time I did this one of the supervisor came stomping over to chew me out, but after he looked at the target and after satisfying himself that I had hit it. He said "Gosh-damn that was fast!"

I loved this and it was rock and roll. I tell you this because it might help you with the decision to take the law enforcement career choice. If it doesn't do anything for you, or you don't enjoy firing weapons, then you probably are not cut out for this type of work. If the above is boring or uninteresting then don't become a cop. Stupid. I know but you have to have a big kid living inside of you to enjoy this line of work.

I remember one time in the Army when I was deployed on a hillside, and an aggressor was sneaking into our lines at night. I saw the guy moving through the field sage, so I motioned to Sam who was sitting beside me in the rocks.

Whispering I said "Put it on full auto…and wait for me to shoot."

He nodded. It was nighttime, and we could see the enemy soldier's silhouette against the bright moonlight sky. We, however, were backed into the hollow of a hill side and shaded by a single tree on the hill side. The soldier moved up and was almost on top of us. We were in the shadow of a little slump in the hillside, so it was like we were in a little cave or room. I opened up on him, and Sam did too. It was like a strobe light in a disco. The soldier only a few feet away screamed like a little girl and fainted. Sam and I looked at each other confused for a moment. We had fired and laughed like madmen. This was before the high–five, but we were feeling that way. As we emptied our weapons, I took a look at Sam; he had the same look as me. Did we just scare the guy to death? The guy was lying somewhere in the field sage and he was not moving.

I said to Sam, "Let's finish him!"

As we clicked our 30 round magazines into our M16s, the soldier scrambled to his feet.   "No. No. I've had enough. You can't kill a dead man!"

I was disappointed because I would have loved to have emptied another clip into him on full automatic. *Sooo goooood!* When he recovered from the shock he came up to us and got our names and said that he was going to report us to headquarters. He asked us who had told us to put our weapons on full auto. For a moment I thought we were in trouble and couldn't help but think that Sam had gotten me into another fine mess.

I told him. "It is dark. I wanted to make sure we killed you."

He said, "Well you nearly did. That was outstanding!"

This doesn't have anything to do with the game warden business except that perhaps it might help you decide if you are the right personality for the job. An adventurous big KID. Who likes to rock and roll on full automatic....so....soooooo goooood!

Well, as we got the sweet Berretta .40 caliber pistols, we also got our first batch of female officers. They were determined lot and didn't have any significant problems with the pistols. And thanks to them my wrist no longer got abused by that old cannon.

Hand to Hand

Believe it or not, the Department taught the game wardens 'Bushido.' It is true and during my fifth year, a mandatory continuing education program was passed nationwide and all law enforcement had to receive 12 hours of annual training. I guess the 'southern attitude' shined through because the powers that ruled decided to invest in techniques for 'Whoop ASS.'

No, I am just kidding, our hand to hand techniques evolved from simpler methods of control such as pressure points, head locks, and take downs. Later we began to get some serious training for survivability, which included techniques for getting an assailant off of you, or protecting your weapons and body if the guy got you pinned on the ground. Now you are all familiar with the new sport called *Ultimate Fighting*. Two guys get into a ring and can use any method to take the other guy out or pin him and make him 'tap out.' These matches don't last but a few minutes or seconds. I remember thinking during training that some of the moves are just the exactly opposite of what you should do, but the really worked.

One little move was a special choke hold that was made when you reached around a guys neck and drove your shoulder under his other arm. You locked your hands together in a strange hung, and then pushed your shoulder into his armpit pinning his free arm against his neck while the arm lock pressed against his other side of his neck. It knocked the sucker out…cold. After I doubted this, Klaus, the sadistic trainer made me let him get the hold on me and then the sick fucker knocked me out. Okay. I was highly upset about this, but I was convinced. And I actually did get to use this technique one time.

Larry and I were in Saraland, and we were going to arrest a guy on a warrant. We knocked on his door and he met us in his pajamas. We told him that he was under arrest, and that he had to put his hands in the cuffs. The guy turns and starts running down the hall. Without thinking I dive after him and make the head lock. I crank down and he stops moving. I let him go and he sinks to the floor. I stand up and look at Larry.

"What happened?"

"I think you killed him." Larry replied.

"Hey. Did you see me do that choke hold 'thingy' move on him?"

"Yep. That was real cool."

"Hey that shit really works."

We just stood there looking at the guy who was lying still in the hallway.

"What do we do now?"

"I don't know…I was one of the guys in class who got knocked out…I have no idea how to wake him up. Hell I was unconscious during that portion of instruction."

Larry stepped up and taped the guy in the ribs with the toe of his boot.

"Well, on World Wrestling channel after they do the sleeper they set the guy up Indian style and then stomp on the back of his neck or slap the shit out of him."

Sounded like a good idea.

I grabbed the guy and pulled him to a sitting position and prepared to slap the shit out of him when he hollered.

"I'm awake don't hit me."

Darn. I never got to try that move.

We really did get some excellent training even if it was from some sick bastards.

As I said one of the sick bastards knocked me out and thought that it was pretty funny. My problem has always been that people don't think they can hurt me. If you see me you just assume that I can take a punch. And if you listen to me talk you probably think that I have already taken a lot of punches to the head.

Every training day, I got volunteered to be the dummy for the practical demonstration. This all culminated at the Tuscaloosa Firing range by a duck pond. Old Klaus was teaching us tactics for defending against a knife attack. He volunteered me to stand in front of him and come at him with the knife while he stood with his back to the pond. I posed for him with the knife up, and he acted like he was teaching a class and then grabbed my collar. While talking, he abruptly dropped down and tried to throw me over his body and into the pond. Realizing what he was up to, I pushed off as hard as I could and did a flip. I landed in the pond, but on my feet. My shin struck a short metal retaining wall bruising it, and my back felt like a cable had snapped. Most importantly, I was humiliated as I walked out of the water. Boy was I pissed. Mike Jackson came over and asked if I was okay.

"That was a cool flip thing. Pat," he said, trying to make me feel better.

"Yeah, I guess so but that shit aint right." Boy was I pissed. I was steaming mad. *It was totally 'on'.*

And, no, we didn't receive any instruction in this type of Judo, so I was sure it was only for their personal amusement. These guys were supposed to be professionals, but they were just jerks. I wasn't going to take this shit again. Period.

When I got home I began plotting my revenge, and about two in the morning I was still stewing and watching a late night infomercials. I was drinking pot after pot of coffee. I watched a No Money Down Real Estate commercial and ordered it. After my revenge I might need a new career. And then at three in the morning, a tired little Japanese guy came on the TV with Danny Bonduce. It was a self-defense video using a move this tiny little Asian guy had developed.

"Are you tired of getting your ass whooped?"

"*Yes.*"

"Are you tired of being bullied?"

"*Yes.*"

"Do you need to put someone in their place with a very discreet move?"

"*Yes.*" I looked around my room for video cameras.

The little Asian guy proceeded to beat up a few people with a couple of simple moves. Danny Bonaduce was impressed. Hell if it was good enough for the *Partridge Family* then it was good enough for me. That's it! I will defeat the bad men with KUNG FU! *Now come on. This aint page one, by now you know me well enough to accept that I would think that this was a brilliant idea!*

I ordered it. A week later it came and I learned one simple move. The little oriental guy was Master Tsai, and he had a powerful move. It was a throat strike. You made a V with your thumb and index finger and struck the opponent in the throat. You hit it with just enough force to allow you to grasp that corrugated tube in the throat, and then you clutched forcefully. It seemed too easy to work, but I was a maniac. I located an old mannequin torso. It was a slim chick, but I cut strips of those floats kids use in the swimming pool called noodles. I duct taped strips of the foam to the mannequin to simulate muscles on the chest. To create a throat area, I took the plastic corrugated hose from an old vacuum hose and duct taped it to the neck of the mannequin. Take a moment and reach up and choke your neck; you will feel that rough tube. It is just like a vacuum hose. I needed some muscles, so I cut some of the float noodles (pool toys) into strips and placed them along the side of the vacuum hose. I duct taped this all together and it looked like a muscular neck covered with duct tape skin. More importantly, it really felt like a human throat. I practiced my strike daily, both in the morning and at bedtime. I got cobra fast, and could smoothly strike with just enough power to allow my fingers to grasp the air tube. Oh but that wasn't enough.   Remember the poor squirrel. I was going to do this right. I bought those little spring hand exercisers and started working out until I could close them with my thumb and index finger. Surely there has got to be some reason for giving you all of these details. There is a story coming and in the end you will agree it's is worth it. *So hang in here.*

It had to be at least six months later when we were told to meet at the Selma police academy for training. Now the odds are that all my fanatical training would never get a chance to shine except that I was dealing with assholes. Consistent pricks. I had planned that when they selected me for the demonstration that I would choke the shit out old Klaus.

We got to the old, dilapidated gym and after shooting the shit for a few minutes, we went inside and the instructors asked us to take off our weapons and boots. Oh shit! Sure enough it is fixing to get physical. He says that we are going to learn some strikes. I am hiding in the back and he points over the crowd.

"Pat, come here."

"No."

"Pat get over here."

"Hell, no. You almost broke my back when you put me in the pond."

"Well then go home. Just leave." The asshole hollered.

I walked out and stood in front of him. I was going to kill the bastard. I looked him in the eye and he smiled like he was a Kung Fu master, and then he said, I can't believe he said this.

He said "CHOKE ME."

My left hand shot up like a snake.   The V shape formed by my thumb and index finger splayed around his throat and sunk into his neck just like I had practiced. The impact was hard and deep enough so that I could easily curl all my fingers around his wind pipe. I mean I was holding his windpipe with all my fingers wrapped around it. I squeezed just hard enough so that he couldn't speak.

His eyes bulged as he choked.

Now please understand when he said, 'Choke me,' he wanted me to come at him with both hands classic old movie style, Frankenstein Style. I knew what he wanted but I also knew what I wanted. Klaus pulled at my arm and I tighten my grip and that voice from hell slipped out. BE STILL!

I stood there effortlessly choking him. My fingers where strong enough to crush steel from six months of exercises.

The other instructor came up and asked what the move was called

"It is the cobra strike." I said calmly.

Meanwhile Old Klaus is just dangling at the end of my arm unable to tell me to quit choking him. I wasn't about to let him go until all the spit and vinegar had left him.

Now the other instructor was asking questions.

"What is the defense for this move Pat?"

"There is no defense." I continued "If you strike my arms it will crush your windpipe. You have to hope that the guy who has you isn't going to kill you."

Old Klaus is still choking.

"Cool." The other instructor was impressed.

It was wonderful. *Old Klaus was twitching and choking at the end of my arm like a little rag doll.* If you have ever been bream fishing with a cane pole, you catch a big one and lift him out of the water. You watch him twist and turn on the end of the line suspended in the air.

I could see Klaus' blood vessels bulging in his eyes, and his knees where shaking so I released him and walked away. They demonstrated with someone else after this. It was just perfect.

Have you ever had dealing with some guy and you just wanted to kill him? Really choke the shit out of him? What are the odds of Klaus asking me to choke him? I was above reproach. I could have hurt him and blamed it on him. I had ten witnesses. I have to thank God for handing me the arrogant jerk and Master Tsai for giving me the tool to fix him.

In the end, you have a problem when dealing with bullies. THE PROBLEM IS THAT YOU ARE NOT A BULLY. You can pretend to be, but when you get to the killing or neck snapping you aren't going to be sick enough to finish the job so in the end you have to find a better way of dealing with them. The guy who shot at me got a reprieve and so did the guy who tormented me for years. So you really have to blame your parents, if they had put cigarettes out on your skin, beat you, or had been just cruel lousy parents, then you could deal with the assholes on terms the bully will respect. Instead, you will just have to do the right thing and be satisfied that your momma is proud of you.

They say that old dogs and elephants have a long memory, but they are nothing compared to memory and persistence of a game warden. Old Klaus took early retirement and never trained another warden.

Lady Wardens

I remember watching Lana, who was one of the first ladies hired; qualify with the 12-gauge shotgun. God bless her, she only weighed about 109 lbs. All the guys were watching, and of course the silver haired ones where bitching.

"What the hell are they thinking? Women working this job?"

Just then Lana fired the 12 gauge shotgun I swear it lifted her off the ground and she landed square on her ass. *Ouch.* I mean she hit hard. It would have made a great *You Tube* video, bone crunching hard. This was a timed event, and you could tell it hurt like hell but she just pumped another shell into the chamber and blasted the final rounds into the target. I was impressed, not with the fact that it knocked her down but with the fact that she reloaded and finished the firing round. I looked at old Harvey.

"I think they will do just fine."

He just nodded.

It was obvious that while they might not be strong enough to handle violators just exactly like the rest of the brutes that I called buddies; if they were determined they would be okay. My ass hurt just watching her hit the ground. Tough lady. The only real difference is that the vehicles started smelling a lot prettier.

Hiring

At the time that I hired on, the Department was still pretty much run by old white guys who dated back to the George Wallace administration. They had their own way of doing things and stubbornly resisted change. When I hired on I had just got out of the U.S. Army and received an extra 5 veteran points on the employment register.

People who wanted a job began by signing up to take the department test, which was comprised of reading comprehension, judgment, and basic gun skills. The test is the first step for getting a position. The same test is used for Marine police, as well as Conservation Enforcement officers, and it is only given every few years to build a register pool of applicants. The year I took the test, over 5,000 people signed up for the testing. The pool was so large that they had to give it in several different locations on different dates.

There was an exam to be offered in Marengo County where I was living, but I was excited and wanted to take the first one which was being given in Selma at a public high school. The site was your typical old wooden style 1960-style school with wooden floors and the smell of Comet. I got there early and talked with some of the other people. Oh, it was so depressing because there were so many applicants, and many had taken the test several times. Some had even gotten to the third phase which was the interview. One guy had flown in from Alaska to take the test. I had no idea that people where so determined to get one of the game warden positions. I was disheartened and getting hired seemed unlikely

Employment Test

Regardless of the competition, I was determined to do my best in the test.

The test was over 100 questions and timed. I remember one portion consisted of a reading of Marine boating law, and then questions beneath it could be answered if you understood what you had just read. It was like an open book test. I think the one I got was regarding boat registrations. The complete section from the Code of Alabama was provided. Below this material you would find questions like "Does a non motorized sail boat have to be registered? Does a non motorized sail boat used as a livery boat or rental vessel need to be registered?" You didn't need to know the law but you did have to be able to read it and apply it to situations.

Another section had a handgun with numbered parts, and you had to pick the proper nomenclature for multiple answers. These questions covered basic stuff actually. I finished the test quickly and looked around, and everyone else was still working on it. This scared me so I went through the whole test again question by question, and by this time a couple of people had finished so I turned in the test. In the hallway, I talked to a couple of people that were smoking, and we talked about some of the questions. They couldn't remember the ones that I was curious about. They acted like they had a different test. I left feeling pretty confident about the test, but doubting that I would get an interview because there were simply too many applicants.

A month later I was notified that I was number 16 on the list of applicants for the openings in the department.

The next phase was an interview from the nearest supervisor who was a captain. He came to my apartment and asked me numerous questions. Have you ever been arrested before? No. His eyebrows went up. I went scrambling around my head trying to figure out what he was up to…

"I did have a ticket for a broken tail light, but I repaired it and drove to the city police and they dismissed the ticket for free."

Evidently that was what he was talking about because he replied "Well there is always a record of it." He added.

He then asked me how long I had wanted a game warden job. I told him that I had always been interested in it, but thought that it would be impossible to get a job because I was poor and didn't know anybody. He grunted. I obviously had pissed him off. I was raised in Choctaw County and the game warden there was the brother to one of the largest landowners. He said the guy's name, and he nodded his head up and down without saying anything. I had definitely blown the interview with the response, but after I added the Choctaw County information he understood that I was just being honest, not just a smart ass. I would later find out that the mentioned game warden was considered to be a lazy, drunken, ass kissing loser. He only managed to stay in the job because he was drinking buddies with the commissioner who loved to turkey hunt on his brother's property. Lucky for me, this supervisor that was interviewing me had sore feelings for the fellow and overall had a very low opinion of the guy. The background check was pretty thorough because he had talked to my high school principal and teachers and several other people. I was shocked when he said they all thought the world of me! The next phase was an interview in Montgomery, where the Department Chief and Chief of Enforcement interviewed me. It was pretty intimidating, but I got the feeling that it was just a final check. It was over quickly, and I was lead out by my new supervisor who gave me directions to the supply warehouse. I was not familiar with area but Mike, who was also hired and would be working with me, knew the directions and helped me find it. Once there, we literally crawled around a pile of clothes and accessories that smelled like baloney looking for uniforms and boots that fit. It was like a Salvation Army thrift store but with less organization.

Well, I want to get back to employment subject, so while I was there I talked to a guy from Alaska who had been trying to get a job for ten years. He knew all the folks in the Montgomery Office by their first names. I was ranked 16 on the list, and had scored a ninety nine percent on the test. With my 5 veteran's points, I had a total score of 105. He explained that probably the first 50 people had scored 99 or better. The problem with this was that it pretty much meant that the people hired were white, male veterans. I think that there might have been one more hire using this method before they went to a band system.

A personnel advisor briefed us on the new employment system. They would create bands of candidates instead of just scoring them based on their raw score. They would, instead, group test takers in hundreds or thousands depending on other requirements. This method allowed the department access to women and minorities that would not necessarily appear on the top of the list. I asked how the band size was determined, and she said that it depended on the needs of the department. You have to understand that the department had to meet the goals of Affirmative Action. They were also being sued by black law makers. I don't have an opinion on Affirmative Action because I agree that the Department's demographics seem wrong when you consider that state population is half female and half black. Clearly a department with all white male employees is clearly not representative of the population, even though they did represent the majority of folks interested in hunting and police work.

The problem with the new banding system is that it allowed the employment based on who you knew. Yep. Now a senator's pet who was scored, say 1500th on the test could be interviewed. This looser, who should never have gotten an interview, could now be included in the top level or band. I am sure you are saying now that I am just a bitter old warden. How you could know this? I know this because of the bizarre quality of the candidates.

They began hiring the most inept uninterested 'players' you could imagine. Maybe they scored better? NO. NO. NO. NO. This could not be true because I personally knew many competent applicants, females, black, and whites who had tested and been placed in the same band as the tattooed, drug seeking, ear ring wearing, thug losers that now got hired. Many of these not hired were already in law enforcement. I would have thought that they were 'shoe-ins,' but they never got an interview. This banding system allowed for the very corruption that it was supposed to be protecting against. Now every politician with a loser of a nephew could get his kin hired.

At first you would think that maybe the old Wallace Administration was selecting the candidates that would quit after the first confrontation, until you saw the awful effort they made to retain the new hires. One guy was morbidly obese, so they bought him a huge all terrain vehicle so that he wouldn't have to walk. I never saw him in uniform until his third or fourth year because no one made a uniform to fit a morbidly obese game warden. I would see the guy from time to time at district meetings, and he would be in blue jeans and khaki shirt. His partner said that the captain could never find him. It was just disgusting. The first batch was a disaster, and one of the cadets used his State of Alabama credit card to call his girlfriend, racking up severally hundred dollars worth of charges while in the police academy. The department didn't fire him, but they said that he had to reimburse the department. He refused, even after considerable effort and begging from the supervisor. He could have paid his phone bill for a couple of hundred dollars; instead he got fired from a state job starting at 35,000 dollars a year. Are you kidding? Another whom I had met was berated by everyone for being stupid. I don't know because I never worked with him, but to keep him they promoted him to lieutenant and put him at a little desk in the radio room. To the supervisors it was a joke, but I wasn't laughing. I never worked with the guy but I knew he had some trouble at the academy. Now suddenly he was my superior…*SHIT*. The system fell apart for all categories of applicants.

I was asked to ride around with a new white warden in Greene County. I was shocked that he was hired because the department was recruiting blacks and women. No kidding, I had to go to the local high schools and look for possible minority cadets. I was shocked to hear that a white guy had been hired and expected that he must be a really smart guy with Army special operations experience. Instead, I found that he was a middle aged tattooed pot- head idiot who talked like a Valley Girl. Oh my God!

We were doing a stake out for night hunters, so we had a lot of time to get to know each other. He had a band aid over his ear, and I asked him if he had cut it shaving.

"Oh no. I hide my ear ring."

Oh no he didn't.

He pulled it off and sure enough he had an ear with a piercing with a tooth pick sticking through the hole.

"Put the band aid back on it!" I insisted. Later he began to talk about drugs and how he was working undercover for the feds.

I asked, "Why are you working for the Department of Conservation if you are undercover…are you supposed to be telling me this?"

He stumbled for an answer, "Ugh, well you know."

"No, I don't know. What are you saying?" I pressed him.

"Your okay."

"I know I am okay but are you sure you are supposed to be telling everyone that you are undercover? Doesn't that defeat the purpose?"

He continued to babble and lie the entire evening, and I found a reason to get the hell away from him. He left me with the impression that he was a druggy and was paranoid that he was going to be caught with some dope. He would later have an early morning accident and get a brain injury. Well, everyone in the department said he had a 'new' brain injury. I did see him after the accident, but he was talking that same bizarre undercover stuff, although it did seem amplified. He insisted that he had been given a date rape drink at the bar where he finished drinking. *Date rape drug?* I can't imagine the sad state of affairs at a club when a short, potbellied, balding, middle aged hippie 'wanna be' is date raped. I guess in his mind he was God's gift to women. Talk about delusional. I am not sure what happened to him. The department goes all hush and signs confidentiality agreements when employees start being processed, OUT. The district was onto his bullshit.

CONCLUSION

So Long *Batman*

If you read this you have to wonder why a huge authentic kid like me would ever quit such a job. For me, it was several things. I was changing, but the main reason was that an event struck home for me.

To get promotions you had to take a test, and even as a young officer we were encouraged to start taking the exams for experience. I skipped the first couple because I knew that I was simply too green to be a serious candidate, but after several years I did take one. I remember how we all met at the public elementary school in Linden. Everyone was nervous and hopeful, and we began after the administrator started the timer. After 10 minutes a big fellow hopped up and left. Everyone noticed, and we would later joke in the parking lot that he must have said "Fuck it and left."

I mean it was a simple test, but it was written in the 1960s and had questions about laws such as 'Provocation'. In those days you could arrest someone for 'giving you the finger.' That law interfered with the civil right for expression and was struck down by the Supreme Court. So here you are with a 1960s test about laws in that era, and you are left wondering about the answer key. Has it been updated to reflect the changes? By all rights the question on the law was wrong because it wasn't a law anymore, so for heaven's sake, which wrong answer do you select? I was really upset about the test. It was just a joke. The big guy who left the test first scored highest and was promoted first. When I heard this I physically felt a snap. It was as if I was lifting something very heavy and something popped inside my chest. It was clear to me that he had done something wrong. From the conversations with others, they felt it was obvious too, but nobody was going to make a stink about it. I asked my supervisor about it, and he said that if I wanted to get promoted to: "Try to find good turkey hunting places for the Department heads.

Are you kidding me? It was all a big joke, even though we were talking about people lives and futures. My supervisor was right on because the big guy at the test would later be caught turkey hunting in the state vehicle and possibly while on duty. He had to write himself a ticket.

I wasn't done with the job, but something in me believed the job ended at a 'dead end'. I know that's not true, but for me it was a core change about the job. It is really hard to explain. I wasn't upset, I just felt different about things. I decided to start looking for another career. I didn't even realize that this shit was important to me. Who'd a thunk it?

Fate had moved for me and this is so silly. Remember the night that I bought the Kung Fu video? Well, I also bought the real estate video. This is the reason that *Batman,* or maybe his alter ego Bruce Wayne, started investing in No Money Down Real Estate. I used this ridiculous video to quickly build a million dollars in real estate equity.

Looking back, I have no regrets. In truth it's not a couple of jerks that caused me to quit. If I had wanted it I would have stayed, but the fact was I was getting bored with the stuff that made up the fabric of the warden's life. Four times people had pulled the trigger and clicked or missed instead of killing me. I was bored? Catching an alligator was a drag? Are you kidding? *The job had become routine.*

In my life I have always bitched about being so poor that I had to clean motel rooms as a little boy, join the Army and end up in a war to pay for college, and countless other jobs to make ends meet. Now I know that each one gave me something special. Perhaps it was simply a new skill, a new interest, or more courage to face the next challenge. I think that the ultimate truth I learned while a game warden is that we are each a hero and each a villain. For example, if a PETA fanatic saw me transport an injured owl across the state then I would be a hero. If the same PETA fanatic saw me gut hook an alligator, or walk through a crowd of citizens only to bash an injured deer in the brain with a claw hammer as low budget euthanasia, then I would be a villain. When you see a policeman climbing into your burning vehicle to save your life… well you know what he is, but ask his second ex-wife and from her point of view he is cheap asshole and a terrible father who is late on the child support payments!

It is the truth when we examine ourselves: policeman, fireman, school teacher, coach or anyone, we are each less and more than we think. Each of us is not quite the nice person that we tell ourselves, but neither are we the loser that we hate when down on ourselves. We are something in the middle.

And old Klaus, the prick, when not bullying he worked as a volunteer on the ambulance and saved lives every weekend. You would never know it just talking to him, and he wouldn't even mention it. He didn't think it was a big deal. It was just what he did. He is a real hero. He was a better man than me and probably you. Be kind when you judge others, and especially when you judge yourself. After all, in the last moments of your life and as it flashes before your eyes, in that lonely moment it will really only matter what you think.

I had out grown my crime fighter stage, but I had met some amazing characters. I can't help but smile thinking of my buddies and the messes we got into. They are real men and women who had the guts to stand shoulder to shoulder and make a noble stand.

I do miss the laughter. When I think of my game warden stories I always remember the grown men laughing in the cabs of dusty state vehicles. Tears running down our faces while begging for air and clutching our aching sides. I don't know what the future holds for the wardens, and my prayers are with them. I am proud to have worked with these fascinating people. Personally, I am determined to make some new 'boring' friends, right after I get through spear fishing today!

The adventure is over for me now but perhaps there is hope for the future. Perhaps there are 'would be' heroes waiting to take the *Batmobile* for a spin. What about you? Want to take her for a spin? She is parked outside and the keys are in the ignition. No? Maybe another, perhaps there will be a new hope for this alliance.

Hand them a chocolate chip cookie and back away slowly. What? No cookie? God help us all!!!!

Other Works by Carlos Patrick Reid are now available at Barnes and Noble, Amazon.com and other fine stores:

Rent Money
The Untold Story

Rent Money offers you a real opportunity to look behind the scenes of what is involved with collecting rent. Collections are a must whether collecting for a business or as a secondary source of income from an investment property. It is not an easy task and you will be amazed by reading some of the stories in this book as to what this couple had to endure to pay their bills. Successful land lording requires a different job description each time you answer the phone. So prepare yourself...think your coworker or neighbor is creepy or smells funny...you have no idea! Murderers, wife beaters, crack dealers, child molesters, con-artists, dead beats, mama's boy...closer than you think. Witness the birth of a new super hero..."Lord of the Cockroaches". P.S. Go wash your hands right now!!!

ISBN 978-0-615-25640-5

ALABAMA
MERCENARIES:
PIRATE SEASON

Carlos Patrick Reid

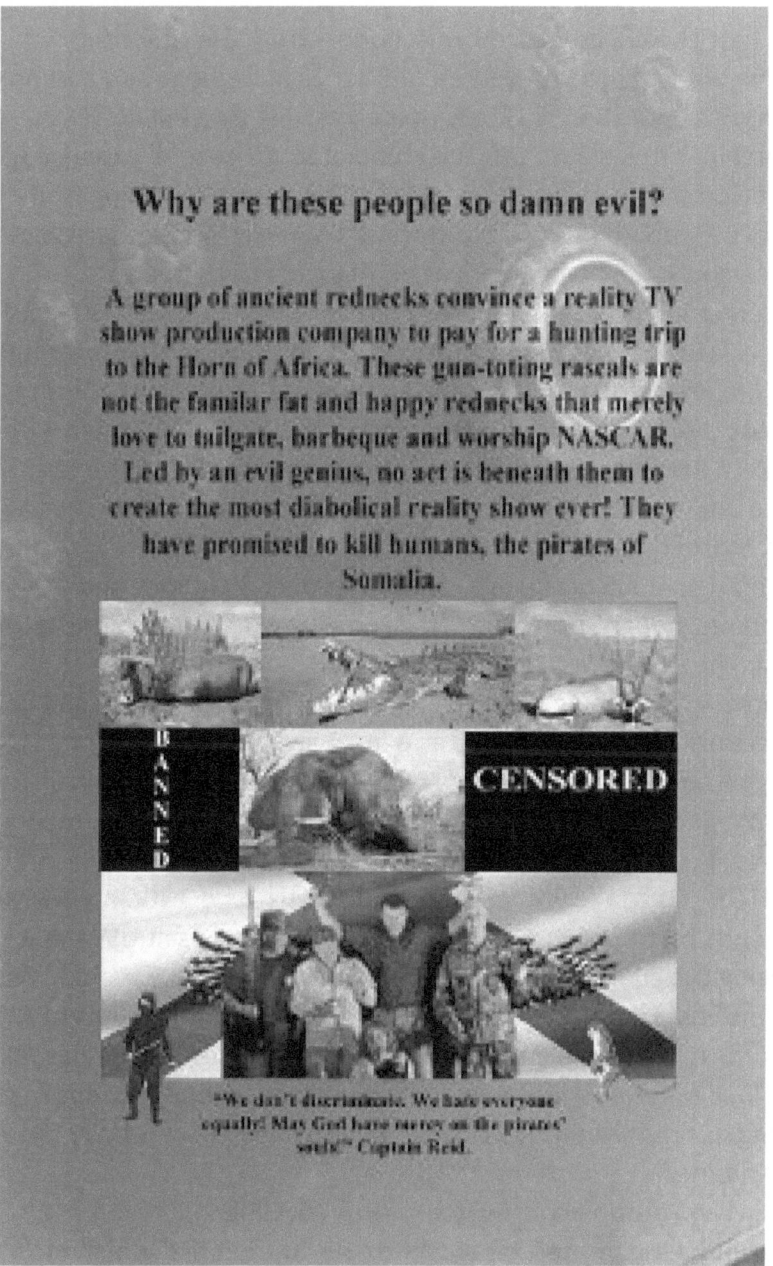

Why are these people so damn evil?

A group of ancient rednecks convince a reality TV show production company to pay for a hunting trip to the Horn of Africa. These gun-toting rascals are not the familar fat and happy rednecks that merely love to tailgate, barbeque and worship NASCAR. Led by an evil genius, no act is beneath them to create the most diabolical reality show ever! They have promised to kill humans, the pirates of Somalia.

"We don't discriminate. We hate everyone equally! May God have mercy on the pirates' souls!" Captain Reid.

ABOUT THE AUTHOR

Carlos Patrick Reid graduated with honors from the University Of Alabama with a Bachelor Degree of Science in Geology and a minor in English. His education was only made possible by a full ROTC scholarship. After graduating, he completed a 3 year all expense paid tour of Germany courtesy of the U.S. Army. Upon returning from Europe, he worked in the laboratory at Chemical Waste Management. Two years later he began work as an Alabama Conservation Enforcement Officer where he worked for 15 years thus: *"Stalking the Warden."* (Holds an informal state record for most murder attempts on his life; exceeding six times at the time of this posting). During his Reservist Obligation, he was deployed to Riyadh, Saudi Arabia with the 324th P&A Battalion Headquarters. He was promoted to the rank of Captain and awarded and Army Commendation during the 1991 War, Desert Storm thus *"SOUL LESS"*.

He retired in 2005 at the age of 40 with over 80 homes and apartments bought using the "No Money Down" method, thus: *"Rent Money: The Untold Story."*.

He enjoys spear fishing, paintball, motorcycling and boxing, and gold prospecting. He prides himself as a 'mad scientist' and has one U.S. Non-Provisional Patent which is being prototyped by the University of Alabama, and several Provisional Patents. As an inventor he made a dramatic 4 minute appearance on the ABC show "THE AMERICAN INVENTOR" http://www.youtube.com/watch?v=oON0Cm-ZWHM

He spends his time by taking creative writing classes at UWA and practicing Mixed Martial Arts, Bushido in Tuscaloosa, Alabama. As a part time Ninja, he has appeared on THE AMERICAN NINJA WARRIOR SHOW for two years in a row with disappointing results. He has fallen in the first water obstacle twice. He blames his friends for not pointing out that Ninjas have to be able to jump. "Somebody should have told me."

http://www.youtube.com/watch?v=9swYoyjZ8IE

When not killing pirates, he works on his 'bucket list' which includes playing the Reality TV show, SURVIVOR.

In October 2011 he was awarded BEST NEW PROSE by THE SUCARNOCHEE REVIEW for his work short story, *"F IRVING!"*

Current projects include the movie production of his novel *"THE ALABAMA MERCENARIES: PIRATE SEASON, THE UNITED STATES OF EUPHORIA (a zombie movie) and KUNG FU BALLERINAS (a children's book)*

www.ingramcontent.com/pod-product-compliance
Lightning Source LLC
Chambersburg PA
CBHW061407280526
45784CB00001B/402